WOMEN AND
SECOND LIFE

T0130887

WOMEN AND SECOND LIFE

Essays on Virtual Identity, Work and Play

Edited by
Dianna Baldwin *and*
Julie Achterberg

McFarland & Company, Inc., Publishers
Jefferson, North Carolina, and London

"My *Second Life* as a Cyber Border Crosser," by Carleen D. Sanchez, was originally published in May 2010 in the "Metaverse Assembled" issue of the *Journal of Virtual Worlds Research*, vol. 2, no. 5 (2010), http://www.jvwresearch.org.

LIBRARY OF CONGRESS CATALOGUING-IN-PUBLICATION DATA

Women and Second Life : essays on virtual identity, work and play / edited by Dianna Baldwin and Julie Achterberg.
    p.   cm.
    Includes bibliographical references and index.

    ISBN 978-0-7864-7021-1
    softcover : acid free paper ∞

    1. Second Life (Game) — Social Aspects.   2. Internet and women.   3. Online indentities.   4. Women — Identity.
5. Computer games — Social aspects.   6. Virtual reality — Social aspects.   I. Baldwin, Dianna, 1960–   II. Achterberg, Julie, 1970–
    GV1469.25.S425W66 2013
    794.8 — dc23   2013004729

BRITISH LIBRARY CATALOGUING DATA ARE AVAILABLE

On the cover: Second Life avatars Steorling *top* © Julie Achterbert and Zoe *bottom* © Dianna Baldwin (Second Life/Linden Lab); *background* (Photos.com/Jupiterimages/Thinkstock)

Manufactured in the United States of America

McFarland & Company, Inc., Publishers
  Box 611, Jefferson, North Carolina 28640
   www.mcfarlandpub.com

Contents

Preface

DIANNA BALDWIN *and* JULIE ACHTERBERG

Dianna

The first time I logged into *Second Life* I was unceremoniously dumped on a sim known as Orientation Island, and here I was supposed to learn the very basics of *SL* such as walking, running, flying, teleporting, interacting, and the list goes on. What I remember most about that experience is just standing right where I had entered the world while others' avatars logged into the exact same location and kept landing on my head and bumping me around. I recall being virtually paralyzed, unable to move left, right, forward, or backward. It wasn't that my controls didn't work, but rather a feeling of sensory overload. What finally got me moving was the sensation, both real and virtual, that people were knocking me around. I am very fond of my personal space, and this was my first experience with how things in virtual spaces can affect you in real life as well.

Julie

My first experience in *Second Life* wasn't too dissimilar. After orientation you worked your way through help island and then sort of "accidentally" discovered the one sign on the whole island that teleported you to the mainland. In "my day" that meant a teleport to one of several freebie warehouse environments and new player "camping" areas. Within my first three minutes I had a Russian named Red stalking me around the freebie place repeatedly sending me 30L and insisting that I needed to "Buy Gooder Shoes." Within three hours I'd written two reports for obscene and harassing behavior, been teleported to a rape room, discovered that the only "group" in *SL* searchable from the interface for the word "teacher" was one devoted to teachers having sex with their students, and fallen through a trap door in a freebie mall floor into a huge room devoted to creating a roman/space opera orgy for nekos, *SL*'s human-cat hybrid avatars (*SL* has its own non-rules for cultural remix-

1

ing). Had it not been that I came into *SL* to act as a go-between for an educational conference and really needed to create a human-appearing moderator out of the default avatar, I wouldn't have logged in again.

Thankfully, I did have that requirement and 6 years experience in MMORPGs to help me navigate the learning curve of the user interface, social and chat environments, and search tools. That "required" three weeks before the conference was supposed to occur, I discovered my first poetry reading, my first free building classes, my first *SL* Live Music concert, my first *SL* art gallery, and met my *SL* mentor. Six years later my *Second Life* has taken me to Montreal and the Netherlands to meet friends as real to me as any in my first life, it's given me the unique experiences of being a musician's manager and poet, it has allowed me to grow aspects of my identity that simply wouldn't be possible in real life and given me a second culture while stretching my technical and creative skills beyond the demands of anything I would experience otherwise and even led to working on this book.

Dianna

When Julie and I first began discussing a book written by women about their experiences in the virtual world of *Second Life*, we envisioned a text that included many different voices and perspectives on what it means to live and work in a virtual world. We knew our own experiences to be extremely diverse, so we believed we could find other women willing and excited to discuss their own unique virtual lives. This book is the result of that belief. Here, the reader will discover essays that deal with a wide range of topics, and while all of the authors have academic credentials, the essays they have written are in a variety of styles. Some are written strictly academically, some are a combination of an academic and creative style, and still others are more creative with an academic undertone. This is the type of book Julie and I strove to put together.

As such, the contributing authors explore topics like the creative process in *Second Life*, issues of virtual identity, replication and creation of culture in virtual environments, education and work in these spaces, and many others. With such a wide array of topics, Julie and I believe that there is something in this text for just about everyone. Whether you are interested in how virtual worlds can be used in education or maybe how identity is created and sustained in these spaces or perhaps how people create in *SL*, you will find something of interest to you here.

As with any endeavor of this size, it would not have been possible without the help and support of friends and loved ones, you know who you are. Julie and I would especially like to thank the authors who contributed their stories and experiences to make this text possible. Without their willingness to share their unique *SL* lives, there would be no book. We would also like to thank them for their dedication and patience throughout this process. A project that includes so many voices is never easy to put together, and certainly not quick. To that end, we would like to thank my graduate research assistant, Simone West, for her perseverance with putting the book together and getting it to the publisher by the deadline. I would personally like to thank Dr. Cynthia Selfe, Dr. Cheryl E. Ball and all the folks at Digital Media and Composition (DMAC) for inviting me to be a visiting scholar in 2010. It was there that the initial book proposal was hatched, and I am grateful for their support and encouragement.

Introduction:
The Big Bang Theory,
or the Creation of *Second Life*

DIANNA BALDWIN *and*

JULIE ACHTERBERG

SL began as a computer program, originally known as *Linden World*, created in 1991 by Philip Rosedale. Rosedale founded the company Linden Labs in 1999, and the beta version of *Second Life* was released in November 2002. It did not go live to the public, however, until June 23, 2003 (Rymaszewski, et al., 1). *SL* began by using a tax structure that charged users based on certain criteria; however, a crackdown on tax evaders that created havoc inworld began what Michael Rymaszewski, et al., refer to as "a grass-roots social movement.... Within a few weeks, a revolution was underway. In December 2003, the revolutionaries won: an entirely new tax system based on land ownership ... was introduced..." (1). This has since morphed into the current free basic membership, which restricts residents from buying property from Linden Labs, and paid premium membership, which allows residents to own land for which they then have to pay a monthly maintenance fee.

Hence the birth of the metaverse (a term originating from Neal Stephenson's 1992 sci-fi novel *Snow Crash* that describes a world with humans as avatars, interacting with one another via software) that is *SL*. This metaverse, according to all accounts, was not Rosedale's intention. According to Wagner James Au, "building the metaverse wasn't even the company's main goal when it began in 1999..." (407–11). Perhaps it was not Rosedale's main goal, but most texts on *SL* refer to it as the metaverse, a world created in words by Stephenson and brought to life virtually by Linden Labs.

Really, What Is a "Second Life"? How It All Began

How is one born into *Second Life*? First off, one starts by creating an avatar for herself/himself, and avatars are not limited to being either male or female; in fact, humanity is not even a requirement as there is an entire community of avies. Avie (AV) is short for avatar, which is the cartoon persona one creates for oneself when entering into a virtual environment. These are often customizable once inworld, or can be changed completely. They include those who call themselves Furries and walk around in *SL* as animal-type avatars as well as robotic or mechanical avies. Even if an avatar one sees is one sex/gender or the other, the real person behind that AV may not be the same sex/gender, and *SL* contains a wide array of gender bending avies. Not only is diversity prevalent, but the possibilities to disrupt traditional norms and roles allow for the collapsing of normal hegemonic power structures that exist in most environments — both real life and online.

With the ability to be someone different comes the very real likelihood that boundaries are crossed or shattered. The hegemonic power structure that keeps men dominant over women, whites dominant over minorities, and the rich dominant over the poor can be reversed, changed, or become non-existent. Here, residents find the freedom to explore power structures and find themselves empowered to do things they would never venture in real life, making *SL* an ideal place to question power structures without the fear of repercussions. Kathleen Fortney notes:

> virtual worlds can enable learners to put on a new persona in a manner that goes far beyond traditional role playing. Consider, for example, the possibilities for delivering diversity awareness education where learners enter as a particular type of avatar to experience firsthand the feeling of being "Different" [85].

Jessica Bennett and Malcolm Beith also argue that *SL* is "a potent medium for socializing — it provides people with a way to express, explore, and experiment with identity, vent their frustrations, reveal alter egos" ("Alternate Universe"). The possibilities in *SL* seem endless, so Julie and I began to wonder how women utilize this environment. Before entering the conversations within this text, though, it is imperative that the reader first understands *SL* as most inworld residents do.

Second Life *Is Just a Game, Right? Actually, It's More Like a World*

Dianna experienced culture shock when she first entered *SL* at Orientation Island, which felt strangely familiar from the computer games she had played throughout life where one learns how to maneuver inside the game. Beyond Orientation Island, however, *SL* is nothing like a game. Dianna has lived and worked in several different countries, and she likens the culture shock she felt in *SL* to what she experienced in the third world country of Angola. Anytime we travel to a new country there is much to learn about the geography, economy, traditions, religions, people, and more. Peter Ludlow and Mark Wallace claim that *SL* "is less a game than a parallel world unto itself" (75). *SL* consists of Welcome Island, Orientation Island, Help Island, Private Regions, Open Spaces, and the Mainland Regions; these are what make up the geography of *SL*. In fact, according to Brian A. White as of January 2007 (now six years old), "*SL* contained virtual land that is the equivalent of over six times the size of New York's Manhattan Island" (5).

It is important to understand that *SL*, like any country in the real world that has its own method of trade — whether it is some form of currency or a barter system — also has an economy. Unlike the various currencies in the real world, *SL* has a digital currency, the Linden dollar, with a single exchange.

Anytime a discussion concerning the economy of *SL* arises, the conversation usually ends with the other person replying, "But it's all just play money, right? Like Monopoly money except you have to buy it using real money!" The normal reply to this is, "Can you take your Monopoly money and exchange it for U.S. dollars?" As White notes, "*SL* has an economy and a currency, the Linden dollar, or L\$. There is an established exchange rate, which allows you to convert real-life currency to *SL* currency (L\$) and vice versa" (254). Statistics on the economy of *SL* can be found at "xChange 4L\$" (https://www.xchange4ls.com/index.php?) where it becomes obvious that people make, spend, and lose money in virtual worlds.

Residents in worlds such as *Everquest*, *World of Warcraft*, or *The Sims Online* create and sell items that allow other residents or players to level up or advance in the game. Even *The Sims Online* is focused on increasing the player's standing in the community and buying a bigger house or car will help a player to achieve these goals. Money is indeed made in these massively multi-user online worlds (MMOs), but it is made behind the backs of the companies that control these worlds. The terms of service for these worlds clearly state that anything created in the game is the sole property of the companies, not the individual creators.

SL does not operate this way. Ludlow and Wallace argue that "perhaps the most important difference between *Second Life* and most other virtual worlds is that *SL*'s terms of service specifically grant residents ownership of the intellectual property right in their creations" (76). This means that residents of *SL* can build and create anything inworld, retain the rights to the object, and sell it inworld or on a website such as Market Place. But *SL*, as mentioned earlier, is not a game like the other popular virtual worlds such as *Everquest* or *World of WarCraft*. Residents do not level up in *SL*. They do not kill monsters, find treasures, nor attempt to impress the neighbors. There are also no goals to attain. So the questions of what people buy and why are valid ones to ask.

For many, the answers to the questions above seem fantastical and unrealistic. If *SL* is not a game and there are no levels to show progress in the world, why would anyone want to spend real money and how could people make real money in this environment? Julian Dibbell begins to shed some light on these inquiries when he writes that *SL*:

> with its wide-openness to user-created architecture, objects, and other in-world content, and its whole-hearted embrace of the real-money trade in virtual properties (...) is striving mightily to leave the games market behind and become, instead, the next-and perhaps final-generation desktop — a globe-spanning virtual realm in which everything from social lives to business plans to artistic movements unfold [107].

Linden Labs, at least in the beginning, understood the concept that "players do not just consume, or act as passive audience members, of the game but instead are active co-creators in producing it as a meaningful experience and artifact" (Taylor, *Play Between Worlds* 133). This world, unlike the others, not only encourages residents to use their creativity to build in this environment, but to actually *live* a second life by participating in a culture that is not so different from our own, regardless of where we reside in real life (RL).

As hinted at by Dibbell, *Second Life* is more than just making and spending money. It is also a creative outlet for many artists, musicians, poets, and others. Nashville, Tennessee's famous Bluebird Cafe streams live video and audio into their *SL* cafe. A search for live music on December 5, 2011, retrieved more than 198 live performances. Several locations, such as Open Mic Poetry Recitals at The Azure and Pagan Poetry offer live poetry readings frequently, and artists display their work in organized events such as TOC Art Gallery. White reports that Circe Broom, a well-known music promoter, states that she is in *SL* "for the music and to help musicians get a break. I was there once and I love music. They need and deserve some help and it makes me feel good!" (qtd. in White 336). *SL* is a place where unknown artists, whether it be musicians, poets, quilters, or someone else with creative flair, can get their work into the mainstream of *SL* and even into RL.

Who Lives a "Second Life"? The Residents of the Metaverse

Often, the first reaction to the residents of *SL* is that the RL people behind the avies have to be die-hard role-playing gamers (RPGers). It does not take long, though, to realize that these assumptions and attempts to stereotype the residents of *SL* are inaccurate. Rymaszewski, et al., devote an entire chapter to twelve *SL* residents and allow them to tell their stories in their own words (196–210). The one characteristic that is strangely missing from these autobiographies is the word "gamer." In fact, the one avie who mentions games, Frank Freelunch, discusses his love of the classic game *Space Invaders* and the fact that he spends time in *SL*'s game emporiums playing these types of games, hardly your typical RPGer. Most of these twelve residents mention every day dreams and desires that they pursue in *SL*. One loves cars and so creates them virtually because she cannot afford them in RL; another created a nineteenth-century island where *SL* residents flocked to live; still another discusses her desire "to set a standard for taste, manners, and a life well-lived while building a personal community that I can be proud of" (Rymaszewski, et al., 203). None of these residents refer to *SL* as a game: no true resident would.

What the residents of *SL* have created for themselves is a community, a culture uniquely their own that matches Bonnie Stone Sunstein and Elizabeth Chiseri-Strater's definition of "culture as an invisible web of behaviors, patterns, rules, and rituals of a group of people who have contact with one another and share common languages"(3). Subcultures also exist in *SL*, ranging from vampires to furries, but it quickly becomes apparent that the overall culture of *SL* is one that Henry Jenkins calls a participatory culture, or one where experiences are turned into "a rich and complex" culture (486–93).

The participatory nature of the culture in *SL* gives everyone a sense of belonging, regardless of the subcultures to which they might belong. In *Textual Poachers*, Jenkins discusses fan culture, in particular the subculture of television fans, and he asserts that this culture "cuts across traditional geographic and generational boundaries and is defined through its particular styles of consumption and forms of cultural preference" (113–17). The same can be said for the residents of *SL*. Its culture transcends the hegemonic boundaries of RL and offers all who reside there a sense of belonging, regardless of any RL attachments.

Women in the Metaverse

The question of gender in the metaverse has been central to a great deal of research on *Second Life* from the beginning. Whether from the perspective of the Girls Game Movement or the Tech Gap and Math/Science Gap research, *Second Life* has been studied as one of the exceptions to the seemingly unbreakable dominance of the male in gaming. Throughout its existence, *SL* has enjoyed a female presence estimated at between 40 and 50 percent of logins

(Philip Rosedale's TED Talk and e-mail from Peter Gray at Linden Labs). In a culture rife with gamer stereotypes that include pimply-faced teenagers and 30-year-old failures-to-launch still living in their parents' basements, the participation of women in any game or platform community is still viewed as atypical and worthy of study.

From Julie's perspective there are several major problems with this presupposition about women, gaming, and the metaverse. First, there have been girls and women in gaming since the beginning. Julie first cut her online gaming teeth in an MMORPG back in 2001 when *Anarchy Online* started their free trial program and by the estimation of her female gamer friends who had been in *EverQuest* for years, Julie's *still* a newbie. (Though she usually retaliates with tales of *Temple of Apshai* from way back in Commodore 64 days.) It was not a casual association she maintained either, as she was a general second only to the president in three different player in-game organizations and played for well over eight years. This was, in fact, the experience that allowed her to navigate *Second Life*'s technological and social environments so easily to start; she had already learned most of the skills necessary in *Anarchy Online*.

The second problem is that *Second Life* isn't actual gaming. In fact, Julie has yet to meet a hard core "gamer" in the traditional sense who didn't run from *Second Life* screaming in frustration after their first login. *Second Life* isn't a game because there's no structure that allows for linear progress toward an end. There's no way to "win" *Second Life*, no levels to navigate, no character skill trees to conquer. *Second Life* is a digital space and has more in common with the chat rooms of the 1980s and the social networks of the last ten years than any genre of digital gaming. *Second Life*, and all virtual worlds since, are essentially 3-D chat rooms melded to a content creation framework. This seems to be, in fact, the reason behind Linden Lab's recent unveiling of *Linden Realms*, a "game" within *Second Life* catering to those who require traditional game structure to interact with the platform.

The fact that so many women participate in *Second Life* compared to traditional MMOs and standalone games has been studied by gaming companies and academia and there are almost as many explanations as research studies. It's become all too easy to assume that women are simply more social than men so a social platform is attractive to women, particularly when looking at larger patterns of gender demographics where women are the dominant presence in both social networks and social gaming. Other explanations of *Second Life*'s female population have included female aversion to competition (Taylor, "Becoming a Player" 51) and freedom from the violence and misogyny endemic to MMOs and standalone games catering to the male gamer stereotype. Also noted has been the less technically demanding user creation tools available to women in the worlds of *Second Life* and *The Sims Online* franchise; to become the designer of your own world doesn't require a graduate degree in coding languages. Is it the ability to "design" and make money or the shopping that appeals to more women? Without the ability to systematically poll *SL* users about their gender and reason for entering the metaverse at each login, there's plenty of room for speculation based on small samples of respondents and anecdotal evidence. In addition, the fact that these reasons are dynamic is often overlooked. A woman logging in to *SL* for the fifth time has radically different reasons than one logging in for her fifth year.

Perhaps most disappointing in all this contemplation of women's participation in the metaverse is the scant information available from women about their own experiences and thoughts about life, work, and play in digital form. While there are studies about what women want in games and even how they behave in virtual environments, there are not nearly so many women explaining their own participation in *Second Life*. Yes, there are respected women in academia studying gender issues in *SL* and other digital spaces in an effort to understand women in gaming and beyond, but few voices from inside the community seem to make their way out to tell us what's really going on there. It's the hope of those contributing here that there might be a few of those voices that make it out ... without filter or interpretation from outside.

Essay Overviews

An exploration of women's involvement in the virtual world of *Second Life* required that our call for papers be open enough to allow for different genres and styles of writing while maintaining an academic tone. To that end, this collection is comprised of essays written by women about their experiences in *SL*, and these essays span a variety of topics and contain everything from poetry and a two act play to more traditional essays. The topics also vary greatly, so we have divided the book into four sections that we believe captures the tone of the essays in that section. The reader will notice, however, that some essays could span across two or more sections, and when this has been the case, we have chosen the section which seems to best represent the overall piece.

The sections are divided as follows: *Life as Avatar, Gender and Race, Work and Education,* and *Culture.* In *Part I: Life as Avatar,* the authors examine how their lives as avatars began or evolved and even, in some instances, how their virtual lives affected their everyday real lives. These essays give a unique view into what it means be a virtual woman. *Part II: Gender and Race* addresses how two women address these very difficult real life topics in *SL,* from creating their avatars to dealing with what it means to be a virtual woman. In the next section, *Part III: Work and Education*, the authors investigate how real life work can be accomplished in a virtual environment both educationally and as a means to enhance one's life. Finally, in *Part IV: Culture*, the first author looks at how one cultural phenomenon is both reproduced and recreated in *SL* while the other author discusses how she achieves a culture of creativity through this virtual space.

PART I: LIFE AS AVATAR

In this section, Christine Ballengee Morris (aka Rain Winkler), from The Ohio State University, writes a dialogue play as response to her own personal ventures in *SL* in which she utilizes a reflective process with an avatar persona. Julie Achterberg (aka Steorling Heron), a high school teacher in mid–Michigan, writes about the role of "digital geisha." J. A. Brown, Meg Y. Brown, and Jennifer Regan, students and former students from the University of Kentucky, pay special attention to the fluidity of "body-building" in this virtual world.

PART II: GENDER AND RACE

Concerning the complicated issues of race and gender in *SL*, Carleen D. Sanchez (aka Adventurette Constantine), an associate professor of anthropology from Austin Community College, addresses the experiences of women of color attempting to "perform" their ethnic identity. Jennifer J. Reed (aka Jamie Pluvences), a doctoral student at the University of Nevada, Las Vegas, examines the experiences of women of color attempting to "perform" their ethnic identity, as well as the gendered (re)production of emotion work and feeling issues of *SL*.

PART III: WORK AND EDUCATION

Women's experiences with work and education are also well represented with Dianna Baldwin (aka ZoeB McMillan), associate director of the Writing Center at Michigan State University, recounting both the excitement and frustrations of taking her first-year composition students into *SL*. Kara Bennett, Ph.D. (aka Dancers Yao), and Susan Patrice, M.D. (aka Kasuku Magic), explore ways virtual world environs can encourage learning about the importance of including human rights in health care. Phylis Johnson, professor at Southern Illinois University, examines the world of news media in *Second Life* through the lens of those women behind the bylines and in front of the camera. Suzanne Aurilio, director of Technology Enhanced Instruction and Faculty

Support in the College of Extended Studies at San Diego State University, investigates the potential for *SL* in teaching and learning.

PART IV: CULTURE

Finally, the book will cover the topic of art and creative writing in *Second Life*. Amanda Grace Sikarskie (aka Ione Tigerpaw), a doctoral student at Michigan State University, investigates the art of quilting, while Patricia A. Facciponti (aka Franchella Milena), former associate director of public information at Lafayette College, investigates poetry as a creative process to describe her experiences as a female avatar in the metaverse.

The Future

The death of the *SL* metaverse has long been rumored, and the truth is that many things have changed about this virtual environment since the beginning of this project. Things such as no longer offering educators a discount to purchase islands at a time when most colleges and universities are experiencing deep budget cuts has not helped those educators embrace the possibilities of *SL*. The Linden Lab Company also decided to do away with their teen grid and open up the main grid to anyone 16 or older. It also seems as if Linden Labs no longer wants users to know the statistics of the online environment. At one time, stats such as how many people were logged in when you went to sign on and how many users were registered were displayed, as if proudly, on the main log in screen. Now, however, such stats are nearly impossible to find and some, such as users logged in during the past 60 days, are no longer available online, and current stats are nearly impossible to find.

Would the demise of *Second Life* mean the end of all metaverses? Not likely. Once the popularity of *Second Life* became apparent, others began to replicate and alter the original design. The world of *OpenSimulator* or *OpenSim* (opensimulator.org) soon sprang into existence where one could download and install their own virtual world on their own servers and not have to pay anyone to own a world, much less an island. The main issue with *OpenSim* is that it is much harder to connect with others outside of your own server(s). While something known as the hypergrid does exist that allows users to connect to others servers, the options are limited and finding others online at the same time can be difficult.

Another option available to those who truly want to experiment and play with virtual environments like *Second Life* is *InWorldz* (inworldz.com). The first thing one will notice about *InWorldz* is that their website looks very similar to the original *Second Life* website. Here, it is completely free to set up an avatar, as it is in *Second Life*, with the main difference being that one does not have to have a premium paid account to buy land. The second major difference is that the cost to buy and maintain land is much cheaper. The world itself, however, looks much like that of *SL* and is slowly gaining new members.

This book focuses on the experiences of women in *Second Life*, but that is only because other options at the time this project began were somewhat limited. For anyone wanting to do more than build or create, *SL* is still the virtual environment that offers the most in terms of social interaction and experiencing what it means to truly live a second life.

Works Cited

Au, Wagner James. *The Making of Second Life: Notes from the New World*. New York: Harper-Collins e-books, 2008. eBook.

Bennett, Jessica, and Malcolm Beith. "Alternate Universe: Why Millions Are Living Virtual Lives Online." Newsweek Web Exclusive 2007: n. Page. Web. 01 Aug. 2007. <http://www.newsweek.com/id/32824/page/1>.

Dibbell, Julian. Introduction. *Alter Ego: Avatars and Their Creators*. London: Chris Boot, 2007. Print.

Fortney, Kathleen. "Using *Second Life* to Provide Corporate Blended Learning Solutions." *Second Life* Education Workshop, *Second Life* Community Convention. Chicago Hilton, Chicago, IL. 24–26 Aug. 2007. Print.

Jenkins, Henry. *Textual Poachers: Television Fans & Participatory Culture*. New York: Routledge, 1992. eBook.

Ludlow, Peter, and Mark Wallace. *The Second Life Herald: The Virtual Tabloid That Witnessed the Dawn of the Metaverse*. Cambridge: MIT Press, 2007. Print.

Rymaszewski, Michael, et al. *Second Life: The Official Guide*. Indianapolis: Wiley, 2007. Print.

Sunstein, Bonnie Stone, and Elizabeth Chiseri-Strater. *FieldWorking: Reading and Writing Research*. 3d ed. Boston: Bedford/St. Martin's, 2007. Print.

Taylor, T. L. "Becoming a Player: Networks, Structure, and Imagined Futures." *Beyond Barbie & Mortal Kombat: New Perspectives on Gender and Gaming*. Ed. Yasmin B. Kafai, Carrie Heeter, Jill Denner, and Jennifer Y. Sun. Cambridge, MIT Press, 2008. Print.

_____. *Play Between Worlds: Exploring Online Game Culture*. Cambridge: MIT Press, 2006. Print.

White, Brain A. *Second Life: A Guide to Your Virtual World*. Indianapolis: Que, 2008. Print.

A Rainy Afternoon:
A Reflective Process
Utilizing an Avatar Persona

CHRISTINE BALLENGEE MORRIS

In this narrative inquiry, the lived experience comes from both a virtual space (*Second Life*) and real life. The avatar (Rain) and the maker (Christine) explore identity construction, aesthetics, and notions of aging and appearance. This research is expressed in an arts-based format, a play, so that the process of internal dialogue is revealed through two characters and serves as an example of valuing the multiple voices that are within each of us. This play investigates the nature of societal influence and its impact on one's identity, recognizing the facets and roles in all of us, and transformative power. This type of presentation and self-exploration serves as an example for epistemological and ontological positioning and curriculum possibilities.

Prelude: Text Play as an Arts-based Research

Narrative inquiry is influenced by the Deweyan notion that life is education. Connelly and Clandinin were first to use the term *narrative inquiry* as a research methodology that through story construction, life experiences (textual and/or visual) can form "theoretical ideas about the nature of human life" (3). Narrative inquiries require one to explore and relate personal practices and reflections to social theory and systems. I chose to tell a narrative within an arts-based methodology because I believe this approach encourages a more critical form of reflection and introspection of my experiences and emotions. Carol Ellis, an educator and narrative inquiry theorist, recently stated she chose a narrative, dialogic representation because it illustrated the debates that were happening in her mind about "the process and ethics of writing

these stories" (3). She further explains that a narrative inquiry that is intro-
spective reveals "...vulnerable, muddy, and ambivalent process of making ethical decisions in qualitative research" (3). In her article, she explores her two
inner voices through a conversation format with her ego and alter ego. It was
her desire that through this methodological approach and writing process her
thoughts and positioning would be clearer for her and provide an opportunity
for readers to view her thought process as she worked out issues. It is this
type of narrative methodology that I utilize to explore my ego (Christine)
and alter ego (Rain) in relationship to society's concepts of aging and the
internalizations of those concepts that Christine and Rain act out in this arts-
based drama.

Arts-based research theorists Tom Barone and Elliot Eisner identify an
arts-based approach to inquiry as having "the presence of certain aesthetic
qualities or design elements that infuse the inquiry and its writing" (73). Arts-
Based Educational Research (ABER) has the potential in its poetic, narrative,
and/or visual presentation of research to engage its audience to revisit their
positions and assumptions toward, in this case, embracing the psychological
and physicality of aging. Barone contends that exploring ideas within a "novel
outlook, perspective, paradigm, and ideology" provides opportunities to view
one's thoughts differently (173). Taking Barone's idea into consideration, a
dialogue approach between my alter-ego avatar and myself reveals my virtual
identity construction, as well as my assimilated social assumptions about aging
and my preoccupation with looking backward to move forward syndrome.
This type of narrative play format also provides readers an opportunity to
experience from vicarious positions and stimulates self-exploration.

Stories, according to Daniel Pink, are the methods by which we as human
beings "are freer to seek a deeper understanding of ourselves and our purpose"
(113). Transformation and dialogues that occur between self and self, and self
and others, demand a dialogic presentation that arts-based methodology provides. In this text play, I explore my self as self and self as an avatar, through
personal reflections of creating and performing my avatar and as I work out
several voices within the virtual space exploring concepts of aging in the real
world. As a tool for self-reflection and alter ego, the avatar has its own voice,
persona, and perspective, which I use to voice my perceptions of aging. Since
the avatar is created by me, my multiple voices as a Cherokee, Appalachian,
middle-class, wife, mother, grandmother, sister, daughter, professor, dancer,
and artist, to name a few identifiers, and the issues of voice and silence, impact
my perceptions of identity. A key to this is the idea of perspective (place in
the world, identity, and worldview), which perspective/position is in effect,
and the inter-play. The text play is also a pedagogical approach that I offer
as an example, and conclude this presentation of my narrative inquiry with

a discussion of the implications of such an approach to learning and teaching about visual culture and gender constructions. I utilize a standard play format.

ACT 1, SCENE 1

(Rain's Inworld.[1] *It is a bright sunny morning — no clouds in the sky. Sitting outside of a café, by the pool, Rain begins reflecting with her creator, Christine, and several close avatars, one being Brooke.)*

RAIN

My name is Rain Winkler, and I live in *Second Life* (*SL*). I am forever young, tall, and curvaceous. I dance, watch movies, teach, and visit exhibitions. Life is without stress, and for the most part, I concentrate on me. I was born February 2007. I have had hundreds of transformations. My appearance began as a standard template avatar until I graduated from Orientation Island.[2]

Christine and I have explored our process of developing as an avatar and what that means in Real Life (RL). She is especially interested in the idea of visual aesthetics in relationship to *SL* and RL identities. My part in her research is to provide alternative experiences that resist social constructs around aging — avatars can stop the clock — the sun can always shine — life is without stress, pain, and poverty.

(In RL, Christine sits in an antique rocker, at a very old library table, with photos of her family surrounding her laptop. She stares at her Cherokee regalia that hang on a wall and a collage of grandson images that brings a smile to her face. She watches Rain dance around in her world and proceeds to express herself in her academic voice by writing, pausing every once in a while to command Rain to dance one more time).

CHRISTINE

As an avatar creator, I have spent time contemplating the impact and possible applications of a virtual space like *Second Life*. The company, Linden Labs, is headquartered in San Francisco and employs 250 people across the United States, Europe, and Asia. *Second Life* is a three-dimensional virtual world that was launched in 2003. Ondrejka stated:

> From the shape of their avatars to the design of their homes, from how they spend their time to what types of affinity groups they form; *Second Life's* design was focused on fostering creativity and self-expression in order to create a vibrant and dynamic world full of interesting content [1].

The designers' vision of *Second Life*[3] was to create a space where a person can build an avatar and spaces that function as in the real world. The hundreds of thousands of residents from over 50 countries have opportunities to interact among 12,000 virtual acres that include a variety of activities and members. According to the explanation online, "*Second Life* is a free online virtual world imagined and created by its Residents. From the moment you enter *Second Life*, you'll discover a fast-growing digital world filled with people, entertainment, experiences and opportunity" (Linden Lab 20).

Second Life provides opportunities for participants to create identities that could be free from societal and physical limitations of ethnicity, gender, geography, sexual orientation or status, and yet key to this virtual world is its capitalist and sexual overtones. When I started this research in 2009, Linden Labs, the company who developed *Second Life*, stated that "There are hundreds of organizations currently in *Second Life*, including many Fortune 1000 companies and government institutions" (Linden Lab 20). Companies such as *IBM, Starwood Hotels,* and *MTV* have virtual stores, but there are also small businesses, theaters, art galleries, social clubs, universities, and even an international art education association in *SL*.

Many of the cultural constructs within *Second Life* appear to be Western manifestations. To purchase items in *Second Life,* money (Linden dollars) must be earned or can be bought with RL money. Capitalist consumption possibilities are available around every corner. Some individuals challenge the capitalism mentality by offering for free items such as body parts and home furnishings. I do not buy items. I find it more interesting to obtain my items for free or to make my own. But actually that is how I am in RL—second hand stores are favorite hunting grounds.

Through the process of building virtual embodied lives, with accessories such as pets and homes, there is a possibility that boundaries and a sense of self and identity challenge the concept of reality. Virtual worlds provide opportunities to transcend beyond the realities of RL human flesh through customization and to face the temptation to build an ideal body that becomes the preferred self.

(Christine reviews what she has written and is tired of talking about SL. *She quickly sneaks a peak of her lovely grandson and goes back inworld.)*

(Rain and Brooke are lounging around on Brooke's Island. Brooke's maker sends Christine a snapshot of herself and then settles into a conversation with Rain.)

RAIN

While I was attending a film premier at Sundance, I met Freeze. He said that some of the big corporations that are in this world are collecting research so that they can apply what they learn in RL. Buying habits and styles are emerging interests. Oh, I also learned that many avatars want to talk about their identity construction and development. One of my friends, Brooke, communicated her thoughts about virtual identities.

BROOKE

My creator purposefully made me the way she would like to look in RL. So, I suppose as you look at me, you can think of the opposite and you will be able to picture her — except the gender of course. She says that no matter what she does, she has a hard time overlooking the fact that she is female. I do have a brother though. Tinderbox Ember is my creator's male avatar. My identity — hmmm.... I'm powerful as evidenced by my stature. I am many races, but primarily I am of the earth, (albeit virtual, I know ... this world is full of contradictions! Don't you love it?).

RAIN

(To Christine) As she states, Brooke is the fundamental nature of her creator. Gender choices in *SL* are limited to male or female; since Brooke's creator desires to explore both genders, she is forced to create two avatars — one female and one male.

(Rain shifts her conversation from Christine to Brooke.)

I am very female. Brooke, the template used for me was a female club dancer. My body type choices included height, breast and hip size, short to long legs, hair, skin color, eye shape and color, make-up and dance moves. My creator challenges herself by having me behave and think in ways that are not available to her in the real world. I am her alter ego, unlike your creator viewing you as the fundamental nature. I also have a male brother called Snow, but his physical appearance and personality have not been developed. Our maker has not identified with him yet. My persona, unlike my creator, is spontaneous, playful, and youthful. As I move through *SL* I am not concerned with daily chores, schedules, responsibilities or obligations. If I feel like dancing in the middle of a meeting, I do. If I feel like leaving, I do. I am about being — Christine refers to this as her teen philosophy for living.

(Sipping on club soda and lemon, Christine contemplates Rain and Brooke's stated experiences and how much their experiences align with other avatars.)

CHRISTINE

(Softly ponders) What is it about Rain that resonates with me? What role does she play? Don't I have enough cultural indicators that I desire a virtual one or two? Gender exploration is a part of the original movement within *Second Life*— not being constrained by the norms that are present in RL and yet, those who can't let go, maintain inhibitions in *SL*. Hum, am I doing that?

(As she begins to write, her Mac makes the "you have mail" sound, and she sees that it is an article that she has been anticipating by Christine Liao.)

I have just finished reading Liao's article in volume 3 of the *Visual Culture & Gender*, "My Metamorphic Avatar Journey." She attempted to create a gender ambiguous avatar. In the beginning of her research, she was exploring the technical inabilities of creating a genderless avatar. Her inworld experiences, which included ridicule from other avatars to being kicked off a site because she was gender ambiguous, led her to emotional and personal explorations. She found that in the process of becoming genderless, she tried to detach herself from her avatar. She states:

> However, the more I tried to separate my feelings from my avatar, the more I felt the impossibility of doing so, if the avatar body were nothing to me, I would not care about how it looks. But I do. I realize that I did not want other people to see my avatar with a gender ambiguous body [Liao 31].

Pamela G. Taylor, B. Stephen Carpenter, and I explored avatar development in an unpublished manuscript and in a presentation at The National Art Education Association Convention in New Orleans, 2008. We contend that the virtual body becomes a part of the participant's identity. When referring to her avatar, Taylor uses the pronoun "I." Carpenter refers to his avatar by name — "Metaphor," whereas, I move back and forth between first and third person in referring to my actions and thoughts, and those of my avatar Rain. The three different relationships we have with our avatars reflect the complex discourse of identity and the relationships faced by users and their avatars in virtual worlds. As Liao concludes, we as creators care about the visual representation/identity of our avatars.

(The sun is changed to a noon light and Rain is transported to an SL *library. Rain proceeds to explore identity development and social presence theory. Lounging under her favorite tree, Rain contemplates and continues the dialogue.)*

RAIN

Christine, as my creator, you seem to be motivated in the making. For others it is the social aspect, but you seem to want to know the possibilities, and I demonstrate what those are in *SL*. At the Communication and Information Technologies mini-conference of the American Sociology Association in *Second Life* on August 12, 2007, identity was explored and defined by Magallan Egoyan. Egoyan explained that social presence theory is the process by which someone comes to know and think about other people's characteristics qualities, which can lead to a better perception of oneself and others (9). This is considered one of the first theories of communication media, which explores interpersonal involvement. *SL* identity is viewed as performative and is determined by the quality of interactions with others and its relational capabilities and interpersonal exchanges. Attendees discussed identity as a related concept that is intertwined with presence and how avatars relate to other avatars or makers. Some stated that since humans are transformative through culture, we are virtual and virtual is essential to the real.

CHRISTINE

I often think that identity in *SL* is performative; therefore, it lends toward the first/third social presence. How does one synchronize one's real life and second life? I read on the Learning Technologies Conference Blog on the backlash of *Second Life* and Chester and Breterton conclude "cyberspace is not a virtual world without connection to the rest of people's lives. What we do and who we are online are shaped consciously and unconsciously by who we are offline. The Internet is, after all a part of our real life" (Learning Technologies Conference Blog 9).

BROOKE

Rain, my creator likes the making and prefers to merge our identity into one. But we are performative in a limited basis, since the Island is invitation only. We enjoy creating, which is a solo act for us sometimes.

RAIN

Christine is always fussing and making sure I receive attention from the other avatars. So, although she states it is the creating, there is always a desire to meet and greet. Now, I would like to get back to my book. By the way, I am wearing a pair of Prada-like shoes, a skirt and top that Christine designed for celebrating a great political year. (Whispering) I have matching thongs and wings (to illustrate my flightiness), which a friend gave to me.

(Wishing that she could spend a day laying in the grass and reading a book, Christine continues writing and realizing that she is beginning to go to a place that is uncomfortable. She goes through her iTunes and decides on listening to a collection of songs that are calming and proceeds to write.)

CHRISTINE

Very few avatars illustrate age beyond 30, excessive weight, receding hairlines, and etcetera. Most strive for an ideal of beauty that focuses on being young, toned, and white. In Steven Holtzman's book, *Digital Mosaics: The Aesthetics of Cyberspace*, he explores examples of cyber-art and the aesthetic principles utilized, which focus on nonlinearity, disruption, and autonomy. Endless possibilities and timelessness of experiences and narrative are key components of cyber aesthetics. The term *virtual aesthetics* explores the idea that one can create new conceptions of reality, identity, and sexuality that actually explores or ignores issues in one's RL. Virtual aesthetics is also interactive, relational, and centers on exploration of self and others through dialogue and sharing of stories, space, and experiences. Through Rain, I learn about areas of my self that remain silent in RL. Through careful analysis, I can identify emerging themes in RL that are explored in *SL*. Since I was four, I understood ethnic difference, cultural borders, and bi-tri-cultural understandings, which strongly influenced my identity development and career choices. As my life chronologically progressed, the volume or silence of the internal voices of each role and identity entity was expressed according to external needs. Through Rain, I remain young, in great shape, free to be spontaneous without guilt, and have relationships with others that span multiple communities. The difference between my RL and *SL* experience is the ability to manage one's identity and social presence in *SL* due to the lack or rejection of outside interference.

(Christine pauses and realizes that she has arrived at a place that requires further examination about aesthetics and the virtual place. Rain is transported to Brooke's Island, since she is an invited guest and decides to relax in a lounger within an environment that encourages contemplation. Christine does an Internet search and finds a few sites to share.)

CHRISTINE

In one, Lev Manovich states:

> Another aesthetic feature of virtual worlds lies in their peculiar temporal dynamic: constant, repetitive shifts between an illusion and its suspense. Virtual worlds keep reminding us about their artificiality, incompleteness, and constructedness. They present us with a perfect illusion only to reveal the underlying machinery next [par. 10].

He continues his exploration with an example of his idea of virtual aesthetics that connects some Residents (members of *Second Life*) needs to duplicate the RL, the relational component, and the capitalistic foundations of the site:

> The best place to experience the whole gestalt is in one of the outdoor cafes on Sunset Plaza in West Hollywood. The avatars sip cappuccino amidst the illusion of 3D space. The space is clearly the result of a quick compositing job: billboards and airbrushed café interior in the foreground against a detailed matte painting of Los Angeles with the perspective exaggerated by haze. The avatars strike poses, waiting for their agents (yes, just like cyberspace) to bring valuable information. Older customers look even more computer generated, their faces bearing traces of extensive face-lifts. You can enjoy the scene while feeding the parking meter every twenty minutes. A virtual works is waiting for you; all we need is your credit card number [par. 15].

RAIN

I've been there but I don't have an agent — they cost money. Well, I hate to interrupt your academic contemplations, but the other day, Brooke and I were talking about this, and for her it is the possibilities that are important to Brooke's aesthetic and identity development; she said:

BROOKE

Well, even though I vehemently proclaim ... why represent RL exactly the way it is in a virtual world? I understand that there needs to be recognizable metaphors, or people would simply be confused all the time and not be able to maneuver through this virtual world. That said I like to use the fact that the constraints of the real world do not limit us in this virtual world — for example, gravity, weight, oxygen. I love building in the sky and underwater — I love participating in art exhibits that literally transform me into another being or another place or literally tie me in knots.

RAIN

Brooke is an example of the virtual disruption and possibilities that Holtzman states are elements that define this type of aesthetics, which serve as an attraction to be a part of this world as a creator.

CHRISTINE

Timelessness is a creative motivator for me. I struggle with the idea of aging in RL, and the idea of being able to escape the gray skies in *SL* is enticing. And possibly the word *escape* is not correct, but actually an obsession with *transcending age* is better stated. As a middle-aged woman and a grandmother of 4, the idea of being *sexy and desirable* seems to be fleeting with every ache and pain with which age rewards me, so an ageless, forever-young avatar is alluring and eases me into accepting the inevitable.

RAIN

I could be a grandmother, but in *Second Life* wearing one's age is not mandatory. Identities are easily transformed and transcended, but there is a limitation regarding how old I can be or how heavy I can be due to technology.

CHRISTINE

I was reading the *International Herald Tribune* when I was in Japan on August 11, 2008, and Aaron Britt wrote, "*Second Life* avatar does and is precisely what the player wants, not just a little Mario who can be made to run and jump or a shapely diva gyrating of her own programmed will, it comes far closer to being a full-fledged virtual persona" (10).

RAIN

I heard that there was a conference this past August in the Netherlands at the Royal Academy of Arts and Sciences, and the participants explored identity in virtual worlds. I understand that the central focus was that spaces, such as *Second Life*, give those in RL the possibility to become someone completely different or, conversely, expose oneself to the world. One can explore questions, such as: How is identity created in virtual worlds? What does it mean for privacy and self-image? Does the virtual world have an influence on our real world? Why are people using different identities, anyway? All of these questions are what you ask, Christine.

CHRISTINE

You are right, Rain, I have explored some of those questions already, but the one that intrigues me at this moment is the impact that virtual worlds have on real worlds. For me, one of the attractions is that it has a parallel or alternate reality; for instance, although the language is *SL* or RL, I approach my avatar and myself as interchangeable (at times), meaning we become WE. The appearance choices within *SL* are hypersexuality and agelessness. In RL, I have been as transformative and disruptive as this world will allow and have embraced as many age defying tools as my checking account will support. From green, blue, hazel, and gold eyes and from black to blonde hair, Botox, skin rejuvenations, peels, and scrubs, I have struggled to maintain a dewy but "aging-gracefully" appearance. In the virtual world, it is much cheaper to maintain your youthfulness, Rain. The difference is that in the virtual world, one can transform with a click of the mouse. However, creating visual identities within *Second Life* can also be time consuming. I have spent up to six hours designing clothes, hair, makeup, and shoes.

RAIN

This sets up a value towards an avatar's identity. The more time we spend with our avatars, Heim posits, the more meaning and value we place on them (51). Our virtual body, like our real one, is judged by our appearance and then how we perform. I have had up to eight shades of skin, eyes and 60 hairstyles in a month's time. My makeup and hair color are frequently changed, depending upon the outfit Christine has created. I have a variety of clothing and shoes that reflect my activities, such as swimming, ballroom dancing, disco, political activities; I have casual looks to attend movies and wild inventions that have yet to find the right event, but I wear them anyway, everywhere. I often send postcards to RL that capture my looks and the places I visit. With an easy push of a button that shutters a snapshot in the virtual world, I can be transported to a new space; I can capture the Kodak moment and share in RL.

(And with a click, Rain transports to a gallery and stops and talks with a few of the avatars that she sees at other galleries. Rain flies over the gallery to find a more private space and lands on top of a nearby building. Looking down onto the road, she reflects more deeply.)

CHRISTINE

The impact of aging and the struggles with remaining young are significant in my identity development, which means I have not escaped the power of media representation and its construction of "reality." Why are standards of beauty (and age) imposed on women? Research indicates that the roots are economic. In the Quebec Action Network for Women's Health in its 2001 report *Changements sociaux en faveur de la diversité des images corporelles,* "Age is a disaster that needs to be dealt with. By presenting an ideal difficult to achieve and maintain the cosmetic and diet product industries are assured of growth and profits" (21). Was it the Barbie I played with and had hoped that I would be as beautiful one day as her? The models that I see every day in magazines and television become younger while I become older. Sandy Landis conducted an analysis of media representations and some of her findings included:

> In the May 21, 2002, issue of *Family Circle,* of the approximately 185 identifiable faces in illustrations, 15, or 8 percent, were conceivably over 55 years of age. Of fifteen representations, four were part of the same story, and seven, nearly half, were connected with products or services to help with the "problems" of aging: arthritis, anemia, incontinence, and wrinkles [21].
>
> Of the approximately 177 identifiable faces in the June 2002, issue of *Better Homes and Gardens,* 22, or 12 percent were feasibly over 55. Of these 22 "old" faces, three appeared in a single movie ad, and five were advertising health products for the elderly [21].
>
> In the June 2002 issue of *Good Housekeeping,* of the approximately 159 identifiable faces, only ten, or 6 percent were likely to be over 55. Of these ten older faces, three appeared in one advertisement for an upcoming film release and four were advertising health remedies for the aged [21].
>
> In the June 4, 2002, edition of *Woman's Day,* 24 of 229 identifiable faces, or 10 percent, were possibly over 55. Of these 24 older faces, ten appeared in a single photograph and five were advertising health products for the elderly [21].

(Humm!) But can this really be just about appearance?

RAIN

I live in a world without age, which functions as an equalizer, which is empowering. Christine, you have had to work so hard to be seen from a position that gave you voice, position, and playfulness. It seems that in RL, those elements are hard to combine, while in *SL* it is easy.

CHRISTINE

You are right, Rain. My earliest power struggle in wanting to express myself was when I was 4 years old, and I wanted to pick out my own outfits. My mother told me "no." Well, I packed everything I could fit in the empty, round oatmeal container and set out to run away. I got to the corner and realized that it was as far as I could go because I was not allowed to cross the street. As I turned around, I saw my mother waiting and I ran to her crying. It was a big step for me and for her. She negotiated a deal where I could lay out my outfits every night, and she would approve. Soon, I gained her confidence, and my empowerment began. But it hasn't always been that easy to maintain, even in areas of appearance (which seems shallow, at times, to talk about). I remember when I went through a stage of my life when my hair was streaked with unusual colors for RL, like pink, fire engine red, green, purple or blue. I was also an administrator. I could see people looking at me and knew that my playfulness with color was disturbing. People would say with mock admiration, "Gee, I wish I could be that colorful." When the provost also asked me about my pink highlights, I stated they were cultural. But I understood these questions and the not-so-subtle messages that they carried. So I changed the hair to a more realistic color to conform. My creative and playful voice was tucked into an internal space, and it has taken *Second Life* to bring it back out.

RAIN

Do you think, when you stated it was cultural, that your answer had elements of truth in it, and you just thought you were being a smarty-pants because your job was working with diverse groups of people as an advocate?

CHRISTINE

Well, Rain, you may have something. Cross (75) suggests that identity is a cognitive map that functions in a multitude of ways to guide and direct exchanges with one's social and material realities. Through MMORPGs (Massively Multiplayer Online Role Playing Games), aspects of our personal cultural identity are shared through stories, with different social groups that creators choose. The power is that there are choices — autonomy. A person's existence and participation within these groups are often the bases for positions of power and, like RL, can lead to violence or discrimination.

(Christine realizes that Rain serves in several roles that are deeply connected to the identities that remain partially invisible in RL. Leaning back in her rocker and turning the music off, she glances at the clock and realizes that this self-exploration must end.)

CHRISTINE

The question becomes, is this type of learning transferable? Can I, as a creator, learn from the process of creating the avatar? Isn't that one of the questions that the conference in the Netherlands asked?

RAIN

Yes it is. You mentioned Cross (76) and in the same article, he contends that, from birth, the individual mirrors behaviors; maturation results from continued human interaction through images and language.

CHRISTINE

Well, according to Cross (76), the effects of images and language shape the innate characteristics of identity development. Judith Butler contends that identities are perpetually performed and are never fully complete or stable, but they are continually becoming and repeatedly enacted. *SL* is one way of performing and transforming.

(Rain stretches her body and transports to an undisclosed Island and decides to float in the pool).

RAIN

I have been told that there have been several researchers within *Second Life* who have argued that the use of games in the classroom engage and provide opportunities to explore identity development that transfer to RL.

CHRISTINE

As you know, Rain, I have taught in *Second Life* through you. In an unpublished manuscript with Taylor and Carpenter, I wrote about this project. You are eloquent in your description; could you restate it?

RAIN

We teach a course that explores identity, race, sexual orientation and gender that occurs in *SL* and RL. My students document and analyze their avatar development in *SL*. As I lecture to the students inworld, Christine demonstrates how to create avatars, and she has her students record each decision, from type of avatar to eye color. She asks them to explain how close their decisions were based on their real appearances. They journal as they proceed through Orientation Island and meet other new avatars. I encourage the students to talk to other avatars, particularly about their avatar construction process. Once the students join *SL*, I take them on field trips to places that specialize in exhibiting race, gender, and sexually oriented visual culture. Through interactive spaces and film presentations, they explore such recreated concepts as stereotyping in *SL*. Interestingly, discussions in *SL* seem to flow more freely and openly than in real life. After only one week in *SL*, students felt comfortable enough to explore difficult diversity issues that would typically take almost 6 weeks for students to feel safe enough to discuss in a real life classroom. Scholars in *Second Life* state that one reason for this openness is that students remain anonymous inworld — only the professor/teacher know both identities.

CHRISTINE

Thank you, Rain. This type of exploration takes virtual aesthetics to a deeper level based on the belief that *SL* can transfer knowledge to RL. Nakamura used the framework of "visual culture studies to focus on the ways that users of the Internet collaboratively produce digital images of the body ... in the context of racial and gender identity formation" (5). Further, Nakamura urges scholars to consider the Internet "as a popular environment for representations of identity" (5). The social, cultural, racial, gender, age, sexual, and other contexts through which identity is constructed, interpreted, and negotiated all find new territory and relevance within virtual worlds such as *SL*. Constructing an avatar, analyzing the decisions that are made, creating dialogic opportunities with self and others about the context of identity formation such as in the form of a play in RL or *SL* can encourage knowing truths through paradoxes and juxtapositions.

Other opportunities that *SL* provides encourage global connections and collaborative projects because travel is a click. On the educational page of *Second Life,* it describes the educational opportunities as:

> Hundreds of leading universities and school systems around the world use *Second Life* as a vibrant part of their educational programs. Linden Lab works enthusiastically with education organizations to familiarize them with the benefits of virtual worlds, connect them with educational peers active in *Second Life,* and showcase their inworld projects and communities [Linden Labs 21].
>
> A large, active education community — with hundreds of K–12 and higher education members — are engaged in *Second Life.* The Open University, Harvard, Texas State, and Stanford are just a few of the many universities that have set up virtual campuses where students can meet, attend classes, and create content together [Linden Labs 21].
>
> *Second Life* has also proven a valuable professional development medium for educators. Organizations such as the NMC have fostered shared learning among educators and are networking, running inworld seminars, conferences and symposia on learning and creativity related to virtual worlds [Linden Labs 21].

Engaging with *Second Life* challenges educators and learners with different sorts of questions and experiments that, in addition to being more relevant to today's digitally literate students, trigger meaningful critically reflective teaching and learning practices. In other words, working in *SL* makes us constantly question, think, and imagine. And isn't that what art education is all about?

RAIN

I have had a great time exploring all of this with you, but I must go. One of my friends has sent me a calling card, and I really want to go to check out the new educational Island. Bye.

(And with a click, Rain transports to TELR Island and begins socializing with other educator avatars. A sunset is added so that the two worlds are in sync.)

CHRISTINE

We cannot stop the clock — almost, but not quite. So is a space that allows that illusion the next best space? What does that really say about society?

What does it say about me? It is not really the age that bothers me but mortality. I enjoy life, as many of us do, and I can't imagine life without me and me without life. I will miss it; and possibly, for a little while, it will miss me too. Until then, I will continue looking backward to move forward, my exploration of transformation and the endless possibilities of creating in a space that seems timeless and forgiving. And possibly, I'll find ways to bring back my humor and lighthearted ways of behavior in RL. With a click *it* was gone and with another click *it* can be born.

> *(Christine quickly saves the document and playfully names it "A Raining Afternoon: Growing Younger and Wiser." She pushes the sleep button and lowers the laptop's monitor, which reveals another snapshot of her grandchildren; she smiles. She rocks out of the chair and stretches her legs, arms, and neck, hearing slight cracks, and she moans. She slowly walks to the bathroom and stares at the image, running her hand through her hair.)*

CHRISTINE

Maybe I will darken my hair a little, since summer is almost over. Darker hair will go better with the new blue contacts.

Epilogue: This Experience

I found that in participating in a dialogue with myself, which we do privately, but rarely publicly, the process allowed me to consider other possibilities, issues, and avenues that were not necessarily written down in this document. This narration first surfaced this fall in two venues that became a part of the dialogue. The first was the interaction with Karen Keifer Boyd and Deborah Smith, editors for *Visual Culture and Gender Journal*. It was their critical eye and deep understanding of visual worlds that pushed the ideas in this paper and led me to understand that this play was a slice of time. The second showing was in Beth Thomas's class. This play was used in her art education course and then I became the blogging professor for a week. The dialogues revealed resistance to visual worlds as an art form or educational space. During the week, we explored thought processes, critical thinking, games and the relevancy, development of self and ideas of reflexivity, flexibility, and change. This clearly models identity in that our identity is momentarily a set of constructs that change constantly due to multiple variables — many, which are not in our control. A reflective process, like this, can provide a way to understand the complexities and ambiguities of identity and culture. It was my desire that through this methodological approach and writing process my thoughts and positioning would be clearer in relationship to society's

concepts of aging and the internalizations of those concepts that Christine
and Rain act out in this arts-based drama.

Notes

1. This term is used to designate when one is in *Second Life.*
2. Orientation Island is where all new avatars can go to become introduced to the skills
of walking, flying, scripting, and policies in *Second Life.*
3. See http://lindenlab.com/

Works Cited

Barone, Tom. "The Purposes of Arts-based Educational Research." *International Journal of Educational Research* 23.2 (1995): 169–180. Print.
_____, and Elliott Eisner. "Arts-based Educational Research." *Complementary Methods for Research in Education.* Eds. R. M. Jaeger and Tom Barone. Washington, DC: American Educational Research Association, 1997. 73–98. Print.
Britt. A. "*Second Life.*" *International Herald Tribune* 11 August 2008: A10. Print.
Butler, Judith. *Gender Trouble: Feminism and the Subversion of Identity.* New York: Routledge, 1990. Print.
Connelly, F. M., and D. Jean Clandinin. "Stories of Experience and Narrative Inquiry." *Educational Researcher* 19.5 (1990): 2–14. Print.
Cross, William, E., Jr. "The Psychology of Nigrescence: Revising the Cross Model." *Handbook of Multicultural Counseling.* Eds. Joseph G. Ponterotto, Juan M. Casas, Lisa A. Suzuki and Charlene M. Alexander. Newbury Park, CA: Sage, 1995. 93–122. Print.
Egoyan, M. *Web 2.0 and Beyond: The Sociological Significance of Virtual Worlds Supplanting Cyberspace.* 2007. Accessed 9 July 2009. Web.
Ellis, Carol. "Telling Tales on Neighbors: Ethics in Two Voices." *International Review of Qualitative Research* 2.1 (2009): 3–27. Print.
Heim, Michael. *Virtual Realism.* Oxford: Oxford University Press. 1998. Print.
Holtzman, Steven. *Digital Mosaics: The Aesthetics of Cyberspace.* New York: Touchstone. 1997. Print.
Landis, Steven. *Survey.* 2002. Accessed 21 March 2009. Web.
Learning Technologies Conference Blog. Second Life *Backlash.* n.d. Accessed 9 July 2009. Web.
Liao, Christine. "My Metamorphic Avatar Journey." *Visual Culture & Gender* 3 (2008): 30–39. Web.
Linden Lab. *Linden Lab.* Accessed 20 August 2008. Web.
_____. *What Is Second Life?* Accessed 21 March 2009. Web.
_____. *Education.* Accessed 21 March 2009. Web.
_____. *Education Use.* Accessed 21 March 2009. Web.
Manovich, Lev. "The Aesthetics of Virtual Worlds: Report from Los Angeles." 1995. Accessed 22 March 2009. Web.
Nakamura, Lisa. *Digitizing Race: Visual Cultures of the Internet.* Minneapolis: University of Minnesota Press. 2008. Print.
Ondrejka, Corey. *Living on the Edge: Digital Worlds Which Embrace the Real World.* 2004. Accessed 2 July 2008. Web.
Pink, Daniel. *A Whole New Mind: Moving from the Information Age to the Conceptual Age.* New York: Riverhead Books. 2005. Print.
Quebec Action Network for Women's Health. *Changements Sociaux en Faveur de la Diversité des Images Corporelles.* 2000. Accessed 21 March 2009. Web.

Taylor, Pamela, Christine Ballengee Morris, and Steven B. Carpenter. *Digital Visual Culture, Social Networking, and Virtual Worlds:* Second Life *and Art Education.* The National Art Education Association Conference. New Orleans Conference Center, Louisiana. 28 March 2008. Presentation.

Digital Geisha

JULIE ACHTERBERG

There have been myriad papers, dissertations, and books written on the intricate interplay in "identity" that comes with avatar creation. I have no intention of commenting on any of them, but I would like to say that every dissection of the psychology involved in the creation and adoption of an avatar persona I've read has managed to de-emphasize the most important point. It's personal. There's no one reason for anything. Some people treat the avatar as a toy to express playfulness and others as a status symbol, constantly in search of the new "coolest" look. Regardless of your approach to creation, we each identify with our avatar to some degree, just not all the same degree, and the connection between avatar and "user" changes constantly, evolving with our experience of the environment and our fellow explorers. As Meadows asserts, "Psychologically, you are your avatar," and I think with any length of use that becomes true. "The avatar is a tool for regulating intimacy" he argues, and "the assumption of the mask" makes avatar users feel emotionally safe because of the physical separation when in fact they are "more exposed precisely because (they) feel this way." What surprises non-users and users alike is that living life as an avatar removes more masks than it creates depending on the degree of self that becomes imbued to the avatar. James Baldwin once wrote, "Love takes off masks that we fear we cannot live without and know we cannot live within." I suppose that's as good (if contradictory) a summary of my experiences as a woman in *Second Life* as I can give. I've lived that life as a teacher, a poet, a live music fan, a stage dancer, a musician's recruiter, a musician's manager, a role-player, but through it all I've also been what I would term a digital geisha.

In traditional lore, a geisha inhabits what is referred to as "the flower and willow world," a place set apart from the everyday and created by two distinct types of women, the courtesan and the geisha (or "entertainer"). The courtesan exists to give sexual pleasure, their eroticism magnified, one facet of the feminine exaggerated in the furtherance of the beauty their world is supposed to represent, particularly to the powerful men who seek their leisure there. The geisha, in contrast, is a non-sexual object of pursuit existing only through the patronage of the men they can entice with the beauty, art, elegance, and culture they are trained to exemplify while maintaining their power and independence by refusing advances. The flower is seduction and indulgence, the willow is grace and resilience. Women outside of this world became wives, responsible for family and household, no time for music or art or finery. This division of the feminine, some would argue, is strictly cultural, a response to an extreme example of a male-dominated society, but there are other forces at work to create the role of geisha that are not strictly cultural. I experienced these in my sojourn in *Second Life*, both from within myself and from those that I met along the way.

Avatar as Self

My avatar went through all the usual growing pains for about three months. Bad prim hair, freebie shopping for clothes, skins, just anything you could find that felt right. When I decided to really start developing my avatar, I realized that I'd been working to create the "me" who might have been had things not gone terribly wrong. This epiphany came as I looked at the shape I'd so carefully created for Steorling over the months I'd been in *SL* (I've never bought a shape, I crafted my own.) and realized she was an age-progressed version of me at 8 years of age. As I thought about this idea, and the origins of my avatars name, I knew precisely who Steorling was to become. She would be me, only ... beautiful.

This was something I'd resolved for myself, a way to escape what I felt at the time were the confines of my RL existence and enjoy myself. What I hadn't foreseen was the conflict that would arise between this wish and my moral compass. The difficulty was that I already had a horribly inconvenient penchant for getting gentlemen friends hopelessly entangled even before I began down the road to making my avatar attractive. I had ranted at my *SL* mentor about the terribly disconcerting way that male friends kept "falling for me" and wanting more than I was willing to give, when I wasn't trying to do anything more than be my authentic self. About the third time I took my aggravation at what I termed "*SL* Psychology" to this very wise friend he informed me I was "just too damn charming" and confided that when we first met he believed I was flirting seriously with him. His observation required a lot of soul searching and was the first I began to really examine what I was doing in *SL* and whether I was contributing to these situations that made me so uncomfortable.

Illusionary Worlds: Flowers, Willows and Second Life

Second Life is, first and foremost, a social platform. Yes, it is a marvelous tool for collaboration, performance, education, art, and e-commerce, but everything going on there is essentially social. What's more, it's social in ways defined by the users. Subcultures flourish and you can spend your entire existence in *Second Life* completely immersed in a single community or shifting from one to another with impunity. Unlike gaming platforms, a virtual world doesn't just offer the illusion of choice, you actually have to make choices as you navigate the virtual landscape. There are a few key choices that people make at some point in their development that are universal choices and moral choices at that. At some point every individual makes a choice whether they will engage in cyber (virtual sex) and whether they will take the social ties in *SL* as far as partnering, a form of mock marriage. These choices can change, of course, but generally if an individual has opted out of one or the other it's going to affect all other choices available to them. You can see this on profiles all over *SL* with phrases like "No cyber, No BF's (GF's)" posted on front pages as though they equated with role-play limits. For women these two choices immediately define their role within the Flower and Willow world as courtesan, wife surrogate, or geisha. Each fulfills a different social need and one individual can move from one to another merely by changing one or both of those choices so long as they are willing to suffer the social consequences.

Being a woman whose moral compass eliminates both cyber sex and mock marriage from her array of choices, my default social role became geisha long before I had contemplated the metaphor. My mentor is fond of saying "avatars are only a pixel deep" and this wisdom along with some understandings I developed about social interactions from my wise best friend (my oneesan, "older sister" in Geisha terms) became the basis for my understanding of the geisha metaphor and my own needs and wants from this virtual world.

There are essentially three major needs that are at work in relationships real or virtual. Men need respect, to know their worth is their most important impulse. Women require cherishing, being held as a treasure. Both sexes engaged in virtual societies are looking for what Baldwin describes in the quote near the beginning of this essay. The masks we can't live with or without need to be removed or, at the least, peered behind by someone trustworthy. You can see these needs expressed everywhere in *Second Life*, whether in Gorean societies or poetry circles, and outside as well.

Take, for instance, the pop culture success of the movie *Avatar*. At the center of the epic romance set on a far away alien world is the indigenous Na'vi understanding of the phrase "I *see* you." At the romantic climax, when the Na'vi heroine is faced with the unconscious avatar (a genetically engineered

Na'vi puppet animated by a human user) of her mate, she turns away from this "mask" and instead seeks and saves a broken human she's never laid eyes on, an alien paraplegic. The first words they speak on seeing each other are "I see you" in the Na'vi sense, the understanding that I see more than what my eyes see. This is, of course, the very simplest understanding of intimacy and it's what all human interactions (particularly between the sexes) are striving for in the end.

How we chose to define cross gender intimacy often makes those two moral choices for women in virtual worlds and defines our role. In simplest terms, the courtesan equates intimacy with sex, the wife surrogate with couple hood, and the geisha with intellectual companionship not only for themselves, but for the men who are attracted to each. The mistake I've encountered with men in *SL*, again and again, is their inability to comprehend that women do not easily swap these choices and roles in response to the level of emotional intimacy pursued with them, so romancing a geisha will only get you more geisha, not a courtesan. Women who are inconsistent in these roles face the social consequences I mentioned earlier and nothing will get a woman permanently labeled a "bitch" faster than a courtesan grasping at a wife role or a wife suddenly turning courtesan, and not just by the men they confound, but other women as well. The Flower and Willow world just can't exist with these flagrant foundation shakings, after all, and even in *Second Life's* more modern jargon the "drama" created by such behavior is often viewed as the worst sin you can commit against the social contract of the metaverse and the essential serenity of the digital geisha's illusionary world.

Becoming Geisha

The recognition that I was a digital geisha came to me one evening while I was recruiting for an *SL* musician and dancing with a new live music fan who for a half hour had been telling me about his induction into BDSM at 15 by a 35-year-old dominatrix and making remarks on the "vanilla" wife he'd married. My best friend (my onee-san) IM'ed me to ask if I was planning on adding him to my dancing harem, the name given to the male friends who routinely danced with me at venues when they knew they'd be ignored occasionally while I did my job. I answered her that I wasn't sure, he hadn't told me yet if he was a dom or a sub, that at the moment I was just feeling like one of those prostitutes who men pick up to talk about the things they can't discuss with their wives because of the emotional ramifications: a talking whore. She just laughed knowingly because you can't be a female having social interactions in *SL* (or any online platform) without having been turned surrogate for wife or mother by at least one male. I thought about it a good deal, looking at my various experiences with *SL* men, and discovered similar patterns over and over.

Essentially, because of my convictions on key points of virtual interactions between the sexes mentioned earlier, I have a Geisha's aversion to any relationship with a male who is incapable of attaining the place of patron. All other relationships stand on shifting sand and while it's interesting to become as mutable as some male friends require, negotiating and renegotiating the basis for the friendship in that not-so-subtle wrangling that goes on in *SL* or RL, it is in the end exhausting. Those instances when male friends shifted into the falling-in-love-with-the-avatar mode were by far the worst. Thankfully, I've only had two names lost off my friends list as a consequence of my refusing to lose my geisha status by relinquishing my convictions, one an angry man from Mumbai with transference issues involving the "white women" he dated while being educated in the West, and a married pastor on an alt who had no business romancing me in the first place. All the rest have remained friends, though generally while moving on to either courtesan or wife as their needs required. Those few who have come through the other side to enter the ranks of my patrons are by far the dearest to me of all my digital friends.

The Art of the Geisha

The art of the digital geisha varies little from traditional geisha. Her first obligation is to maintain the Flower and Willow World's cultural and artistic fabric. The scope of these activities for geisha in the metaverse run from hostessing at venues and events to being creative. In some sense they've taken responsibility for the persistence of the best of this virtual world. Fashion designers, sim designers, musicians, artists, fundraisers, gallery owners, venue and musician managers, group managers, thespians, poets, advertisers, journalists, and bloggers; there are thousands of jobs within the metaverse filled by women who spend their money and energies on what they love of *SL* arts and culture.

A geisha's second obligation is to delight and the most important and social means to delight, both for yourself and those you "entertain," is conversation. My mentor, Phorkyad, once said, "a conversation with you is like walking a meditation path." This was long ago, before I began to realize that the digital Flower and Willow world also hosts the illusions and arts of male entertainers, performers, and musicians just as the world of the geisha did long ago. Being a master of all things theatrical and spoken word, I suppose he is akin to the old *taikomochi* (the original geisha, or art people, being male), the stage masters of kabuki, and the teahouse creators of haiku. He's taught me generou*sly* from his arts and wisdom over the years, and that he ever considered me an equal is a flattering thing to this geisha.

Perhaps due to these corollary obligations, I've observed that Geisha in digital environments would benefit from learning some old wisdom (as well as a little *SL* Psychology). Somewhere between the most rabid tenets of feminism and PC ism we've lost some truths about the feminine that we can relearn in the metaverse. What follows are some guidelines for digital geisha that I've developed over my years in *Second Life* and I'll share them with the understanding that they are drawn from my own experiences, enlightened moments, and epiphanies and will be vigorou*sly* opposed by a few, but have held true for me with such consistency I take them for truth.

CONVERSATION

1. Never tell a man he's WRONG. He may be mistaken, misinformed, even forgetful ... but never, ever wrong. A good geisha knows how to change a mind, if it's worth her time, but she does so by redirection and rationalization not confrontation. Just like striking a bull with the pick, telling a man he's "wrong" always smacks of an attack on respect and just makes him angry. (And usually a lot less rational.)

2. Flirtation is not the same as seduction. The courtesan is expected to be explicit, but a geisha's ability to delight comes from inference not invoking. Just the other night a friend apologized for using the f-word in a hurried communication adding, "I don't even know why I feel it, but I can't say that around you." Telling, isn't it? I've never remarked on a single word choice to him, but he "feels it."

3. Men are visual creatures, even when just looking at your words. Keep them few, a distillation not unlike poetry. Include gestures and inflections even actions. Mark them as your own with personality and voice. What that voice entails, whether smart-alec imp or serene muse, should come from the center of you, otherwise where's the fun in conversing at all? i.e., I have a habit of using the words "sir" and "gentleman" in very specific but contrary ways that have drawn more than a few questions from friends. I also take a twisted delight in mixing metaphors that are only a degree off so that it sounds like wisdom, but can be confusing to those that are too literal. Actually, if you're a literalist you will be finding yourself another geisha. And that's just fine with me.

AVATARS

1. The essential thing about an avatar is that it be a thoughtful expression of self. It does not need to be trendy or expensive. If you enjoy morphing and have all the transmutational creativity of a changeling in how often you reinvent your core appearance, that's fine, but the avatar of a geisha reflects who she is in some manner so that others are drawn to it, and if you can do that with just a little quirk that asks the viewer to wonder on the "why" of it, all the better. No self-respecting geisha is going to have a cookie cutter avatar indiscernible from the rest. What's most interesting in looking at avatars as they develop over months and years is that they begin to reflect their owners RL appearance in subtle and telling ways. If you want to know what a woman loves about herself in RL (or hates, for that matter), look closely at her default humanoid avatar at two years of age.

DRESS

1. Just as with conversation, a geisha is flirtatious and sensual, not explicit. If you want to be treated like a prostitute, dress like one, otherwise wear what conveys sensuality and playfulness without crossing the line. Some truth doesn't change that much over the ages and the truth that men are visual means that it doesn't take a great deal of "skin" to allow them to fill in the rest from their own imaginations, and when it comes to pixels the "full monty" isn't really that alluring compared to what they can dream up on their own, is it? [Traditional geisha understood the "less is more" principle. The elaborate white face make-up of young *maiko* (tea server) geisha in training includes alluring patches of naked skin at the nape of the neck left as the makeup is brushed on in a classic "w" pattern. It's a mark of a sensual nature aligned with the "modesty" of formal attire and make-up that creates the desired effect.]

2. Dressing appropriately to the event or location, particularly when you've been invited and it's a themed event, is respectful conduct. It's helpful to have a few tried-and-true basics in your inventory for any of a number of occasions. i.e., Color themed events (usually red, black, or white), the usual club and music genres (Jazz, Blues, Cyberpunk, Ballroom, Urban, Hip hop, etc.), various time periods (Medieval European, Feudal Japan, Greek/Roman, Ancient Egyptian, Jazz Age, etc.), and any role-play or subcultures you enjoy (fantasy, sci-fi, gorean, furry, steampunk, neko, biker, etc.).

CONDUCT

My personal codes derive from a Christian ethic and understanding, so the first rule of behavior is always to love people where they are. Discernment is a virtue, con artists and hate-filled individuals are always to be avoided, but judging them beyond simple avoidance is for God alone.

As an extension of the first principle, and in the role as delighter, a geisha always attempts to make people comfortable and at ease, shielding them from embarrassment and never drawing attention to mistakes or flaws publicly. We all have them, and no one likes having theirs critiqued openly. This is particularly important when you've been allowed behind a mask or two by those who have given you their trust.

Keeping confidences is critical, and there are those who consider every word spoken in IM personal. Know where peoples' privacy boundaries are and respect them both in what you speak and what you don't. Traditional geisha were renowned for their discretion and ability to keep a secret and that same trustworthiness is what makes digital geisha confidantes to male and female friends alike.

PROFILES

1. What you write in your profile can not only draw interest from like-minded individuals, it can also deter the undesirable social contacts. I can tell you without reservation that having two or three marvelously desirable gentlemen of patron status gracing your picks section with accompanying praises *really* cuts down on the number of times you're likely to be hit on by strangers with lines like "Do you wanna *uck?"

2. The groups people belong to often give more information about them than their words. An avatar with three sexgen groups or club memberships beginning and ending in a lot of X's is going to be trouble to anything but a courtesan. (Groups are blockable, after all, so just consider everything there advertising.)

3. Another observation about profiles that I've made is that their attraction does wax and wane with how many more social connections you desire. When I first entered *SL* I read them religiously. After recruiting for a year and a half, opening profiles at lightning speed for just one piece of information, I started to lose interest. The pendulum is swinging in the other direction a little, now that I've left live music management, but I suspect the actual reason is about how many friends I miss and how many I still feel I have to make.

GRACE

Some trifling things to consider....

Strange as it may seem, there is room in the metaverse for the geisha principle of essential grace ... that almost ritual performance of even the smallest task. In *SL* that translates to knowing, for instance, whether you get up from a couples dance poseball first or he does. I have two gentlemen friends who have opposing pet peeves about this and I've actually marked it in the Notes section of their profiles in case I should ever forget which is which. Bling, annoying gestures, particle poofers, we all have little things that make us grind our teeth at times. If you just accept that and take note, it goes a long way to letting people feel valued and *known* to us. (And, even if your core expression of identity is a sim crashing particle "nuke," you can at least apologize to a friend you know it sends into blue screen technically or otherwise).

Let me clarify, in case you've gotten the wrong impression from the guidelines above, I do not believe virtual worlds exist purely for the pleasure of men as is often assumed of the RL geisha's illusions. As logging in is a voluntary activity by either of the sexes, women must be getting something out of this platform or there wouldn't be so many. I would argue, however, that women fulfill their own social needs by playing these roles, and some curious *Second Life* lore bears that out. First, there is something called the 80/20 rule (or in some cases the 90/10, depending on who you ask). This is a common observation by citizens of *SL* that their friends list tends to be heavily weighted toward the opposite sex (or those they would find sexually compatible, perhaps). Another phenomenon commonly alluded to is the 10 year gap. The average difference in age of your closest friends, regardless of sex, will tend to be plus or minus 10 to 15 years. (Mine are as high as 22 years different, younger and older.) These observations indicate a good deal of surrogate and mentor behavior is going on in *Second Life's* socializing and that women find their roles as attractive to fill as men find them to patronize particularly when you consider that real life age is often the *last* information you get about another person in *SL*. For this reason, and the fact that *SL* is a global community spanning many cultures and ethnicities, I contend that the role of digital geisha exists, not due to the pressures of a male-dominated society (as the traditional geisha of Japanese culture are presumed to be), but the complementary social needs of men and women.

Wives and Courtesans

So what of the other roles women play in virtual worlds, those that have made other choices in defining intimacy on digital platforms? The courtesans are ever present in *SL*, but the curious thing is that according to Lindens' own research, vast numbers of the "working girls" in *SL* are actually created and animated by men. It's an accepted fact of *SL* existence that the more highly sexualized and anatomically exaggerated a female avatar is, the more likely it is to be designed and animated by a male. So how many RL women are actually participating in the culture of the Flower and Willow world in the role of courtesan is difficult to determine. At one point a few years ago there was a great deal of controversy over the numbers of new players being "forced into the sex trade" by the platforms economic system. The argument was made that players who didn't want to put any U.S.$ into the metaverse found escort work to be the most lucrative alternative for newbies, but it was sensationalized to the point that no useful data was ever produced on the phenomenon. The argument also had substantial holes in it from the perspective of *SL* veterans as a successful escort avatar requires a large amount of upfront investment and there are enough other avenues of employment and economic gain that escorting is seen as the job of last resort even if you don't have any moral objections. Anecdotally, real life women acting as *SL* escorts exist, of course, but in actual numbers I'd have to conclude it's a small population in comparison to all women participating in *SL*. It's also important to add that not all courtesans are escorts, quite a few are what might be considered "party girls," the digital equivalent to spring break co-eds. Interestingly, in the larger community there are just too many that have earned a bad reputation by being hustlers, con artists, and drama inciters, so the social consequences of choosing that role drive these individuals to try to legitimize their sexual behavior via partnering or RP/BDSM "bonds." There's a social stigma developing against these serial and multiple partnerings in the same way casual sex might be viewed in the real world. Just recently a woman on the forums asked Lindens to create another level to partnering by creating a "marriage" designator to reflect the ties between those with what she termed "serious" relationships (Allie McCallen https://blogs.secondlife.com/message/76742#76742). It's a classic example of a wife surrogate asserting that she's "not one of those girls" and it generated some interesting discussion about partnering.

The choice to engage in partnering would seem far easier to gauge simply because it requires registration of the fact within the platform, but as of this writing I've discovered no trustworthy numbers published by Linden Labs (NWN had a bot survey posted at one time which had estimated the number of partnered avatars at 6 percent, but I think most people would consider that a bit low). In my four years on the platform I've been to three partnering ceremonies, six weddings, and witness to 18 other "partnerings" of one variety or another. I've known people who've left *SL* when their partner has found an RL girlfriend/boyfriend, RL married men and women who've come close to adultery in RL with *SL* partners, their emotional betrayal damaging to both relationships. I've known those who have been married in *SL* for all of three days, the partnering a last ditch effort to solidify a relationship that was in meltdown. Of all these pairings only one couple is still partnered ... and one half of that pairing is rarely online anymore. Strangely, all but two couples I know who are married in RL do not partner in *SL* (though several entered *SL* with the same last name when that was possible) and, in one case, a woman I know has both an RL husband and an *SL* husband who socialize together on a regular basis. By far the longest running relationships I've been privy to, outside of those married in real life, are those that are not partnered in any sense. (My onee-san has been best friends with her gaming partner for over eight years on multiple platforms, for instance, though they live an ocean apart and have never met in RL). Not surprisingly, in many instances these long term relationships contain some element of surrogacy for missing or inadequate relationships in at least one of the participants and are significantly more stable when both members of the pairing are fulfilling some need.

Conclusion

If, therefore, the role taken on by women most often is Geisha, does that say something about gender and social progress in virtual worlds? Since *Second Life* is essentially non-procreative, there are no children outside of those role played by adult users, women's roles are defined socially, not biologically. Deconstructing the Flower and Willow World metaphor for just a moment, women have been finding empowered roles to play that also fulfill their needs since the beginning of organized societies. Priestesses, temple attendants, entertainers, artists, midwives; certain women have always found a way to have a level of autonomy while still being supported by the larger culture. In almost every instance, the structure within these worlds is matriarchal and in most instances the power of sex, or lack of sex, has been key. Consider, for instance, the lives of the Vestal Virgins, oracles, and sibyls (and their various interpreters). In each instance, women who attained power and influence did so by limiting or redefining their procreative lives in some sense. These special roles were extremely limited in number, often kept elite by the very women who controlled the matriarchal hierarchy. Within *Second Life* and virtual worlds, however, there are no gate keepers to taking on the role of geisha, no teahouse matrons or formalized apprenticeships to complete to define a woman's place or social interactions beyond her own choices.

Epilogue

As I stated at the beginning of this essay, avatar creation and adoption is personal. Though it's shaped by how an individual sees herself within a social fabric that has its own conditions and quirks as a culture and a technological platform for human interaction, it is linked to our own self-image derived from a lifetime of experiences outside of virtual worlds. While *Second Life* does allow for tremendous creativity and fantasy, we never wholly escape ourselves. It is through this inability that so many of us actually remove more masks than we put on as avatars. The freedom of choice allows the user a limitless palette of possibilities, but at center the roles we choose to live as our avatars are limited by how much of ourselves become imbued to the creation. If approached with an "It's only an avatar" or "It's just role-play" attitude, the avatar can deviate from our own social needs and convictions, but part of what I've just argued is that most women don't find that possible for very long. With time, the avatar becomes such an authentic representation of what we think, feel, and believe, it cannot act independent of our own true character. I *am* Steorling, but what's really surprised me in this journey is the realization that it goes both ways. Life as a digital geisha has profoundly changed my real life perceptions of the world, the people who inhabit it, and my self.

Works Cited

Bardsley, Jan. "Teaching Geisha in History, Fiction, and Fantasy." Web.

Boellstorff, Tom. *Coming of Age in* Second Life: *An Anthropologist Explores the Virtually Human.* Princeton, NJ: Princeton University Press, 2008. Print.

Dalby, Liza. *Geisha.* Berkley: University of California Press, 1983/2008. Print.

Downer, Lesley. "Geisha: The Secret History of a Vanishing World." *London: TLS, the Times Literary Supplement* no. 5097 (2000): 26. Print.

Eggerichs, Emerson. *Love & Respect: The Love She Most Desires, the Respect He Desperately Needs.* Nashville: Thomas Nelson, 2004. Print.

Geser, Hans: "Me, My Self and My Avatar. Some Microsociological Reflections on 'Second Life.'" *Sociology in Switzerland: Towards Cybersociety and Vireal Social Relations.* Zurich, April 2007. Web.

Gray, John. *Men Are from Mars, Women Are from Venus.* New York: Harper Collins, 1992. Print.

Guadagno, Rosanna E., Nicole L. Muscanell, Bradley M. Okdie, Nanci M. Burk, and Thomas B. Ward. "Even in Virtual Environments Women Shop and Men Build: A Social Role Perspective on *Second Life.*" *Computers in Human Behavior,* vol. 27, issue 1, Current Research Topics in Cognitive Load Theory, Third International Cognitive Load Theory Conference, January 2011. Web.

Heider, Don. "Identity and Reality: What Does It Mean to Live Virtually?" *Living Virtually: Researching New Worlds.* (ch. 7, vol. 47) Ed. Don Heider. New York: Peter Lang, 2009. Print.

Jones, Donald E. "I, Avatar: Constructions of Self and Place in *Second Life* and the Technological Imagination." *Gnovis Journal* vol. 6. Web.

Matviyenko, Svitlana. "Sensuous Extimacy: Sexuation and Virtual Reality. Taking on a Gender Identity in *Second Life*." *UC Irvine: Digital Arts and Culture*, 2009. Web.

Meadows, Mark. *I, Avatar: The Culture and Consequences of Having a Second Life*. Berkeley, CA: New Riders, 2008. Print.

Smith, David Harris. "Disintegrating Involvement in *Second Life*." *InTensions Journal* 3 (Fall 2009). Web.

Stites, Theodora. "Modern Love: Someone to Watch Over Me (on a Google Map)." NYTimes. com (July 9th 2006). Web.

N00bs, M00bs and B00bs:
An Exploration of Identity
Formation in *Second Life*

J.A. BROWN, MEG Y. BROWN
and JENNIFER REGAN

The virtual world of *Second Life* has been recognized as a vanguard for online, user-generated avatar interaction. Players have the freedom to create their character as they wish and are not bound to the cultural expectations of visual appearance and behavior that is often found within the real world. This may be a freeing experience for those that feel constrained by society's norms. In particular, this freedom can be regarded as welcomed outlet for women as many have felt the burden of unfounded, gender-based expectations. Thus, the experience of female interaction and identity development within *Second Life* warrant analysis. With the perspectives of Freud, Erikson, and Turkle as a framework, the formation of identity within *Second Life* is explored via narratives. Three novice female players report their experiences: one as an androgynous avatar, one as a female avatar, and the final narrative as a male avatar. Attention is paid to the concept and process of virtual identity with an eye toward self-perceived influences from both the real and virtual worlds.

Real World and Virtual World Identity

Computer-mediated communications (CMC), such as emailing and texting, have become a ubiquitous presence in our modern society and have influenced how we interact with one another. For those that often use various modes of CMC, it not only shapes how one communicates, but the meaning of the content as well. In particular, this includes how the user elects to showcase aspects of their identity. Because CMC is not dependent upon the physical attributes of the user, self-portrayal is subjective and dynamic.

With the advent and continual advancement of CMC technologies, new methods for socialization have allowed users multiple outlets for identity. In most instances, identity portrayed via CMC does not have to conform to the characteristics of the user. The creation of a "false identity" is not necessarily done to deceive others, but to express different facets of oneself within virtual environments. In return, it is plausible that the creation and interaction of such identities influence self-perception — not only within the virtual world, but also within the real world.

Unfettered self-portrayal within a virtual environment calls into question the development of identity formation, given the ease with which altering a persona within the virtual world differs dramatically from that of the real world. With a plethora of opportunities for virtual self-representation, a user must decide how and to what extent they will advertise their identity. This is compounded by the anonymity often afforded within virtual environments. In return, this may further the distance between the real and virtual world attributes of an individual. Additionally, users may choose to alter how they portray their virtual identity at will or even terminate their online persona. Although in real life an individual may alter how he or she appears via clothes, hairstyle, etc., there are still sex-defined physical qualities that can be difficult, if not impossible to conceal.

Depending on the online platform one chooses to socialize, the characteristics of a person's identity are displayed in various ways. For example, on popular social networking sites (such as Facebook or LinkedIn), an individual can be represented by a combination of media preferences (favorite books, music, movies), demographic attributes (age, sex, geographic location), and professional status (academic history, employment, career goals). Online dating sites add a unique dimension to self-representation by showcasing lifestyle and relationship preferences.

Second Life *and Self-identity*

The online world of *Second Life* (*SL*) offers users a virtual community that differs from traditional social networking sites in that interaction is dependent upon the utilization of a user-created and customized avatar within an open-ended virtual realm known as "the grid." Just as an avatar has a bevy of modifiable traits at his or her disposal, so too, the grid supports the creation and display of an untold number of destinations for virtual socialization. Dependent upon the intentions and interaction of the user, *SL* can be utilized as a game, a computer code playground, a marketplace, chat room, sex club, dance floor, fashion boutique, or anything else the user can imagine and create within the grid.

Such an environment can be a welcomed exploratory outlet for individuals from varied cultural backgrounds and perspectives. Like many online social networks, a part of *SL*'s appeal is the opportunity for anonymity, the freedom to portray the self in just about any manner desired. This may be particularly appealing for those that wish to explore a life, albeit virtual, that is completely within the control of the user. Therefore, those that are dissatisfied or feel inhibited with aspects of their real life may find the freedom afforded within *SL* as an opportunity to express themselves without the constraints that are typically present in their everyday life.

Identity Formation Within Real Life

Virtual independence speaks to users' perceptions of self and how individuals choose to portray themselves within *SL*. Although an avatar is in essence a "blank slate" at initiation, it is not devoid of its creator's influence. Creation does not occur within a vacuum, but springs from the imagination of the *SL* user. It is inevitable that the avatar in some way bears the imprint of its maker, as it is a virtual extension of his or her real-life identity.

With this in mind, the concept of identity formation is not confined to the real world. Rather, the creation of additional identities, via CMC, introduces additional aspects for consideration. The following questions merit exploration as we try to understand the dynamics of self-identity. What aspects comprise the process of identity formation within *SL*? How do real-life factors influence this process? How does online identity evolve within *SL*? What role does gender play in this process?

The exploration of the many layers that constitute identity formation is not a new endeavor and has resulted in an abundance of theories. From a psychological viewpoint, one of the earliest speculations on the roots of identity formation originated with Sigmund Freud. Although controversial, he proposed concepts that spoke to identity formation from a psychoanalytic perspective. He shed light on internal drives and external contributors, both of which contribute towards the constructs of the id (rooted in instinct), ego (rooted in perceived reality), and superego (a moral basis) (Freud 88).

Freud's theory of psychosexual development is a foundational component to psychoanalysis, and it addressed stages of development that contributed to self-identity. However, it was Eric Erikson that elaborated upon similar concepts from a psychosocial perspective and proposed that stages occur throughout phases in life. In essence, an individual is confronted with crises at stage-specific points in life and must progress through each to confront the next stage. It is this process that influences the individual's perception of self.

Erikson proposed that the first stage (247), basic trust versus basic mistrust, occurs in early childhood and is a starting point for developing trust by being provided for and safeguarded. If trust is not established, mistrust takes root. Next, autonomy versus shame (251) was proposed to occur within early childhood, when a child begins to develop a sense of independence. Initiative versus guilt (255) is the next stage proposed by Erikson. During this time, a child attempts to control aspects of his or her environment, which can lead to meaningful interactions. The child then encounters the next stage, industry versus inferiority (258). More advanced skills are acquired during this time, like those learned in school, and can be a springboard for the child's sense of competency.

The stage that Erikson proposed to occur during the teenage years is identity versus role-confusion (261). Although the child has been forming his or her identity, much of it comes to a head at this time, as he or she is faced with sexual maturity and the proposition of adult-like roles. The subsequent stage, intimacy versus isolation (263), is a time when young adults are faced with the prospect of developing intimate relationships and building a family. Next, Erikson believed an aging individual confronts the stage of generativity versus stagnation (266), when he or she is faced with guiding the next generation (such as raising a family). Finally, an older person is said to face the stage of ego-integrity versus despair (268); this is a time when a person reflects upon their life with satisfaction or regret.

Because Erikson's theory suggests that development occurs within a psychosocial context, it may be applicable to the development of identity within an online environment, such as *Second Life*. Although his theory has been elaborated upon since its introduction, it may serve as a framework for understanding how anonymous online interaction is initiated and develops for new users.

Identity Formation Within Virtual Worlds

Sherry Turkle has devoted much of her career to examining user perspective of and interaction with technology. Her article, "Who Am We," specifically addresses the multiple identities that one can adopt within a virtual environment. Turkle's dialogue with Doug, a multi-user dungeon (MUD)[1] dweller, highlights a granular quality to identity that is amplified by the split between the virtual and real world. Each piece of his identity is distinct, yet they are parts of a whole person. The use of computer technology amplifies this distinction and gives classification to each of the nuances of Doug's personality—"real Doug," "online voyeur Doug," "online macho guy Doug," etc. (Turkle 5).

While Doug might be any number of wild characters online with very different personalities, it is notable that he maintains the dissonance between these characters and his offline life. He explained to Turkle how addressing different activities (such as tending to a spreadsheet and flirting with a girl) was like turning different parts of his mind on and off. Doug explained how an online inhabitant might regard oneself as having multiple personas.

It is this very notion, the ability to see oneself as multiple people, which is particularly compelling when considering traditional notions of feminine personas. While Doug may be able to virtually embody a macho cowboy while he does work and interacts with friends, sexist myths imply the mutual exclusivity of this feat. In various forms of popular culture, women are portrayed as incapable of holding this delicate balance between being a dutiful co-worker and a good mother, all while maintaining friendships and quality time for themselves. With the boundaries and expectations of online life at best muddled, if not non-existent, it seems that females in particular might stand to benefit from the freedoms that virtual worlds can offer.

In applications like *SL* where one's gender, let alone species, is not a fixed part of one's self, a female is afforded the opportunity to explore outside of conventional boundaries and experience a world where *she* is in control. Such unfettered freedom is an enticing aspect for online interaction and warrants a look into the unique feminine perspective. This chapter provides our (the authors') firsthand account of the contemplations, inner-reflections, and decision-making involved when navigating the virtual world of *SL* for the first time.

The first narrative is of Cupcake Hubbenfluff—a female player's androgynous avatar. Next, the exploration of Piper Carousel, a female avatar, is shared. Finally, the experience of a male avatar, Skyther, provides insight on the perceived formation of "faux-male" identity. In addition, we consider how gender influences our real-world and virtual-world identities. We conclude by presenting common themes and relating our avatar experiences to the perspectives of Turkle, Erikson, and Freud.

Narratives

CUPCAKE HUBBENFLUFF

I hated playing with dolls as a child so it was strange that I enjoyed changing clothes as much as I did in *Second Life*. When playing, I was surprised to find myself spending huge chunks of time working on my visual presence.

I would not even explore the world. I would just sit at home, happily editing my appearance. Would my avatar, Cupcake Hubbenfluff, look better with a sweater or a jacket? Where could I find hair that looked like my own real life hair for free? Was the *SL* hairstyle labeled "Male Bollywood" the closest thing I could get? Had I ever spent his much mental energy on tweaking my appearance in real life?

My experience as Cupcake Hubbenfluff did not begin as a vanity quest. Rather, my research team had set out to explore the dynamic experiences as female newcomers (n00bs) to *SL*. We agreed that it would be best if we all experienced *SL* through different lenses. "We'll try out all sorts of options," we said, "females playing male avatars, females playing female avatars, females playing genderless avatars!" I agreed to hunt down a genderless avatar because I feel so strongly about the role gender plays in stereotyping others. By choosing neither male nor female characters, I was hoping to avoid the kind of unsettling sexual interactions (unwanted flirtations, degradation, etc.) that can occur in real life, along with the assumptions that I should act a certain way. To me, choosing a genderless character was about going beyond a surface understanding of myself as a woman and attempting to understand myself as a person.

As a newcomer to *SL*, I was unsure where to begin in terms of making my genderless avatar, so I relied on the search bar to explore. Using the word "free" in conjunction with other words like "clothing," "avatar," "animals," "skins," and "androgyny," I began my search for a genderless look. What I found is that without a guide, navigating *SL* is a difficult task. I failed to find genderless avatars, and could not afford the pricier (genderless) animal avatars that are available to users for a fee. Determined to complete my portion of the research with some sort of gender-neutral view, I took the hair off of my avatar and dressed androgynously. Still, my curvaceous body was a clear sign of my avatar's gender. I felt frustrated that I had to choose one or the other. Rather than having an experience that would transport me beyond gender roles, I found myself staring into the traditional male/female binary that dictated mutual exclusivity — choose one or the other, you cannot be both.

Dressing my character in clothes labeled for males made me appear less feminine, but I certainly did not look "gender neutral." Though I was disappointed that things might not go quite the way we had planned, I was still determined to have a meaningful *SL* experience, whether or not I could find a particular look for my avatar.

This began a new kind of search — one that I decided would be for a look that was like me. It seemed that if I could not run away from the real world, I ought to see how I interpreted myself in a virtual world. I was still limited by how little *SL* currency I had, so I continued to include "free" in my search terms. My first free find was a body that had been created by another player. The description of the body read, "For those tight ass system skirts." It seemed that the idealized female *Second Life* body was disappointingly similar to the idealized real world female body. Putting my feelings aside, I let curiosity get the best of me. I "put on" the body and my rear end ballooned into a "bootylicious hump." Even if having a glorious rump would earn me a sense of belonging in *Second Life*, there was something about the disconnect between my offline booty and my avatar booty that left me feeling unsettled. Can one have an "inner booty" the way one can have an "inner child"?

The next item I found in *Second Life* was a dress that exposed my right breast. Alarmingly enough, this one cost money. It left me stumped. Why would it cost *me* money to show off my body? I continued my search, this time for free clothes, and found hoards of revealing clothing: tight leather *everything*, short shorts, short shirts, and sexy lingerie. At one of the *SL* shops, I found Furry avatars, complete with nipples.

What was going on here? Although I had come into *SL* with the expectation that I could customize all physical aspects of my being, my body did not in any way feel like my own. I was limited by what was made available to me and I felt a loss of ownership when my avatar's curves originated from an unknown artist. While technically I did have choices, there were many limitations to the kind of body that I could encompass. I was unsure of what made me so uncomfortable with choosing a body that did not look like me, other than the nagging sense that it did not *feel* like me.

It was here in my desperation for customization that I began to wrestle with the "can't beat 'em, join 'em" mentality, thinking that perhaps my avatar should just look unrealistically attractive and downright sexy. I tried not to think about why I suddenly felt this was such a good idea, but inside I knew full well that part of the motivation lay in my unpreparedness to feel alienated because of my appearance, even in an imaginary world. There was almost mischievous pleasure in the thought of picking a wildly mainstream standard of beauty. No one that knew me in real life would be the wiser had I donned a corset or a plunging neckline. I could even sell my virtual body for *SL* currency so I could buy that androgynous body I had been after. How is that for conflicting ideas?

Rather than embracing the ability to hold both notions at the same time, I felt troubled that the very same feminist, whose sensibilities were insulted by the majority of *SL* clothing, was also the same person who wanted to show off her body. Initially, it seemed that the Internet was the perfect place to deal with matters of identity and cognitive dissonance, but it was actually more difficult than I had imagined.

At last, I decided that I would create my avatar to look as much like me as I could, and that I would wear whatever appealed to me, the player behind the avatar. At this point maybe I was not even sure who "me" was, but I thought of Sherry Turkle's aptly named essay "Who Am We?" and considered the complexity of being.

I finally ended up giving Cupcake Hubbenfluff as close to a "normal" (whatever that meant) womanly shape as I could and navigated my avatar to an *SL* store where another player had suggested I could find free clothes. I picked out a tutu and a plaid blazer because I do not have the sharpest fashion sense. Another *SL* player spoke to me and suggested that I check out another store. I teleported there, and found myself back in the 1950s. Exploration led me to a black and white checkered dance floor where everyone was dancing away to the sweet grooves of the decade. The entire front row closest to the DJ was packed full of characters sporting those ubiquitous tight leather "everythings." They were dressed all in black and looking pretty gothic for people doing the twist.

It was here I realized I had been missing the point of *SL*. In searching for all possible meanings in each and every combination of free avatar clothing, I missed out on the fact that a werewolf doing the twist might signify a bolder claim to one's identity than obsessing over what my avatar would look like. Rather than drawing on comparisons to offline visual representations, these players had created something entirely new. I had forgotten that it did not matter what I looked like, online *or* offline. My avatar was just an empty vessel for me to fill with meaning.

Overall, traveling to the last store was kind of like real life … but kind of not. I felt the richness of the experience in my real-life self and was confused, yet I had learned things about myself that were less obvious in my real life. Maybe saying "real life" was more inaccurate than I believed it to be. I learned that even if I was not worrying about making a sexy appearance that pleased others, I still held a very shallow notion of self in *Second Life*. I was so worried about compromising my feminist ideals that I ceased to remember my "shell," the least important part of myself. Had I only interacted with more people, perhaps I would have realized my words could be louder than my appearance. Rather than everybody else, perhaps it was me that was more worried about what my appearance signified.

As I logged off each time, I sensed the single components of myself, so different, and so separate that I could not help but wonder, "Is it really *me* this time? Or is it *us*?"

Piper Carousel

As a novice to the world of virtual environments, it was a relief to embark on this journey as a female avatar within *Second Life*. Although the idea of anonymity was exciting, I was comforted by the notion that at least one aspect of my identity would resonate in this unfamiliar realm. However, it did not take long for anxiety to rear its ugly head, as I realized the plethora of options available for creating my avatar. The first big decision was selecting a name for my avatar. Although a name is not tangible, it is nonetheless a marker for identity. The name "Piper" came to mind, as it embodied a sense of intrigue and panache. I then chose "Carousel" as the last name, which seemed to capture my whimsical side. As a conservative female in real life with a traditional American name, "Piper Carousel" was a great start to becoming a virtual reflection of my alter ego.

Because the freedom of being "someone" other than myself intrigued me, Piper was dressed in a punk style, à la Joan Jett with a hint of Lara Croft. Piper had short brown hair, a black motorcycle leather jacket, a low-cut tank top, jeans, and black leather boots, a far cry from the cardigans and ballet flats of my real life. Normally, my everyday style is a conservative mix of J. Crew and Gap, so dressing my avatar in (mildly) provocative clothing was an early sign that the virtual world would serve as an escape for me. In fact, the only similarities between my avatar and I was our hair color and gender. The idea of embracing this new identity was exciting, yet I was nervous to provide her with attributes too similar to my own. I wanted to enjoy myself without the fear of personal judgment, something that is inescapable in real life.

Despite my initial confidence, it was hard not to worry about the provocative nature of Piper's clothing after teleporting to several destinations. Every time a male or female started chatting with me, paranoia that they had an ulterior motive (i.e. to seduce me) overtook me. Although my avatar did not resemble me, Piper still embodied my personality. My skepticism bled into this virtual world, as I constantly doubted the motives of other avatars, particularly female avatars that might have been operated by men. Clearly, judgment exists in the virtual world just as it does real life. The paranoia evoked by Piper's appearance was unsettling; thus, I decided that a shopping trip was in order. Shopping in *SL* cannot be much different than strolling through Nordstrom, right?

Upon entering the store, it quickly came to my attention that my so-called risqué appearance was actually quite conservative when compared to others in the room. Even though *Second Life* offers a world of infinite possibilities, the promiscuity of the clothing at my disposal was shocking. If women dressed like this in real life, we would all look like Julia Roberts at the beginning of *Pretty Woman*. This made me wonder about the real women behind the avatars. What was prompting them to dress their avatar in such a manner? Unlike myself, were they able to escape the mental shackles of real world judgment by embracing the true anonymity afforded in *SL*? Or, were these avatars an accurate reflection of the real person? The thought that some of the avatars may have been men in real life was inescapable, and if so, what did that say of the owner? Was this a reflection of their preference for feminine garb? I also wondered if the real life persons behind the avatars were like me, the J. Crew and Banana Republic shoppers of the world, seeking a sense of freedom. And if they were, did they, too, experience a sense of self-consciousness upon their maiden voyage of the virtual world? More importantly, it would have been fascinating to know how my fellow "Banana Republicans" learned to transition their mindset and be at ease with their avatar.

As I struggled to navigate the store, the clothing options were overwhelming. Figuring out how to purchase clothing was even more so. Despite my best efforts to step outside of my comfort zone, I still found myself wanting to have and experience something familiar, something that resembled the elements and preferences of the real me. For example, the shopping experience should have been comfortable, yet I quickly learned that even a real world favorite pastime was not the same in *SL*. With this in mind, I chose to stick with my punk ensemble despite being approached by a persuasive saleswoman. To my surprise, we had a friendly conversation and I was taken aback by her kindness. Once again, I found myself questioning motives and the true personality of the real life operator of the avatar. I could not help but think, "Is she just being nice to get a sale? Is she trying to take advantage of me in this situation? Is she a male or female in real life trying to flirt with me? Or, is she just trying to be truly helpful?"

The irony had settled in. I wanted to explore *SL* in an effort to experience an environment that was, I thought, free from judgment. However, this was far from the case. *I* was the judge. The pressure I feel in real life as a woman was clearly evident as I navigated the grid and this bothered me. No one, not even myself, was immune to my skepticism.

It seemed that was the case not only for *whom* "I" conversed, but also *how* dialogue was exchanged. As an enthusiastic texter and instant messager, my digital speech mostly consists of upbeat dialogue with lots of unnecessary emoticons, and many exclamation points. However, when other avatars used a similar style in chat, I was wary to continue the conversation. Again, it was uneasy with not knowing the real person behind the avatar. Although online communication is regarded as a reasonably "safe" means to improve social skills, I felt as if I were compromising my own social etiquette. For example, in real life I would never be so rude as to abruptly cease conversation with someone. Although such behavior is afforded in a virtual environment, such an exchange made me feel uncomfortable. This likely speaks to my identity as a "proper young lady," an ingrained quality to my personality. Plus, I trust my instincts to gauge a person's true nature and intentions by interpreting facial expressions and body language, which are mostly lost in *SL*. I regarded this as evidence that I could not separate Piper from the true me; my attempts to make her my alter ego were failing.

It took time for me to fully realize that the discomfort I was feeling was self-imposed. I had to truly recognize that *SL* was indeed another world, albeit virtual. Perhaps I was approaching that final cathartic moment that captures devotees to the freedom afforded in *SL*. Furthermore, I appreciated the flexibility that *SL* offered a conservative, Caucasian female. In fact, I came to recognize that I alone could place expectations upon my behavior within *SL*, a foreign notion in real life. In real life, I am unable to portray my identity as a sexy, leather-wearing Lara Croft wannabe. Yet, as I learned to embrace that line of distinction between the real world and virtual, I allowed Piper to capture those hidden nuances to my personality.

Additionally, I dared to step beyond those characteristics and keep my judgmental tendencies at bay. In doing so, it allowed me to question the source of those real life attributes and why I had not yet dared to view real life in the same way. If the only thing that had changed is perspective, then why could not my perspective in real life change? I believe this further speaks to the pressures I so strongly feel within real world expectations.

Ultimately, I found that I could emulate any character I wanted within *SL*, such as a murder mystery detective. This sense of freedom allowed my imagination to run wild. I was utterly captivated by the idea that however I dressed and talked, and whomever I talked to, was my own secret. Unless I chose to share my experiences with my family and roommates, the experience was purely my own, and I could do whatever I wanted with it. It was a relief to allow myself as Piper to delve into different aspects of my personality and satisfy my social curiosities without the people I know in my real life judging me.

Although women have come a long way from the expectations of the "dutiful housewife" of the mid–20th century, the freedom I came to find in *SL* was a harsh reminder of the gender differences and inequality that still exist in today's society. In retrospect, I am shocked at how I, as Piper, initially felt like a sexual object. It was not because fellow avatars were making lewd gestures, but because I was paranoid with the situation. I had not yet formed a complete identity because I was placing *myself* within *SL*, not Piper. Yet it took "her" exploration of the world to develop not just a sense of comfort within the new environment, but also a sense of identity.

Overall, this experience prompted me to consider what it really means to embody and exhibit attributes that are markers for identity. Furthermore, I believe the culture of an environment directly speaks to how one behaves, yet is not the determining factor. More than anything, I have learned that *outward* perception, regardless of the environment (real or virtual), is a governing factor for *self*-perception.

Skyther

It was an easy decision to select the sex of my avatar on my maiden voyage through the world of *SL*. As a female I thought it would be fun to be a male for once, even if only a virtual one, and hence, Skyther was born. The ability to decide how my avatar would appear and behave was refreshing, as conventional norms could be challenged.

Skyther was initially presented to me as a rather normal appearing fellow — dare I say handsome for a virtual character? Yet, this was just not good enough; I wanted him to have a unique appearance that set him apart from the crowd. Perhaps this was my rebellious nature coming through — a projection of my true self via the avatar. Originally, Skyther was an average-sized male with dark hair, an athletic build, and a slightly tanned complexion. Of course, these appealing male qualities had to change, as I insisted that he not meet conventional norms for male attractiveness. Thus, before I even learned how to navigate through this new world, I made it a priority for my virtual character to meet my expectations with regard to appearance. It reminded me of how we, in real life, tend to make a point of "looking the part" for the day before stepping foot outside of the house.

It did not take long for Skyther to morph into a rather unsightly character, reminiscent of a mix between a badly aged, booze-guzzling former jock and a transient. I purposely wanted to see what it was like to "be" a person that was unabashedly distasteful. I even wondered if his pathetic appearance was the manifestation of some kind of subconscious passive aggressive attitude towards men (doubtful), or if it was my way of exhibiting the desire to defy the Barbie mentality of physical perfection (more likely).

Skyther began as a scraggly, overweight avatar. Not surprisingly, I felt self-conscious upon initial exploration of my new environment. Soon after his induction into the *SL* world, I noticed other "n00bs" walking around him; some even seemed to steer clear of his direction. They looked like deities compared to Skyther; each appeared to have fantastic facial features and flawless physiques. Clearly, Skyther stood out.

Despite discomfort from this mild embarrassment, I navigated Skyther through introductory tutorials so that I could learn how to maneuver him within the *SL* grid and interact with others. All the while, I felt more and more like an outcast. In retrospect, it is difficult to pinpoint if that was just my imagination, or if others were truly trying to avoid him. This experience mirrors that of a teenager walking into the cafeteria on the first day of school.

There was the need to look calm and cool, as if the thoughts of others were of no consideration. Yet, there was also a sense of desperation to find another like soul to befriend. How was Skyther going to make any virtual friends if he looked like he just stumbled out of a dumpster? Does appearance, even in a virtual environment, really matter that much?

Although I wanted to reflect my bold female attitude that does not care about the opinions of others, I succumbed. I was embarrassed of my virtual vanity. Am I secretly like this in real life? What happened to the strong woman that typically shuns unfounded social expectations?

This need to appear "cooler" made me consider the origin for such a strong desire. Although I wondered if it was my interpretation of society's standards for outward appearance, I considered if it was an inner need to fit in, even in a virtual world. I have carved out a comfortable niche in real-life that supports my happy-go-lucky personality, where I do not have much concern for "fitting in." However, this was clearly an issue for me in *SL*.

This identity crisis bothered me on two levels. First, I found it disconcerting that I cared about what others thought of a fictional character's appearance. One of the benefits of *SL* is the freedom of anonymity, but I could not seem to mentally embrace the notion. In that brief amount of time that passed in the initial creation, I found myself immersed within the development of Skyther and therefore, somehow identified with the character.

The brilliance of allowing a player to design his or her own avatar within *SL* was no accident. It sets the stage for the player to experience exactly what was occurring to me at that moment, a feeling of emotional connection to the avatar as if it were an extension of the self. There was a time when this concept was novel, but it is now more of a ubiquitous feature in online environments and digital games.

Next, the fact that I found myself so quickly caring for Skyther's appearance speaks volumes about the pressure a person may feel to showcase him or herself in an acceptable manner. More importantly, I wondered if females experience this more acutely than males, thus creating a strong desire to fulfill expectations. Whether this pressure derives from common sources such as popular media or not, it is undoubtedly there. Therefore, it could be posited that my need to meet those standards were being mirrored by Skyther.

After slimming him down, giving him a head full of lush dark hair, and ample height, I believe I satisfied my virtual vanity. However, there was an unavoidable sense of guilt. What does it say for my (and society's) opinion of men who may have some of the physical qualities originally displayed by Skyther? In addition, what does this hasty change in appearance say about the female perception, for example, of men that carry extra weight, measure under 5'7", appear advanced in years, or are balding?

Skyther's new body was, by mainstream standards, more appealing, and I was eager to find out to what extent that would affect virtual communication. I decided early on that all of my dialogue would be via typed text, as I did not want to disclose my true female identity with live speech. I recall the first time an avatar "spoke" to Skyther, I responded with a long pause. My initial reaction was to reply with apologies for not wanting to join a social group and thank it for asking.

However, I somehow felt empowered as I began to recognize myself as "male," even if only virtually. This realization somehow gave me permission to neither apologize needlessly nor exhibit courtesy and graciousness at every opportunity, as is common practice among females in my real world community. No — it was okay to walk away. It felt good, *really good*, to do so. Plus, there was no need to explain my matter-of-fact behavior. So, when Skyther was approached again in other similar situations, he either walked away in an attitude of disinterest, or responded with a simple, "No, thanks."

By doing this, it was as if for the first time I felt "okay" about behaving in a manner that was true to my *real* emotion. Southern congeniality and manners are a part of who I am. Or are they? This made me question the extent to which my social skills are also a product of real-life influences — similar in nature to the socially driven fashion standards I regularly mocked. Are my "pleases" and "thank you's" a verbal name-brand pair of jeans? Either way, I relished how I (as Skyther) could behave in a manner that mirrored my real-life preferences.

This experience was also eye opening, as it was a clear demonstration of what I apparently believe is acceptable or common as male behavior. For example, I do not believe that the average person aims to portray him or herself as rude. In particular, I never thought of men as social brutes, yet perhaps I have believed it was more acceptable for them to behave in a more forthright manner. With this in mind, I believe this experience prompted me to consider the gender-specific expectations that society may have regarding appropriate speech mannerisms and behavior.

In addition to choosing a communication style with Skyther, I had to also take into account how I was going to use him to interact with others and explore the *SL* grid. I further enhanced his identity by deciding how he was going to approach others. This could not have been addressed before I was sufficiently confident with his appearance and speech.

Initially, it was difficult to find locations where other avatars congregated. Nonetheless, I eventually discovered hot spots where others, usually female, welcomed me. Again, due to my beliefs regarding Skyther's gender, I felt more comfortable with taking my time to respond. Surprisingly, this was never an issue, as I would think it to be in real life. For example, if I were to speak to somebody in real life, I would expect a response in a timely manner that indicated interest and respect. If not, then I would regard them as rude. Thus, it is interesting to consider if my delay was deemed acceptable because of Skyther's gender and pleasing appearance, or if that is typical behavior within *SL*.

It was also amusing to observe female avatars' behavior when around Skyther. Some would walk in my direction, stand near, and even make flirtatious gestures. It was as if they were expecting Skyther to be the initiator of conversation. I would position him in their direction to acknowledge their presence, but was never the first to speak. I wanted to see how this would affect the dynamics. Every time without fail, the female would give up and walk away. Although we live in an era where it is perfectly acceptable for women initiate conversation, this did not seem to be the case within this scenario that played out numerous times. Therefore, based on those experiences, it seems clear that gender roles are very much present within *SL*.

Discussion and Conclusion

COMMON THEMES

The analysis of our leap into the virtual unknown has produced several common themes. Despite the different perspectives we brought to the analysis, we all found that our playing experiences overlapped with our real lives.

We began our journey by analyzing the appearance of our avatars as a reflection of our real selves. We questioned our "look," described ourselves in depth, and expressed our desires to be more visually appealing. It was evident that we deemed such aspects as clothing choice, body shape, and hairstyle with great importance. As stated earlier, the purpose of these experiences was not a "vanity quest," but to explore the boundaries (or lack thereof) of our femininity within *SL*.

Perhaps our initial reliance on the development of the physical aspects of our avatars mirrored a self-conscious feeling that resembled real life. Since we were all eager n00bs to *SL*, we could not quite shake the feeling that our avatars' attractiveness would somehow lead to acceptance and success. We were all too aware of the power, or at least the myth, of first impressions.

We found the objectification of women in the game displeasing. We were both uncomfortable, and a little angry, that we were encouraged to create sexy avatars. Even though Skyther was a male avatar, he also came up against sexual expectations. It seemed that he was expected to perform heteronormatively and to act as a dominant male.

One common theme that came as a great surprise to us was how much

Second Life led us to question our behavior. We struggled to figure out the influences on our *SL* behaviors and our reactions to them. Sometimes we experienced moments in which we wondered, "Why did I think/do that? That's not me! Or is it?" While we may have been agonizing over what was happening in a virtual world, we were each prompted to question our true identities.

The Perspectives of Turkle, Erikson and Freud

Although there is no single, widely accepted identity theory, similarities between our online experiences and the ideologies of Turkle, Erikson, and Freud became apparent.

For Cupcake Hubbenfluff, her cohesive sense of being was challenged by trying to adopt a physical presence that was in conflict with her real life body. Similar to Turkle's MUD dweller, Doug, who presented various persona characteristics, Cupcake's creator also found such multidimensionality a more difficult task than initially anticipated. While Cupcake's creator had been in Doug's position in real life, (that is, multitasking work and participating in offline *and* online social interactions), being in *Second Life* was different. She was impersonating someone she was unfamiliar with. It wasn't just that Cupcake Hubbenfluff was a virtual representation of her creator, but with all of the focus on her physical appearance and search for accessories, Cupcake felt pressed to re-prioritize what she wanted to get out of playing *SL*.

Cupcake Hubbenfluff's experience was also complicated by conflicting values. Originally, she believed that she could use the Internet to portray herself as someone very different. When the time came to shape her avatar, it was no longer just dissonance from physical attributes that disturbed her — it was also the implications behind those attributes. Choosing to search for an androgynous avatar was a deliberate choice to eliminate certain real-world biases, and when Cupcake's creator thought about making an avatar that more closely resembled mainstream media's idealized feminine body, she grappled with the message that body would inadvertently send to others. Unable to separate *SL* expectations from offline expectations, she feared her appearance would cause others to judge her by offline standards. It was when she encountered the juxtaposition of werewolves and sock hops that she realized that offline standards were not necessarily applicable.

After reflecting on the various feelings and desires of herself and her avatar, Cupcake Hubbenfluff was intrigued that a single human being could be comprised of so many complex, and sometimes conflicting, ideas. She began to view *SL* as a prism, separating one body into a radiant array of colors.

As Piper Carousel delved deeper into the unknown world of *Second Life*, a clear correlation could be drawn between her experience and Erikson's eight stages of psychosocial development. As an amateur to gaming as a whole, Piper Carousel entered the arena with far more distrust than trust in both the game and her peers. Whether it was choosing a name or choosing an outfit, it was evident that Piper was deeply ingrained in the first stage (trust versus mistrust). Piper's feeling of mistrust seemed to be overcome through her encounter with the kind salesperson. Although brief, it combated her unshakable feeling that every *SL* player had a surreptitious agenda. After achieving the virtue of "hope" in Erikson's first stage, Piper entered the second stage of "autonomy versus shame and doubt." While Piper began to embrace her independence more, she was never able to fully advance beyond the second stage. According to Erikson, the third stage of initiative versus guilt, is when the child begins to fully understand the world and had Piper's experience not been cut short, perhaps she would have progressed and been able to attain her own "purpose."

Finally, the virtual interaction that contributed to the identify formation of Skyther could be likened to the primary constructs of the psyche, as proposed by Freud. The development and expression of the id, ego, and superego speak to the identity of an individual and, potentially, an avatar. The instinctual drive that is associated with these components were evidenced in Skyther's questioning of appropriate behavior with other avatars. Although she recognized the reality of the situation in that she was anonymous and could behave in any way she wished (ego), she was reared to conduct herself in a certain socially accepted manner (superego). Nonetheless, she relished the notion of behaving without regard for others (id) by behaving in an instinctual manner, void of social opinion. This struggle prompted sincere thought as to the origin of influences, whether from society or the self.

Regardless of the degree of reality applied to the *SL* experience, the identity formations of Cupcake Hubbenfluff, Piper Carousel, and Skyther sheds light as to how a female in today's society makes her way into any sort of environment. Her never ending sense of exploration, ever-evolving journey, and responsibility of creating an image are fraught with implications, and reveal the kind of battle she comes up against when creating her identity.

Notes

1. Howard Rheingold explains MUDs as, "Mutli-User Dungeons — imaginary worlds in computer databases where people use words and programming languages to improvise melodramas, build worlds and all the objects in them, solve puzzles, invent amusements and tools, compete for prestige and power, gain wisdom, seek revenge, indulge greed and lust and violent impulses." (149)

Works Cited

Erikson, Erik H. *Childhood and Society.* New York: Norton, 1950. Print.
Freud, Sigmund. *The Ego and the Id.* London: Hogarth, 1927. Print.
Rheingold, Howard. *The Virtual Community: Homesteading on the Electronic Frontier.* Cambridge, MA: MIT Press, 2000. Print.
Turkle, Sherry. "Who Am We?" *Wired,* Jan. 1996. Web. Dec. 2011.

My *Second Life* as a Cyber Border Crosser

Carleen D. Sanchez

> *Overhead blimp: A new life awaits you in the off-world colonies, the chance to begin again in a golden land of opportunity and adventure. New climate, recreation facilities...—Blade Runner* 1982
>
> Second Life *is an online 3D virtual world imagined and designed by you. From the moment you enter* Second Life, *you'll discover a universe brimming with people and possibilities.... Enter a world with infinite possibilities and live a life without boundaries, guided only by your imagination. Do what you love, with the people you love, from anywhere in the world.—*What Is *Second Life?* Second Life *Website*

Introduction

As noted by Boellstorff (144), issues of race and ethnicity have been under-researched and under-theorized with regards to cyberspace and virtual worlds. And, *Second Life is* a place where race happens (*sensu* Nakamura 2002: xi). The development of *Second Life* has allowed participants to engage in fantastical as well as banal social interactions through new technologies once heralded as the antidote to the ills of the post industrial age. Options abound in *Second Life* for "trying on" new identities as easily as trying on new clothing—seemingly without experiencing the consequences of violating social propriety. Yet virtual worlds are constructed out of the cultural and historical templates already in existence and thus replicate relations of power that mirror those found in the real world. As a creative construct, *Second Life* emanates out of a political economy and cultural milieu based on a Eurocentric model of the world (see Blaut 1993) that privileges a limited set of subjectivities.

Consequently, there has been a tendency to conceive of virtual worlds as largely under the purview of whites; and whiteness is the "default" assumption unless otherwise indicated (Boellstorff 2008: 144). Yet, as Cornel West

(2001) has demonstrated, race *does* matter, even in virtual worlds. Similarly, Anzaldúa (2007), and Moraga and Anzaldúa (2002) have theorized the borderlands inhabited by *Chicanas* (i.e., Mexican American women) to call attention to the rich terrain of cultural production that is otherwise neglected by mainstream society and feminism. Life on the racial and ethnic margins presents myriad obstacles, difficulties, and stereotypes that must be overcome in order to participate in cyberworlds as fully enfranchised beings. As a Chicana engaged in *Second Life* I have found that cyber border crossings are as salient as crossing real borders of nation, race/ethnicity, gender, and class. The primary border to be crossed is between real life and *Second Life*. While no passport is required, passage into *SL* requires cultural, technological, and financial capital that is concentrated in the hands of white, educated, middle class people.

My experience in *SL* has demonstrated that *avatars of color* (e.g., non-white, non-western, non–European) experience harassment, verbal abuse, marginalization, and cyber violence in the form of shoving and ejection. These experiences were disturbingly borne out by Mohammed (2009) when her avatar was "killed" while wearing a *hijab*. While Castronovo (2003: 2) indicates that "avatars can be seen as bundles of attributes," avatars of color are identified by their "phenotype" created through the conscious efforts of the user rather than genetics. Visible markers of race and ethnicity are reflected in skin color, hair styles, wardrobe, and body shape. Performing race and ethnicity complicates avatar identity in that individuals can choose to embody their actual racial/ethnic identity or engage in racial "tourism" by "passing" as a member of a different group (Nakamura 2002). As such, cyberspace is perceived as a post-racial location (Boellstorff 2008) and performing race/ethnicity is an option open to any player. What is not widely acknowledged, however, is that white privilege allows white players to engage the virtual world without the need to be cognizant of underlying racist tropes that permeate real and virtual life. This privilege is not, however, equally open to women of color unless we construct avatars that can "pass." In this article, I will explore the way that race and ethnicity intersect with gender as a woman of color that engages in various *Second Life* activities. By relying on the work of critical race theorists, feminist borderlands theorists, and post-colonial theory I will examine *Second Life* to reflect on the degree to which the color line and ethnic boundaries are replicated in virtual settings.

Envisioning the Virtual

In the cyber noir film *Blade Runner*, earth is a wasteland occupied by extinct animal species replaced by genetically manufactured copies and humans unable to qualify as off-world colonists. As a dystopian view of a future in Los Angeles, Ridley Scott projected a decadent and decaying society comprised of non-whites and other socially marginal groups (e.g., Goths, Hare Krishnas) that merely exist while entropy degrades culture and language into a patois of Chinese, Spanish, German, and English. Those members of society that are not the "little people" are signposted in the film primarily by their whiteness. Escape from the nightmare that earth had become was possible through emigration to off-world colonies; new lands that offered opportunities and adventure. Dystopic science fiction of this nature reflects anxieties that whites experience today in reaction to contemporary shifts in U.S. demography, politics, and perceived eclipse in the global arena.

Second Life, however, is more commonly associated with ideas set forth in Neal Stephenson's novel, *Snow Crash* (1992). Also principally set in Los Angeles, *Snow Crash* concerns the lives of people that move in and out of a three dimensional virtual *metaverse* within which their avatars are able to club, conduct commerce, and even "die" in combat. As in *Blade Runner*, the Los Angeles of *Snow Crash* reflects a dystopian view of a society broken down under the anarchy of unrestrained neo-liberal capitalism. Pizza delivery joints are run by the Mafia; the most dangerous man in the world is an Aleut assassin leading a floating refugee city towards the Pacific Coast of the former USA. The main character, Hiro Protagonist, is a racial/ethnic hybrid: ½ Korean and ½ African American. Evocative in its elaboration of a virtual world wherein nearly anything is possible, *Snow Crash* itself crashed out of the constraint of the printed word and became the inspiration for the development of computer based virtual reality.

The Matrix relies on similar notions found in *Blade Runner* and *Snow Crash* in its portrayal of a ravaged world in which humans live plugged into a virtual reality. While humans are enslaved to extract electricity from their bodies for use by their robotic masters, those few that have awoken and been ejected from the matrix include a rag-tag ensemble of racially/ethnically diverse people. Indeed, the film *Matrix III* focuses on the protection of "Zion," an underworld community of hybrid, multi-ethnic people that look to Neo, the "One," for salvation. Again, whiteness and multi-ethnicity are underlying aspects of the characters that populate the matrix and "reality."

With this very brief synopsis of these significant works of cyber fiction I wish to draw attention to the fact that for many, the imagined future and cyber worlds are constituted as places signified by the presence of non-white, hybrid, and defective peoples. In these dystopias, whiteness is used to mark superior beings (e.g., Deckard and the Replicants of *Blade Runner*, the Agents of the *Matrix* franchise). But, these representations of whiteness are those left behind — simulacra of real whites that either left earth behind or no longer control what is left of earth. Imagery of this type serves as a cautionary tale of what unrestrained miscegenation might produce — a world out of control [of whites].

In contrast, the creators of *Second Life*, Linden Lab, organized their virtual world as a utopia; a place where individuals are free to do and be as they wish. "...we're building a new world" (Guest 2007: 60). Significantly, *Second Life* and official Linden discourse are devoid of references to race, ethnicity, disability, or any other type of salient identity that might interfere with Linden Lab's vision of a perfect world. Indeed, there is a pervasive blindness to color which has negative rather than positive effects for people of color. This (color) blind spot is so ingrained that demographic profiles for *Second Life* and other virtual worlds provide little more than age and gender breakdowns (e.g., Spence 2008). As a result, it is not possible to know the ethnic or racial background of virtual world residents (although it is possible to break down participation by nation or language). Yet the primary message about avatars in *Second Life* is that choices abound that allow residents to create, consume, and engage in almost any activity as long as it doesn't violate the terms of agreement (Rymaszewski, et al., 2008). The ideal of a new world where new relationships and a new social order is reflected in the statement "This time, though, our new lands have no indigenous inhabitants to dispute our claim to the territory. Virtual worlds are empty except for us, and are shaped entirely to our desires" (Guest, 2007: 6). No more messy business of colonization — that project has been completed. But we do take our colonial imaginary into virtual worlds with us.

3D(ementia-nal) Living

"Your avatar choices say a lot about who you are..."—Rymaszewski, et al., 2008:10

My *Second Life* began on October 25, 2008. After more than a year of residence in *SL*, my avatar has settled into a very specific look and routine. She is humanoid, female, and bears some physical resemblance to me. However, in real life the markers of my identity as a Chicana are significantly more apparent than in *Second Life*. For Latinos, who are classified on the basis of ethnicity rather than race, group identity is constructed out of a complex integration of shared history, language, ancestry, culture, geography, and religion. This complex mosaic of culture and history is difficult to encapsulate into a singular visual representative that can be read and comprehended by other residents. Further, there are aspects of *Second Life* that hinder Latin@ identity construction.

First, *Second Life* surnames are "preordained"—that is, Linden Lab requires new residents to select a surname from an established menu during identity creation. However, non-white "ethnic" surnames are conspicuously absent from the menu. Available surnames have included: Alex, Lamplight, Wardell, Oximoxi, Rembrandt, Sandalwood, Slavicz, Maesar, Leborski, and a variety of nonsense names and random juxtapositions of letters. Names almost entirely reflect American, European, or white identities. I was not able to find a name to convey my Latina background. A limited range of surnames illustrates what I consider Linden Lab's *illusion* of choice.

Finding an appropriate "skin" also proved to be a challenge. The majority of offerings in terms of skin tone reflect the dominant U.S. binary racial classification system (black or white). One of the first tasks in the transition from newbie to more sophisticated resident involves skin upgrading. In my searches for a skin authentic to my aesthetic, I was frustrated to find that skins might come in different tones, but facial features and body contours are nearly uniformly "Barbie doll" white or stereotypically "black." Latina, *mestiza*, and Indigenous appearing skins are sorely lacking. I was able to locate a "Frida Kahlo" skin. Given that she is so very iconic, a Frida skin can really only be worn by a Frida personifier. There is one store, Brazen Women, that offers "older" skins, but skin color and shape fall into the black/white binary. A likely response from a Linden or other *SL* advocate would be that anyone can create the items one needs in *Second Life*. Of course this presupposes the ability to design and create. *Second Life*, based as it is on consumerist capitalism responds to market demands. The lack of items that resonate with Latin@/Chican@ culture and phenotype (of which there are many) may indicate a limited participation by Latinas in *SL* as consumers or designers.

As a result, as I engage in *SL*, I experience a tangible erasure of being. Who I am seems difficult to replicate in *Second Life*. Since I cannot adequately signify who I am, I experience the psychosis of being an interloper, an impostor. These feelings are similar to Chicana/Latina real life experiences—particularly that of not belonging. As a cyber border crosser, I experience the ambivalence of not being of here nor there as Anzaldúa (1999: 99–113) and Moraga (2002: 24–33) wrote about living in the real world. Entering into *SL* creates a distortion, a type of cognitive dissonance, since one's identity as a woman of color is largely invisible, suppressed, neglected, or erased. As a cyber border crosser I may be able to move fluidly across the socially constructed and binding boundaries of race, ethnicity, and gender. But the more important question is, do I want to? As in my first life, my *Second Life* leaves much to be desired. The perpetual immersion in a white-oriented world wears upon the psyche. My Chicana self often looks not for escape in exotic vacations, but rather trips "back home" to the comfort of family, food, traditions, and *raza-ness*. *Second Life*, then, fails to meet my needs for "escape." I believe that this is an important distinction, and one that bell hooks reflects on in *belonging: a culture of place* (2009). hooks reminisces about Kentucky, the home place in the hills outside of the everyday indignities of racism, segregation, humiliation. Likewise, I associate escape with returning home where I can relax away from the scrutiny of white dominated society. *Second Life* strikes my curiosity, meets my need for debate and discussion in Socrates Café on Philosophy Island. I have enjoyed explorations and dancing the night away in techno clubs. But these are proxies for opportunities lost when I moved from the fast paced living of Los Angeles to the Midwest. Additionally, as a Latina with a significant amount of international traveling under her belt, I find tourist sims to be sterile and made to appeal to the timid American traveler too afraid to actually engage with the dirt, poverty, and reality of non-western settings.

Finding Communities of Color in SL

Second Life is known amongst virtual world cognoscenti as a place where members of non-mainstream groups can find like-minded people. The most notable communities are the Furry (avatars that dress/play as animals) and Gorean (Dom/Sub play) groups. *Second Life* has literally given new life to these rather underground real life micro-cultures. While in world sexual minorities are able to enjoy sex play and community secure in the anonymity of the platform.

My search for groups based on racial or ethnic identities has not been successful. A search did reveal more than 360 individuals that used Chicana, Chicano, Latina, or Latino as a first name. In this way, some residents explicitly signify their ethnicity through naming. For Latinos, who can be of any racial group, phenotype is a poor marker of ethnic identity. In the real world, Latino identities are conveyed by language, behavior, social networks, kinship, and to a lesser degree physical appearance. Interestingly, the one Latino community I was able to find was the Furry Latino group (242 members in January 2010). What had originally brought this group together was identification as furry, and secondarily as Latino.

Linden Lab does not record demographic information regarding resident/user race or ethnicity. Interestingly, gender and age categories are considered relevant data points to gather. Indeed, *Second Life: The Official Guide* (Rymaszewski, et al., 2008: 86) light-heartedly revealed that many men have female avatars in *SL*. It has reported that a good percentage of female avatars are animated by men. Boellstorff (2008: 141–142) noted that during his fieldwork it was common for residents to engage in "gender swapping" which allowed residents to more directly experience gender embodiment. Nevertheless, some activities such as shopping in *Second Life* is certainly a more female oriented activity. There is a wider range of skins, clothes, and accessories for females than males. (Rymaszewski, et al., 2008: 15, 256–261).

But, as has been pointed out already, references to race or ethnicity are seemingly taboo. The official guide to *SL* offers "not to be missed" hotspot recommendations (Rymaszewski, et al., 2008: 38–63) and a sample list of communities (44–45). However, none of these communities is organized around shared ethnic, cultural, or racial identities. *Second Life* does boast sims and even regions dedicated to non–English speakers, but are based on national or linguistic terms such as Mainland Brazil or areas where German, Korean, Japanese, and Spanish speakers can congregate. This is an aspect of a globalizing market that must be attractive for Linden Lab to explore. However, national identities or regions for specific language speakers do not address issues of race and ethnicity in the overall U.S. conceptualization of this virtual world.

In terms of studying race, ethnicity, gender, and other "invisible" identities within *Second Life*, proxy measures are required. One must rely on avatar "phenotype" (physical features) and other markers such as clothing, hair, and accessories. However, the difficulty is discerning whether the person behind the avatar is acting out a desire to inhabit the body of a different race or is in fact performing his/her actual identity. Since *SL* is populated by every variety of avatar, it can be difficult to determine what motivates users' choices. I have found that many Black female avatar bodies are highly sexualized and eroticized. Anecdotally, it appears that the more sexualized the body, the less likely the user is black or female. Avatars of this type recall blackface performance; whites are able to enact their projected fears and desires to control the exotic female other in a socially sanctioned performance space called *Second Life*. In my travels through *SL*, I have met avatars designed to reflect the real life identities of their users. For example, at Virtual Native Lands the Director is Nany Kayo, an enrolled Cherokee (her profile states "Cherokee by blood, by custom, by law, and by choice").

Latino-ness is represented by a few sims such as Visit Mexico *Second Life* Ruta Maya and the Smithsonian Latino Virtual Museum. Both, however, seem to be largely oriented towards attracting non–Latino residents. Visit Mexico *Second Life* Ruta Maya recreates popular tourist attractions such as Chichén Itzá, Palenque, Tulum, and colonial Campeche. Created by the Mexican Tourism Board, this sim provides residents the opportunity to engage in virtual tourism "without the cost of staying in a hotel" (*Second Life* Update. com). More importantly, cyber tourism offers travel without the inconveniences of interactions with *real* Mexicans. There are no children hawking cheap souvenirs, linguistic barriers, or concerns about "Montezuma's revenge." Instead, all is provided for the virtual tourist including cyber stereotyping that allows visitors the comfort of their xenophobic knowledge base. Visitors can obtain "authentic outfits [that] are replications of outfits worn by Mayan royalty" (Virtual Mexico Note Card n.d.) Claiming authenticity for these costumes is highly problematic since they neither resemble archaeological imagery of costume (see Joyce 1999, 2000 for a thorough discussion of Maya dress) nor conform to modes of dress by contemporary Maya peoples (Hendrickson 1995). Rather, these costumes are a pastiche of stereotypical "Indian" wear — animal skins, feathers and spears. Regardless of the designer's intentions (Aries Bricklin, who is a skilled *SL* clothing designer), the result is a reification of the trope of Indian as savage. Equally jarring is the audio tour with the voice of a woman with a British accent!

The Fantasy of Transcendence

Some have argued that virtual worlds such as *Second Life* allow individuals to transcend the physical limitations of the body (Jones 2006: 3, Guest 2007: 114). One can style an avatar into any shape, size, or creature (anything from aliens to velociraptors). Transcendence, however, is an unrecognized privilege of whiteness, heteronormativity, ableness, and even perhaps gender. For residents that enjoy white privilege, this transcendence allows them to play out fantasies of performing the other. In this way, whites can dress and act out according to their romanticized notions of ethnicity. They transcend their whiteness by appropriating the phenotype, dress, and stereotyped behaviors of non-whites.

For people of color, however, the notion of transcendence is awkward and problematic. Jones (2009: 4) suggests that *Second Life* is attractive to individuals that wish to be free from social and physical limitations of the body limited by ethnicity, gender, sexual orientation and other markings. Boler argues that computer-mediated communication, while offering the hope of disembodiment, actually "re-invoke stereotypical notions of racialized, sexualized and gendered bodies (2007: 140). Similarly, I question whether those of us with non-normative bodies desire to be set free from these so-called limitations. Do we really want to transcend our racial/ethnic identities? Do we desire the ability to "pass"? Is the fantasy of transcendence real? Do people of color really feel that we want to transcend the body or do we merely desire to transcend the privilege attached to whiteness? People of color are subject to greater surveillance, racial profiling, and racist commentary in everyday real life (Antonovics and Knight 2009; Kivel 2002, Murcchetti 2005). Due to institutionalized racism, skin color itself has been criminalized (Harris 2002: 224) and the costs take a heavy psychological and physical toll (Kivel 2002). Entry into the upper echelons of U.S. society still remains contingent upon factors outside the control of the individual. Be this as it may, individuals that must endure the threat and fear of racist, sexist, or homophobic assault do not necessarily wish they could change their state of being.

I contend that for users of color there are opportunities to play with identity by performing whiteness, fantasy creatures, other genders, etc. However, assuming that virtual worlds allow us to transcend the limitations of the body assumes that our bodies are the problem. For people of color, our bodies are not the problem, rather a history of racism, prejudice, discrimination, colonialism, and oppression is what we wish to overcome. The subtext of transcendence is that white is the norm and that given the opportunity, anyone can engage in *SL* without the problematic of being recognized as colored by look, dialect or dress. The fantasy of transcendence is little more than the colonialist desire to remake the colonized in the image of their white masters.

Transcendence is also problematic in the sense that it offers the opportunity for whites to transcend their perceived lack of ethnic identity and adopt for a day the experiences of people of color. However, should a white user performing blackness with a black avatar experience racism or harassment, he or she can easily shed this other skin and return to the safety of whiteness. For users of color, however, authentic renditions of themselves via avatars means potential exposure to racism and harassment. If I have no desire for whiteness then I must face the consequences of choosing not to transcend.

The subtext conveyed is that people living "defective lives" can be freed through technology and virtual living within *Second Life*. Similarly, poverty, issues of computer access, and the need for technical competency are not addressed. *Second Life* is in many ways a virtual gated-community that protects a cyber-suburbia from direct interface with marked and marginalized *real* bodies. Yet, for the "ethnic curious" (akin to being "bi-curious") whites can presume to experience "blackness" by wearing a black skin and virtual bling or play out fantasies of being an exotic erotic Asian. Should the experience prove too real or too uncomfortable, escape is a quick avatar appearance edit away. But for users that must continually be hyper vigilant within white patriarchal capitalist sexist society (bell hooks), there is no easy edit. The question is, can a woman of color present her authentic self through performance of an avatar in *Second Life*? *Second Life* does present opportunities for some marginalized or poorly understood micro-cultures to play and interact with relative freedom (e.g., furries, Goreans, etc.). However, these identities are not tied to racialized stereotypes that are part of one's physical being. *Second Life* is a controlled and contained environment where racial and ethnic identities may well be construed as dangerous to the "public" good.

As there are currently no off-world colonies to escape to, people that have become weary of the ennui of the daily grind can enter into a perpetually clean world. For many residents, places such as *Second Life* provide order and safety from a chaotic world (Guest 2007: 76). What would such residents be willing to do or do without to guarantee the illusion of order? Social order is maintained to a degree by adherence to informal rules of "Slettiquette." An example is a rule that states "Just like in first life, no one with self-respect likes a badgering beggar." Code for no panhandlers, please! Through the deployment of polite language and an ethos of "just get alonged-ness" *Second Life* has literally and virtually eliminated the inconvenience of stepping over the undeserving poor. This is but one example of the types of social discomforts that are not allowed in *Second Life*. Behaviors that infringe upon other people's enjoyment of the *SL* are designated as griefing and carry the potential punishment of banishment.

If We Build It, Will They Come?

Audre Lorde (2002) in "The Master's Tools Will Never Dismantle the Master's House" argued against mere tolerance of difference. At the time she was speaking out against mainstream feminists regarding Black women and Lesbians of Color as afterthoughts ... the last point on the agenda (literally). Similarly, any social project that seeks to be liberatory cannot relegate minorities, and especially women of color, to the margins. If we seek to create new worlds in virtual environments, we must fashion such places with new tools and new perspectives. Certainly in the realm of technology, Linden Lab and other developers of virtual reality have made the speculative fiction of the past into today's (virtual) realty. However, given that the developers employed the old tools of the Master — capitalist based, gender neutralized, and from a predominantly (although not necessarily conscious) white perspective — the final product is a world that negates difference because it is too difficult for whites to deal with.

Mohammed (2009: 9) advocates the creation of educational materials within *SL* as a means to apply a "negotiation rather than negation" approach to teach cultural/religious understanding between Muslim and non–Muslim residents. Certainly, increased participation by diverse peoples through the creation of sims, educational endeavors, gatherings, and discussion groups holds significant potential for making non-western, minority, and differently constituted people visible within *SL*. However, this raises the question, if such venues for learning about difference are created, will residents avail themselves of such opportunities?

Examples of educational sims for the dissemination of cultural information include Virtual Native Lands and the Smithsonian Virtual Latino Museum (SVLM). Opened in March 2009, the SVLM required major financial and labor commitments to integrate online museum collection materials with the sim build. The resulting product is of high quality and caters to a wide range of interests. One may spend quite a bit of time examining the various exhibits; clicking on artifacts or panels will link directly to digital archives, sound files, and images. This is an excellent museum with great educational potential. Since the official opening through January 2010, there have been more than 12,000 visitors. Over the course of 2009, the SVLM had the greatest number of visits in April (3106, average of 103 per day) and the fewest in December (339, average of 7.3 per day). By comparison, about 30 million people visited SI museums and the national zoo in 2009 (Smithsonian Institute 2009: 9), which averages out to more than 80,000 people per day. Daily visits to *Second Life* average around 50,000. This does not indicate that the SVLM is an unsuccessful project. Visits were high in November, likely corresponding to Day of the Dead activities that were advertised both in and out world.

Visits to Virtual Native Lands, a sim that offers accurate visual and textual information on American Indians, also seem light. The website for VNL states that it "promotes the use of emerging Internet technologies to create and sustain Native American culture." Similar to VNL is an educational project developed with the USC Annenberg School for Communication Network Culture Project. The project developed in response to "harmful misrepresentations of Native Americans in *Second Life*" (Mayo 2009: 22). The current director of the project, Nany Kayo, has set up VNL as a non-profit educational project designed to serve several needs. I communicated with Nany in VNL in October 2009. Nany took time out of her busy schedule to talk about plans for the upcoming Day of the Dead festivities in coordination with the SVLM. It was clear from our discussion that Nany is a hands on *SL* creator with a passion for the work she is engaged in. According to Nany VNL is the only sim in *Second Life* created by an authentic American Indian. This is a important aspect of the sim. Nany notes that some residents claim to be Native, profit from such claims, but perpetuate stereotypes about Indians in negative ways (Mayo 2009: 23–24). Plans for the future include collaboration with an American Indian college. From VNL, one can teleport to a mall to buy items from American Indian creators such as realistic skins, authentic clothing, and household items. At this mall commerce provides opportunity for education. Visitors can view posters critical of "Caucasian Fantasy," the appropriation of Indian culture in ways that reinforce negative stereotypes of Native peoples.

Will There Be White Flight from Second Life?

If, as I have suggested, *Second Life* is similar to a gated community keeping the riff-raff out, what will happen when the gates break down? Currently, gate keeping in *Second Life* is accomplished by external cultural, economic, and social factors that limit accessibility by women, people of color, the poor, and people with disabilities. While there are certainly increasing numbers of people crossing over the digital divide, what will be the results of greater influxes of the multitudes? Will more and more *SL* residents opt for creating barriers between themselves and perceived *others*? Currently, privacy is maintained by fences and ejection bots. Will segregation be the result of a multiculturalized *Second Life*?

In world, conduct is regulated by the terms of agreement and *SL*ettiquite. The overriding desire for *SL* by Linden Lab and the majority of residents is a calm, tranquil virtual life where one is free to engage in the 3Cs: commerce, combat, or consensual sex. But, if *SL* is like RL, can social movements, protest, political action, and even affirmative action take root? If I am offended by a grotesquely stereotypical racist/sexist avatar — do I have recourse? The answer, at this point is yes and no. Since *SL* is a privately owned, corporate venture that individuals opt into, anyone who encounters difficulties is free to leave. Abuse reports can be filed, but there is no guarantee that Linden Labs can or will take action. Abuse that occurs in private sims are regulated by covenants and may not be punishable.

Au (2006) recounts the experiences of Erica, a woman that spent a month modeling her friend's black skin, who was completely surprised and outraged by the treatment she received as a black woman. Yet, she did not report the abuse, since there are "Better things for Lindens to worry about." This is white privilege in operation — the ability to walk away from racism (Kivel 2002). The subtext is really that she (as a phenotypical blonde in RL and *SL*) had more important issues to deal with than challenging racist discourse within *SL*. For residents and avatars of color, however, the choices are more problematic. One can choose to perform whiteness in *Second Life*, as two of Erica's Black friends do (Au 2006). Or, one can perform as a woman of color and be prepared for racist/sexist treatment, or leave *Second Life* behind. Methal Mohammed's (2009) experience of being singled out and killed without warning in *SL* was so disconcerting that she did not return to *SL* for two months. Further, she became concerned the same could occur in RL.

The anonymous nature of *Second Life* offers people myriad opportunities to explore new skins, new behaviors, and new relationships. This is a positive aspect of virtual world living. However, a negative aspect of anonymity is that racist, sexist, and other hurtful actions can take place with the victim having little recourse. Abuse reports can be made, but in the immediate moment, avatars of color may be so shocked by the attack that they fail to take down information. Regardless of what actions Linden Lab might take against abusers, once a resident has experienced abuse he or she may simply decide to not engage in *SL* again. As long as *SL* persists mostly as an entertainment platform, the larger *SL* population may not consider the lack of interest by people of color anything to be concerned about. However, the *SL* grid will continue to grow and engage with educational and commercial operations that will desire the participation and economic resources of people of color. The issue that needs to be addressed now is will the borders that limit users of color be build up or knocked down?

"Within the interdependence of mutual (nondominant) differences lies that security which enables us to descend into the chaos of knowledge and return with true visions of our future, along with the concomitant power to effect those changes which can bring that future into being. Difference is that raw and powerful connection from which our personal power is forged" (Audre Lorde 2002).

Works Cited

Anzaldúa, Gloria. *Borderlands/La Frontera. The New Mestiza: Second Edition.* San Francisco: Aunt Lute Books, 1999.

Au, Wagner James. The Skin You're In. *New World Notes,* 2006. http://nwn.blogs.com/nwn/2006/02/the_skin_youre_.html, accessed 31 January 2010.

Blaut, J.M. *The Colonizer's Model of the World: Geographical Diffusionism and Eurocentric History.* New York: Guilford Press, 1993.

Boler, Megan. "Hypes, Hopes and Actualities: New Digital Cartesianism and Bodies in Cyberspace." *New Media and Society* vol. 9(1) (2007): 129–168.

Castronovo, Edward. "The Price of 'Man' and 'Woman': A Hedonic Pricing Model of Avatar Attributes in a Synthetic World." *Cesifo Working Paper* No. 957 (2003): 1–45.

Guest, Tim. *Second Lives: A Journey Through Virtual Worlds.* New York: Random House, 2007.

hooks, bell. *Belonging: A Culture of Place.* New York: Routledge, 2009.

Jones, Donald E. "I, Avatar: Constructions of Self and Place in *Second Life* and the Technological Imagination." *Gnovis,* vol. 6 (2006) http://gnovisjournal.org/files/Donald-E-Jones-I-Avatar.pdf, accessed 15 January 2010.

Kivel, Paul. *Uprooting Racism: How White People Can Work for Racial Justice,* rev. ed. Canada: New Society Publishers, 2002.

Linden Research. "*SL*etiquette," http://wiki.secondlife.com/wiki/*SL*etiquette, accessed 15 January 2010.

Lorde, Audre. "The Master's Tools Will Never Dismantle the Master's House." *This Bridge Called My Back: Writings by Radical Women of Color,* ed. C. Moraga and G. Anzaldúa, pp. 106–109. Berkeley, CA: Third Woman Press, 2002.

Mayo, Coughran. "Native Intelligence." *Prim Perfect* vol. 19: 22–24, 2009.

Mohammed, M. "Cultural Identity in Virtual Worlds (VW): A Case Study of a Muslim with Hijab in Second Life (SL)," *Journal of Virtual Worlds Research, 2* (2) (2009), http://jvwresearch.org/index.php/past-issues/22-health-and-heathcare, accessed 1 December 2014.

Moraga, Cherrie L. "La Güera." *This Bridge Called My Back: Writings by Radical Women of Color*, ed. C. Moraga, and G. Anzaldúa. Berkeley, CA: Third Woman Press, 2002.

Nakamura, Lisa. *Cybertypes: Race, Ethnicity, and Identity on the Internet.* New York: Routledge, 2002.

Rymaszewski, Michael, et al. *Second Life: The Official Guide, second ed.* Indianapolis: Wiley, 2008.

Scott, Ridley (Director). *Blade Runner* (Director's cut), 1982. DVD Warner Home Video, 1997.

Second Life Update.com. Visit Chichén Itzá Mexico in *Second Life*—Travel to Yucatan Peninsula Virtual World. 2009. http://www.secondlifeupdate.com/virtual-world-experiences/visit-chichen-itza-mexico-in-second-life-travel-to-yucatan-peninsula-virtual-world/, accessed 15 January 2010.

Second Life wiki. Wikipedia, http://en.wikipedia.org/wiki/Second_Life#cite_note-35 Smithsonian Institute. 2009. Detailed Performance Data Report, Fiscal Year 2000 http://www.si.edu/about/policies/documents/FY2009-Detailed-Performance.pdf

Spence, Jeremiah. "Demographics of Virtual Worlds." *Journal of Virtual Worlds Research* vol. 1, no. 2 (November 2008).

Stephenson, Neal. *Snow Crash.* New York: Bantam Books, 1992.

Wachowski, Andy, and Lana Wachowski (Directors). *The Matrix.* DVD Warner Home Video, 2007.

West, Cornel. *Race Matters.* New York: Vintage Books, 2001.

Gender (Re)Production of "Emotion Work" and "Feeling Rules" in *Second Life*

JENNIFER J. REED

I initially joined the 3D virtual world of *Second Life* (*SL*) in December 2008. As a scholar and a social researcher, I felt intrigued by the possibilities of this new form of online user-created community. I noticed the light blue *SL* logo, the Eye in Hand, prominently displayed next to the words "*Second Life*" on my computer screen. The Eye in Hand icon symbolizes the interactive bond between two vital human functions: (1) the Eye, which represents sensing, observing, and knowledge, and (2) the Hand, which represents doing, acting, and power. How would humans use their knowledge and power in this virtual world? What would they imagine and create here?

I first became interested in the computer-mediated communication (CMC) environment as a potential teaching tool in the mid–1990s. I mention the beginning of CMC use in the classroom now for two reasons. First, computer discussion lists were promoted as a new platform for teaching and learning when the internet revolution began in much the same way as scholars and professionals are promoting 3D virtual worlds such as *Second Life* for their educational potential today. Second, despite the promotion of CMC with the advent of the internet, there was still controversy and uneasiness about what would be created in that new environment much like with 3D virtual worlds like *SL* currently.

The old debate in the CMC literature centered around the type of effect that the new mode of communication had on human relationships. Some investigators argued that people were being alienated or constrained by computer interactions and focused on the negative group outcomes associated with CMC when compared with face-to-face group outcomes.[1] Other investigators focused on the social meanings that emerged in CMC and demonstrated that computer-mediated interactants actively exploited the systems' features in ways that produced a sense of community.[2]

Today, a similar debate has emerged surrounding the newer technology of 3D massively multiplayer online (MMOs) spaces like *Second Life*. Because *SL* users can create their own avatars and are primarily responsible for the content of their virtual world, some investigators argue that it is a liberating and transgressive medium.[3] Still other researchers challenge this proposal and even question whether *SL* users simply reproduce traditional roles and norms found in real life (RL).[4,5] So, is *Second Life* a limitless platform of the human imagination, or is it a space where people reproduce their real world cultural and political ideologies?

Gender, sex, and sexuality are highly politicized issues in the real world. Brookey and Cannon critiqued authors who claim that 3D virtual spaces such as *SL* are unique social arenas used to challenge and transgress traditional gender roles and sex norms (i.e., the "liberatory perspective"). Instead, they argued for a "critical alternative" that takes into account how cyberspace is used to reproduce gender roles and sex norms found in RL. Based on the works of Michel Foucault and Judith Butler, Brookey and Cannon applied the perspective of a "docile body" that has become an active embodiment of disciplinary gender and sexual practices in RL. They used docility to explain why some *SL* users choose to objectify and marginalize themselves in the virtual world. For example, some women choose to construct identities in *SL* that are sexually submissive to men, reinforcing a RL ideology that limits the value of women. Rather than being passive, perhaps *SL* users have internalized these RL ideologies. Liberation from one's physical body in *SL* does not necessarily allow one to escape the RL influences that shaped one's identity. Some researchers have argued that more theories are needed to guide studies in cyberspace, particularly virtual studies of gender, sex, and sexuality (Brookey and Cannon; Consalvo). Brookey and Cannon caution that "cyberspace should not be regarded as an environment that moves the user outside of the political and social matrix of gender and sexuality" (160). What other RL theories could be applied to *SL*?

According to the sociological symbolic interactionist tradition and the sociology of emotions, feelings shape the flow of interaction. Hochschild referred to "emotion work" as "the act of trying to change in degree or quality an emotion or feeling" ("Emotion Work" 561). Hochschild found that feeling rules (i.e., different feeling expectations based on group membership) and emotion work (i.e., in the form of managing one's own feelings in an effort to make relationships run smoothly) vary by gender in RL. In particular, women have traditionally done more emotion work, making a resource out of feeling and offering it to men as a gift in return for the more material resources they lack (Hochschild, *The Managed Heart*). Giddens contended that it is crucial to recognize the correlations and interactions among gender, sexuality, intimacy and love. He proposed that as women gain financial resources over time, men are gaining fewer emotional resources, creating a shift in gender power that can lead to violence, particularly as men fail to manage their emotions.[6]

My research questions addressed in this study are: Do *SL* residents challenge and transgress traditional gender roles with regard to an avatar's gender presentation since there is no way to be certain of the RL person's sex behind the avatar? More specifically, do *SL* residents challenge and transgress traditionally gendered emotion work and feeling rules, or do they recreate them? I set out to answer these questions by conducting a virtual ethnography over a six month period as two different avatars: (1) a female avatar, Jamie and (2) a male avatar, Jamey. Because my RL gender is female, I began the project by creating a female avatar. Given the rather steep learning curve required to gain *SL* technical skills, I felt more comfortable entering the virtual world with my RL female gender identity. Once I gained enough technical ability to navigate around *SL*, I also constructed a male avatar. I had regular meetings with a group of professors and students who were also conducting research in *SL*. We met about every other week—usually in *SL*, but occasionally those in the same geographical location met in RL—to discuss our experiences and exchange ideas. I kept a journal to document my journey.

I intended to collect data through natural and participant observation, informal interviews, and critical self-reflection. However, in an early meeting, group members engaged in a heated debate over the ethics of gender switching for research purposes in *SL*. No one appeared to have an issue with changing any other visual representation of one's avatar, such as age, race, height, weight, or clothing style. Some even argued that to represent one's *SL* avatar as a different gender than that of the RL person was a deceptive research practice. Those who advanced that argument perceived gender as a "master status," which is a sociological term meaning "one status within a set that stands out or overrides all others" (Conley 743).

Two researchers suggested that I conduct interviews only as a female avatar or risk being accused of deceiving research subjects. Moreover, one researcher, Alexx argued that although it was unethical to switch genders with research subjects, it was completely ethical to have virtual sex with them because it's not "really" sex and it involves no deception if you disclose your status as researcher ahead of time. A quote from MacKinnon's famous article came to mind: "Sex as gender and sex as sexuality are thus defined in terms of each other, but it is sexuality that determines gender, not the other way around" (531). Following this discussion, I decided to exclude interviews as a data collection technique. Instead, I chose to focus on my own experiences in *Second Life* from a RL woman's standpoint. As such, I realize that these experiences may not be reflective of others' experiences in *SL* and are not generalizable.

At the time of my research, the *SL* platform itself seemed to reproduce the overriding importance of gender as I was forced to check a box for either "female" or "male" upon creating an avatar. (Now, you begin by choosing a pre-made avatar — that you can later modify — from the following categories: people, vampires, animals, robots, or vehicles. Still, if you start with an avatar from the people category, the choices are labeled female or male and wearing traditionally gendered clothing.) The 3D visual setting of *SL* strongly recreated RL gender norms in terms of the appearance of the standard avatar with which I could start. My initial experiences in *SL* reflected those of Dumitrica and Gaden who wrote, "a heterosexual normativity was suggested ... primarily through the options available for creating and enhancing the avatar, but also through the visual predominance of patriarchal ideals of beauty as stretched by prevailing imagery of the binary male/female" (12). Although I could definitely modify my avatar, it would require a great deal of technical skill and time to make significant changes. Sunden highlighted that since online bodies are "materially grounded in the computer code ... system developers and programmers have the power to set limits for the types of bodies that can be created" (172). Lacking those resources, I chose to modify my avatar by searching for various body parts and clothing that I could acquire at a *SL* store. Although many items were available for purchase with Linden dollars (i.e., *SL* currency purchased via RL credit card), I made the decision to only obtain free items. Despite many choices within *SL* resident-owned shops, I found that "the vast majority remain framed by a particular imagination of gendered beauty and desirability" (Dumitrica and Gaden 13).

Shortly after leaving "Orientation Island" to explore *SL* more fully, my newbie female avatar, Jamie, was gifted several objects by random *SL* residents including clothing items and a small bubble maker resembling a wand. When I "wore" the bubble maker on my hand, it continuously produced small, transparent bubbles all around me. I was also quickly offered many friend requests and landmarks to locations where I could obtain clothing and accessories for my avatar. Additionally, one male avatar offered to speak with me "any time" moments after meeting in a club. A nearby female avatar remarked, "He just wants to be surrounded by all the ladies."

I discovered that the *SL* clothing stores were mostly gendered. Examples of signs displayed at the entrance of female stores included: "NO MALE AVATARS ALLOWED!! SECURITY WILL BAN ANY MAN WHO PASSES THIS SIGN" and "WOMEN'S FREEBIES (NO MEN ALLOWED)." It was interesting to me that there was even some secrecy surrounding the virtual female form.

Female stores often had virtual dressing rooms that were semi-private areas partitioned off for trying on clothes and accessories. Beauty was clearly emphasized. For example, a sign was prominently displayed next to a women's dressing room:

> HOW DO I GET MY BODY NICE? In *Second Life* you need 2 things to look beautiful. 1st you need a high quality body/face shape the shape is the form/structure/size of your entire body and face. 2nd you need a high quality skin color — skin is the outer coloring of your body it attaches to the outside of your body shape.

Shortly after entering *SL*, I began noticing avatars around me with better looking hair than I had. The hair on my starter avatar looked like it was pasted on my head like a helmet. Due to recently improved hair technology, an avatar's hair could now more closely replicate the movement and style of hair in RL. I quickly began to feel badly about Jamie's hair as I saw more avatars with prettier hair. I reflected on this experience as not being "real," and then went to the *SL* store to shop around for new and improved hair. After "trying on" various hair, I chose a style for Jamie. Appearance was definitely important.

I felt good about the new look. However, shortly after spending time improving Jamie's appearance and checking out the multitude of locations *SL* has to offer, I found myself spending more time alone exploring the beautiful created environment and landscape. Boellstorff found that some *SL* residents settle into a pattern of solitude. He called for "a theory of cybersociality that takes into account how some people enter virtual worlds to be left alone" (125). Once I became more familiar and comfortable with the *SL* environment as Jamie, I gravitated toward the impressive 3D graphic representation of places much more than people.

As my male avatar, Jamey, I noticed almost immediately that I was rarely approached or spoken to first. I was also offered far fewer friend requests. At the outset, I felt a sense of relief and freedom from random people trying to interact with me as often as when I appeared gender female in *SL*. However, as more time passed as Jamey, I occasionally felt frustrated to have to work harder to attract attention, yet I generally felt that I was taken more seriously when I did work to establish a connection with someone. Sometimes I appreciated feeling like I had to earn a person's attention and could choose to be left alone more easily. I was also unsure how to respond appropriately in certain situations. For example, I was concerned that my normal RL response to certain situations in *SL* would make people question my "real" gender or sexual orientation. I found that when that happened, I tended to react indifferently because of my uncertainty as to "how to act male" or if gender was even an important distinction. Instead of interacting smoothly, I found that

I was reminding myself that my *SL* avatar was gender male, even though I became increasingly unsure what that even meant socially.

On one occasion, upon teleporting to a new location, my male avatar was taking particularly long to "rez" (i.e., fully appear and come into focus on the screen) which depends on the speed of the computer, the server and the internet connection. Apparently, Jamey's image began to rez on top of a female avatar, Rose, that happened to be in the same location. Even in my limited experience, I noticed that avatars frequently appeared on top of each other when several people were teleporting to the same *SL* location. Sometimes it felt awkward or even a bit embarrassing when one person "showed up" directly in another's virtual visual space. However, during *SL* meetings, our group members just joked about it. In this particular instance, Rose typed via local chat for all in the immediate range to read, "This guy keeps bumping into me." It took me a second to even realize that she was talking about me. I felt extremely annoyed by her implication. My first reaction was to call Rose a name and ask her who she thought she was that I would intentionally bump into her, but then I stopped and thought about it. Would my initial reaction as a female have been the same as hers, especially if it were a new situation? Perhaps she was a newbie to *SL*. Maybe she was reacting to a previous experience of feeling like a male was too close in her space. I could relate to that experience in my identities as both RL and *SL* gender female. How would I effectively communicate with her as a RL female in this situation represented by a *SL* male avatar? All of a sudden, I felt quite confused. Events such as the situation with Rose made me question my choice to gender switch in *SL*. On the other hand, these were the defining moments that convinced me of the importance of my research albeit the uncertainties it created for me in RL.

The only gifted object I received as a male in *SL* was a picture taken of me while dancing at a beach club. A female who had a male partner with her gave me the picture and said, "Put it on your profile." "Thank you," I replied. I felt touched as if she had made a generous gesture by giving me this gift. I had no reason to think that there were any motives attached. That was a different feeling than I often experienced as a female avatar when gifted an object by a male. First, she made it clear that she had a partner with her. Second, she waited until I hung out and interacted for awhile before offering it to me.

I identified two critical incidents that occurred during our *SL* group meetings. After the dispute about gender switching, I always attended our meetings as gender female to avoid further conflict. For our initial *SL* meeting, we convened in a classroom in a prominent virtual university. During the meeting, a random male avatar entered and began talking to a female in our meeting group. Our group hadn't established any norms for dealing with such a situation in a virtual world. "We're having a meeting," Brooklyn told him.

Instead of excusing himself for the intrusion, our unsolicited visitor continued talking. He began asking questions about the meeting and attempting to engage other females in conversation in an increasingly obnoxious display. Rather than deal with the growing hassle of the situation, the professor leading our group teleported away to a new location and sent us teleport requests to join him there. "Where are you going?" asked the uninvited guest as we all began to disappear without warning. Despite the fact we agreed his behavior was disruptive and out of line, four female researchers, including myself, discussed how we felt badly about simply leaving him there alone. We began to ponder why he had behaved that way rather than focusing on the disruption to ourselves and the meeting. According to Boellstorff, when people disappear suddenly from an online environment without warning those nearby, it is often termed "poofing" which may carry a negative connotation.

The second critical incident occurred when we met again as a group, this time in a gazebo in a more private garden area. A male avatar walked up and stood nearby. "Uh-oh, not again," our group leader announced. In an effort to prevent a similar fiasco, I decided to be proactive this time and address our new guest up front. There are two ways to communicate via text in the immediate *SL* area—local chat is text that anyone within the immediate range can read and instant messaging (IM) is text directed to one specific person in range that only s/he can read. I greeted Taylor by his first name (which was displayed above his avatar) via local chat so that the entire group was aware of it. I told him that our meeting group was from a large southwestern university and we were meeting to discuss research in *SL*. "We would be happy to talk with you afterward," I said. As we proceeded with our meeting, Taylor began to leave me angry personal IMs. "You could have just told me that you were having a faculty meeting and that I wasn't welcome," he said. I explained via IM back to him that we were just learning about *SL* and how to have meetings in a virtual space. Taylor responded by telling me how rude I was and calling me names. At this point, I told the group via local chat that he was IMing me. His messages became progressively more aggressive calling me a variety of names. His text was now coming across my computer screen so rapidly that the lines were scrolling down before I could even read them. "Jamie, is he still IMing you?" Jenny asked via local chat after some time had passed. "Yes," I replied. Taylor retorted via IM to me, "Tell your friend (Jenny) she isn't funny." I decided to disengage from the interaction by ignoring his IMs and presence until he left the area. Hochschild wrote that since women are generally expected to do more emotion work through demonstrating warmth and support, a female is more often perceived as cold in the exact same interaction in which a male is perceived as neutral. Would Taylor have reacted the same way in that situation if my avatar was male?

Based on my *SL* experiences as a RL female presenting as both a female and male avatar, I found that residents often applied traditional gender roles to me based on my avatar's gender presentation, even though no one could be sure of the "real" gender identity behind the avatar. In particular, I found that traditionally gendered feeling rules and emotion work were expected of me, also based on my avatar's gender presentation. My female avatar was approached more frequently and, as with the example of Taylor during our group meeting, expected to be accessible and nice or possibly sustain verbal/text assault. I never had this experience when presenting as my male avatar. As Haraway and Twine described bodies in RL, the representation of the female body appears to also be "marked" in the virtual world. That is, meanings are attached and discursive associations are made to possessing a particular bodily appearance — in this case, "being a woman."

Although my limited, exploratory experience appears to uphold the critical alternative of a reproduction of gender roles that is retrograde in RL, I argue that virtual spaces such as *SL* may still be liberatory because of the reflexivity made possible by the relative ease of changing one's physical appearance, such as gender. Nakamura referred to choosing another identity in cyberspace, particularly an identity that differs from one's RL gender and/or race, as "identity tourism" ("Race in/for"). She asserted that role playing is a *feature* of virtual communities and that it is absurd to ask those who play within them to subscribe to their RL gender, race, or other condition of social life. *SL* offers an environment where a person can change characteristics quickly, temporarily, and recreationally with nearly no RL risks, as one can literally teleport away from a location or logoff of *SL* altogether.

Rather than viewing gender as a core identity, Judith Butler discussed gender as a performance shaped by RL discourse and social scripts. According to Butler, a hegemonic gender order is built upon the belief that there are two genders — man and woman — each with a corresponding set of behavioral tendencies called masculinity and femininity. However, she proposed that "gender" is actually a performance — performing masculinity or femininity. For Butler, "there is no gender identity behind the expressions of gender; that identity is performatively constituted by the very 'expressions' that are said to be its results" (25). In other words, "although gendered behaviors are modeled after images of what it means to be a woman or man that we learn from our families and other institutions" (Seidman 37–38), others will likely construe our behavior as expressing an inner gender identity. Gender performativity is "compulsory in the sense that acting out of lines with gender norms brings with it ostracism, punishment and violence, not to mention the transgressive pleasures produced by these very prohibitions" (Butler 22). Performing various identities such as gender in virtual spaces like *SL* allows us to question the essentialness of social categories through simulated experiences where RL risk is minimal. That said, continuing the theatrical metaphor, Hawkes pointed out that even if we perform gender, "performances are also dependent on script-writers, availability of finance, even a supportive audience" leaving them "vulnerable to reactionary influences" (144).

As a RL female presenting myself as a *SL* male avatar, I gained a greater understanding of the constraints as well as the advantages of being perceived as male. Gaining such awareness can translate into increased social intelligence in dealing with people in general, and with men in particular, in RL. I propose that *SL* is not *either* a liberatory, transgressive social arena *or* a place where we reproduce gender roles and sex norms. It is both. Here, we can recreate the dominant RL ideology and power relationships and create revolutionary new ways of interacting that allow us to transform those power relationships. Both of these possibilities point at alternatives to the ideas of postmodern fragmentation and fragmented identities. We have to start by understanding where we are (or have been) if we hope to change. As Foucault wrote, discourse can be both an instrument and an effect of power, but also a hindrance, a stumbling block, a point of resistance and a starting point for an opposing strategy. "Discourse transmits and produces power; it reinforces it, but also undermines and exposes it, renders it fragile and makes it possible to thwart it" ("The History" 101). As such, virtual spaces such as *SL* are both shaped by and, in turn, help shape a rapidly changing wider society. It will be interesting to see if and how younger generations that have grown up with such virtual world technologies interact with the world differently.

Notes

1. For an example of studies that focused on the negative group outcomes associated with CMC compared to face-to-face interactions, see Baron; Kiesler, Siegel, and McGuire; Kiesler and Sproull; Siegel et al.; Sproull and Kiesler.

2. For an example of studies that focused on the positive features of CMC that produced a sense of community, see Bromberg; Hellerstein; Jones; Myers; Parks and Floyd; Rheingold; Turkle; Walther. For an overview of this early debate in the literature on negative versus positive outcomes of CMC, see Reed.

3. For a sample of investigators who argued that *SL* is a liberating and transgressive medium, see Berman and Bruckman; Nyboe; Stone; Turkle.

4. For a sample of investigators that challenge the notion of *SL* as liberating and transgressive, see Bryson et al.; Gunkel; Roberts and Parks.

5. For an example of researchers who question whether *SL* users reproduce traditional RL norms, see Brookey and Cannon; Nakamura, "You Said."

6. Hochschild noted that "'emotion work' refers to the effort — the act of trying — and not to the outcome, which may or may not be successful" ("Emotion Work" 561). Thus, failing to manage emotions can be reflective of a failed attempt or of never even trying to alter one's feelings.

Works Cited

Baron, Naomi S. "Computer Mediated Communication as a Force in Language Change." *Visible Language* 18.2 (1984): 118–141. Print.

Berman, Joshua, and Amy S. Bruckman. "The Turing Game: Exploring Identity in an Online Environment." *Convergence* 7.3 (2001): 83–102. Print.

Boellstorff, Tom. *Coming of Age in Second Life: An Anthropologist Explores the Virtually Human.* Princeton, NJ: Princeton University Press, 2008. Print.

Bromberg, Heather. "Are MUDs Communities? Identity, Belonging and Consciousness in Virtual Worlds." *Cultures of Internet: Virtual Spaces, Real Histories, Living Bodies.* Ed. Rob Shields. Thousand Oaks, CA: Sage, 1996. 143–152. Print.

Brookey, Robert Alan, and Kristopher L. Cannon. "Sex Lives in *Second Life.*" *Critical Studies in Media Communication* 26.2 (2009): 145–164. Print.

Bryson, Mary, Lori MacIntosh, Sharalyn Jordan, and Hui-Ling Lin. "Virtually Queer? Homing Devices, Mobility, and Un/belongings." *Canadian Journal of Communication* 31.4 (2006): 791–814. Print.

Butler, Judith. *Gender Trouble: Feminism and the Subversion of Identity.* New York: Routledge, 1990. Print.

Conley, Dalton. *You May Ask Yourself: An Introduction to Thinking Like a Sociologist.* New York: W.W. Norton, 2008. Print.

Consalvo, Mia. "Hot Dates and Fairy-Tale Romances: Studying Sexuality in Video Games." *The Video Game Theory Reader.* Ed. Mark J. P. Wolf and Bernard Perron. New York: Routledge, 2003. 171–194. Print.

Dumitrica, Delia, and Georgia Gaden. "Knee-High Boots and Six-Pack Abs: Autoethnographic Reflections on Gender and Technology in *Second Life.*" *Journal of Virtual Worlds Research* 1.3 (2009): 3–23. Web.

Foucault, Michel. *Discipline and Punish: The Birth of the Prison.* New York: Vintage, 1975. Print.

_____. *The History of Sexuality, Vol. 1: An Introduction.* New York: Vintage, 1978. Print.

Giddens, Anthony. *The Transformation of Intimacy: Sexuality, Love and Eroticism in Modern Societies.* Cambridge, MA: Polity, 1992. Print.

Gunkel, David J. *Hacking Cyberspace.* Boulder, CO: Westview, 2001. Print.

Haraway, Donna. "Situated Knowledges: The Science Question in Feminism and the Privilege of Partial Perspective." *Feminist Studies* 14.3 (1988): 575–599. Print.

Hawkes, Gail. *A Sociology of Sex and Sexuality.* Philadelphia, PA: Open University, 1996. Print.

Hellerstein, Laurel Nan. "The Social Use of Electronic Communication at a Major University." *Computers and the Social Sciences* 1 (1985): 191–197. Print.

Hochschild, Arlie Russell. "Emotion Work, Feeling Rules, and Social Structure." *American Journal of Sociology* 85.3 (1979): 551–575. Print.

Hochschild, Arlie Russell. *The Managed Heart: Commercialization of Human Feeling.* Berkeley: University of California Press, 1983. Print.

Jones, Steven G. "Introduction: From Where to Who Knows?" *Cybersociety: Computer-Mediated Communication and Community.* Ed. Steven G. Jones. Thousand Oaks, CA: Sage, 1995. 1–9. Print.

Kiesler, Sara, Jane Siegel, and Timothy W. McGuire. "Social Psychological Aspect of Computer-Mediated Communication." *American Psychologist* 39.10 (1984): 1123–1134. Print.

Kiesler, Sara, and Lee Sproull. "Group Decision Making and Communication Technology." *Organization Behavior and Human Decision Processes* 52 (1992): 96–123. Print.

MacKinnon, Catherine A. "Feminism, Marxism, Method, and the State: An Agenda for Theory." *Signs* 7 (1982): 515–544. Print.

Myers, David. "'Anonymity Is Part of the Magic': Individual Manipulation of Computer-Mediated Communication Contexts." *Qualitative Sociology* 19.3 (1987): 251–266. Print.

Nakamura, Lisa. "Race in/for Cyberspace: Identity Tourism and Racial Passing on the Internet." *Works and Days* 13 (1995): 181–193. Print.

_____. *Digitizing Race: Visual Cultures of the Internet.* Minneapolis: University of Minnesota Press, 2008. Print.

Nyboe, Lotte. "'You Said I Was Not a Man': Performing Gender and Sexuality on the Internet." *Convergence* 10.2 (2004): 62–80. Print.

Parks, Malcolm R., and Kory Floyd. "Making Friends in Cyberspace." *Journal of Communication* 46.1 (1996): 80–97. Print.

Reed, Jennifer J. *Social Support and the Self in Computer-Mediated Communication.* MA thesis. University of Akron, 2000. Print.

Rheingold, Howard. *The Virtual Community: Homesteading on the Electronic Frontier.* Reading, MA: Addison-Wesley, 1993. Print.

Roberts, Lynne D., and Malcolm R. Parks. "The Social Geography of Gender-Switching in Virtual Environments on the Internet." *Virtual Gender: Technology, Consumption and Identity.* Ed. Eileen Green and Alison Adam. New York: Routledge, 2001. 265–285. Print.

Seidman, Steven. *The Social Construction of Sexuality.* New York: W.W. Norton, 2003. Print.

Siegel, Jane, Vitaly Dubrovsky, Sara Kiesler, and Timothy W. McGuire. "Group Processes in Computer-Mediated Communication." *Organizational Behavior and Human Decision Processes* 37 (1986): 157–187. Print.

Sproull, Lee, and Sara Kiesler. "Reducing Social Context Cues: Electronic Mail in Organizational Communication." *Management Science* 32.11 (1986): 1492–1512. Print.

Stone, Allucquere Rosanne. *The War of Desire and Technology at the Close of the Mechanical Age.* Cambridge, MA: MIT Press, 1995. Print.

Sunden, Jenny. *Material Virtualities: Approaching Online Textual Embodiment.* New York: Peter Lang, 2003. Print.

Turkle, Sherry. *Life on the Screen: Identity in the Age of the Internet.* New York: Simon & Schuster, 1995. Print.

Twine, Richard T. "Ma(r)king Essence — Ecofeminism and Embodiment." Ethics and the Environment 6.2 (2001): 31–58. Print.

Walther, Joseph B. "Computer-Mediated Communication: Impersonal, Interpersonal, and Hyperpersonal Interaction." *Communication Research* 23.1 (1996): 3–43. Print.

_____. "Interpersonal Effects in Computer-Mediated Interaction: A Relational Perspective." *Communication Research* 19.1 (1992): 52–90. Print.

Zoe's Law for *SL*, or If It Can, It Will, So Expect It

DIANNA BALDWIN

Anything that can go wrong, will go wrong.—Murphy's Law

It was late, I was tired; but I had to figure out what had gone so horribly wrong with my first of two classes earlier that night. Sure, some of my students were resistant to the use of Second Life *in their first-year-composition (FYC) class, but I kept telling myself that change is one of those things that even digital natives resist when it does not meet with their pre-conceived ideas of what something should be. And holding class in a virtual environment was simply one of those things some could not or would not wrap their minds around.*

Zoe's law kicked in from the beginning of class. The students and I logged into Second Life (SL) and convened at our class location. Immediately things began to go south. Students wouldn't sit down, they played with gadgets and accessories they had gathered for their avatars, they wandered around looking at everything around them. It seemed nothing I said or did (virtually) would corral them. When things had finally begun to settle ... it happened.

At first, I noticed something rolling across the circle we were all seated in, and then their appeared in the middle of our circle a big pile of virtual feces, complete with flies buzzing around it. As if this weren't bad enough, the next thing that happened was unthinkable. On every student's screen, as well as my own, appeared a repeated image of a super-sized, naked woman. "Just perfect," I thought, as I calmly directed all of the students to log out of SL *so we could try again.*

Introduction

Second Life, a place where people can experiment, play, and learn in wonderfully diverse ways, is also a place full of trepidation for any instructor who chooses to use it, as one might discern from the above incident. The deciding factor for whether or not *SL* will be a success in any classroom relies heavily on the instructor's preparation (as with any class), but more importantly on how they handle things when they go wrong.

There are plenty of sources that praise the use of virtual environments, or massively multi-user virtual environments (MMUVE),[1] for education, and these sources will give prime examples of ways in which it has worked successfully.[2] Such comments as "there is even evidence that using and interacting with others within virtual worlds improves real-life social skills" (Simon Ball and Rob Pearce 50), the use of avatars in online classes can "increase a sense of presence" or the sense of being there (Schroeder qtd. in Traci L. Anderson 103), and "one unique feature of virtual worlds is the possibility to invite professionals to participate directly in the educational situation at virtually zero monetary cost" (Bjørn Jæger 119) can be very convincing that this is a nearly perfect online space. That's not to say that these articles do not also deal with the challenges inherent in this type of environment, but most never relate the horror stories that often occur as well.

At this point, many may be thinking that I am against educational uses of *SL*: not true. I do believe, though, that a teacher who knows the whole story is more likely to be better prepared and have a more positive experience than one who is not. Therefore, the aim of this article is to relate some of these horror stories and then offer suggestions for ways to best avoid duplicating them, and offer helpful advice for when such occurrences do happen.

The Story Continued

As I logged into SL *near midnight, my mind kept circling back to the thing I had seen roll across our virtual class space. If I could locate that, it might hold the key to the bizarre occurrences we had experienced earlier during class. As the virtual landscape began to rez,[3] I looked around the class area, but saw nothing out of the ordinary. It is possible that what I had seen was simply one of my students playing with an object they had acquired from a freebie shop.[4] Once the virtual space had completely rezzed, I used the camera controls to start searching the surrounding area, particularly under bushes and plant life.*

And that is when I found what I suspected would be the "smoking gun": a small, round object under a bush I knew I had not placed there. I took a deep breath, held it, and quickly right mouse clicked the object, squeezing my eyes tight as I did so for fear of it virtually exploding in my pixelated face. I half opened one eye to see, with relief, that the only thing that had occurred was the appearance of the pie menu for the object. My breathe exploded from my lungs. "Wow" I thought out loud, "I'm taking this a bit too seriously."

After a couple of clicks on "more" in the pie menu, one of the options that appeared was "Inspect." I clicked. What appeared was information concerning the object, such as who created it and when it was created. But the only thing that interested me was who OWNED this object because that was the person who had placed it here, and that was the person who was responsible for griefing my entire class.[5]

Armed with the name of the person who had placed the object in my class, I went to the search feature and entered the woman's name. One button click later I had her profile on my screen and I clicked to send her an instant message (IM) informing her I would be reporting her to Linden Labs for abuse.

The disruption that occurred in my class was indeed a griefing episode by another *SL* resident, but I was also partly to blame. Having never taught in an MMUVE before meant no prior experiences from which to draw and make changes. I was flying blind and making plenty of mistakes to prove it.

Perhaps my first mistake was in the belief that these were all college students, and therefore, mature and ready for the challenges of college life. Well, I was mostly right. They were indeed college students, and most were also ready to face challenges head-on; where I erred, however, was in the maturity level required to handle this new environment, as the following chat exchange shows. The first line, or "You" in this chat, is me attempting to give instructions to my students.[6]

[2007/09/13 15:15] You: I thought all of group 1 would look at each other's locations.

[2007/09/13 15:17] Mildrad Pinklady: haha its so much fun watching the macho guys take each other out

[2007/09/13 15:17] Tyson Sawson: no shit

....

[2007/09/13 15:18] Hailey Shelford: we should all take our clothes off haha just kiddin

....

[2007/09/13 15:18] Zao Roux: tyson's getting his ass kicked

....

[2007/09/13 15:18] THERealRomeo Flow: we can hailey my place 6:30 bring a friend

[2007/09/13 15:18] Tyson Sawson: shell bring me

[2007/09/13 15:18] Tyson Sawson: ill take you out

[2007/09/13 15:18] THERealRomeo Flow: and i'll beat your ass

[2007/09/13 15:18] Aska Kungfu: you all are CRAZY

....

[2007/09/13 15:19] Hailey Shelford: haha do u even have a house here romeo

....

[2007/09/13 15:19] THERealRomeo Flow: not on this Island

[2007/09/13 15:19] Aska Kungfu: oh, snap now we are claiming people

[2007/09/13 15:19] Mildrad Pinklady: r they fighting over u hailey?

[2007/09/13 15:19] Hailey Shelford: thanks tyson ur too sweet

[2007/09/13 15:19] Zao Roux: so, a father says to his son, "if you dont stop masturbating, you will go blind!" The son replies, "dad, im in the other room"

....
[2007/09/13 15:19] Tyson Sawson: your gay zao

....
[2007/09/13 15:20] Zao Roux: you just cant handle a real body like mine

....
[2007/09/13 15:20] THERealRomeo Flow: imma have to spit this pimpin
[2007/09/13 15:20] Velleos Nakamori: and so the internet in effect destroys the english language [Qtd. in Baldwin Pg 113–15].

It is obvious from this exchange that the furthest thing from the minds of most of these students is a college level writing course. Although one student is aware enough to comment at the end of the chat on the state of the English language as it is being represented in textese/chatspeak and dialect. My level of frustration during this exchange, combined with the griefing incident that occurred earlier in the night, was off the charts. Again, I could not lay all of the blame on the students.

Remember Zoe's Law for *SL*: if it can, it will, so expect it. It could, it did, but I was in no way prepared for it, nor did I completely know how to handle the incidents that occurred on this night. I knew that if I were ever going to have any degree of success in these classes I needed to reflect on how I had setup the class space and prepared students for this experience. I also had to delve deeper into the research available to try to understand not necessarily why these events occurred, but what it meant.

The Class Setup

One of the greatest things about *SL* is its globalness. People from all over the world live as residents in this world. Many work in *SL*, making real world fortunes, they play in *SL*, and they create relationships that often last for a lifetime and even bleed over into real world marriages and children. I wanted my students to be able to interact with these people and learn from them. As Bryan W. Carter points out, "*Second Life* encourages engagement, communication and interaction with ... other residents on the same level if not more so than that which occurs in the real world" (103). Therefore, when I went in search of a place to call home for my two classes, I had very specific requirements in mind.

As noted in the introduction to this anthology, *SL* is primarily made up of the mainland, opensims, and private regions. I ruled out creating a space on the mainland for a couple of reasons: (1) buying land on the mainland requires a paid membership in *SL*, (2) renting land on the mainland, versus buying, is also expensive, and (3) being on the mainland would also be very distracting to the students. My next thought was to rent land on an opensim, but this would mean little to no traffic through the land, and I felt it would isolate my class from the residents. The third option then, to rent land on a private region, seemed the most appealing. The class would have other shops and businesses around and could interact with others who were not in our small class nor even in the same geographical state (Tennessee) as the students. I spent a month searching for a location that I felt offered a good balance of diversity without being over stimulating.

I then spoke with the owner of the land I wanted to rent and obtained permission to hold class twice a week. This was only fair since the more avatars there are on one parcel of land equals a greater amount of lag.[7] The owner of a private region has to ensure that the businesses renting from him do not experience too much lag because it will hurt the business. Once I had finalized the rental agreement, I began introducing myself to the locals.

When I set the land up for class, I did not create any ban lines or require that residents be in our class group in order to enter our parcel. I wanted regular *SL* residents to feel free to drop by and observe our class sessions. The following chat session is one example of why I wanted this.[8]

> [2007/09/13 17:43] Nexus Whiteberry: Howdy. Class time now? I just noticed you all down there and the parcel and your profile.
> [2007/09/13 18:28] ZoeB McMillan: yep, we are now Island hopping
> [2007/09/13 18:29] Nexus Whiteberry: I'm next door-ish, working on my new store. Feel free to IM sometime. Happy to chat and learn more about what you're doing as an educator in *SL*.
> [2007/09/13 18:30] ZoeB McMillan: thank you, i appreciate it.
> [2007/09/13 18:30] Nexus Whiteberry: :-) ["*Second Life* Chat" 13 Sep. 2007].

Brief encounters like this were not uncommon and served as proof that everyday residents in *SL* were interested in those attempting to use the virtual environment for educational purposes rather than financial gain or pure pleasure. They also meant possible contacts for my students when they began researching *SL* as a culture. Even with all of this forethought and planning, however, Zoe's Law for *SL* still took control.

Student Preparation

I believe my biggest failure in this endeavor was in the preparation, or rather the lack thereof, of my students for attending class in a MMUVE versus other online environments. Most of my students heard class in "*Second Life*" and assumed they would be participating in an online game. *Second Life*, however, is anything but a game. Online gaming worlds such as *World of Warcraft* (*WoW*) are known as MMORPGs or massively multi online role playing games. In games such as *WoW*, *Everquest*, or *Rift*, the object is to level up your character in the game by accomplishing quest, joining guilds, participating in raids to tackle the larger monsters or obstacles, and eventually reach the highest level (at least until another expansion pack is released).

Second Life has none of these features. It is impossible to level up your character in *SL* unless you are participating in a sub-culture of gaming within world. As Mark Meadows relates, "*Second Life* ... may look like a game, but that doesn't mean it is. It's a virtual world, but a world nonetheless. *Second Life* is more like a continent or city than a game. It is a landscape, one that is populated by avatar cultures as distinct as human cultures" (26). What I had done was asked my students to enter into a new culture without having any prior knowledge of what they may find there, and I then asked them to treat it seriously and to get down to work.

When we travel to new cultures in real life, the first thing we typically want to do is experience the culture. We want to observe the locals, find out the best places to eat, drink, play, and experience firsthand what it means to be a part of this culture, if only briefly. In essence, we want to play. Play, however, was not something I had planned for or even realized as a necessary part of the experience. According to Sherry Turkle, college used to be a moratorium for youth, but it is no more. She goes on to suggest that "if our culture no longer offers an adolescent moratorium, virtual communities do. They offer permission to play, to try things out. This is part of what makes them attractive" (xiii). This element of play was completely missing from my schedule of *Second Life* activities. I had expected the students to enter the environment and go straight to work on studying the culture, with no thought to letting them become accustomed to the new space and allowing them time to "play." The students, however, were one step ahead of me and made time to explore and cut-up in a way they would never do in a regular classroom. When our classes were strictly brick-and-mortar, the students behaved in a socially correct and accepted fashion. The experience of finding themselves in a new and foreign virtual space literally brought out the still very much inherent kid in most of them. Only the older students refrained from the playfulness the others exhibited.

One might think that the exchange mentioned above is a bad thing. That was certainly how I felt on the night that it occurred. Upon further research and reflection, however, it was clear that something very unique and unusual took place that night. The exchange that happened was among students who really did not even know each others real names yet. All in-class communication up until this point had been very limited between the students. Yet in this virtual space, they allowed themselves to have a voice, even if it were not exactly what I expected. This is an attribute of online personas that can be and often is very useful.

I actually experienced this difference the very first night of class. After introducing *SL* to the students, I logged in from home and noticed a student wandering around our class area. We exchanged greetings, and before I realized it, we were having a discussion. Following is a part of our chat ("You" here is my part of the conversation).[9]

[21:00] You: good. so how ya feeling about class

[21:00] Alex: really? i felt like i was going to throw up when you told us we had to write a essay. but i like the virtual idea

[21:00] Alex: math is more my thing

[21:01] You: ah, so computers are right up your alley

[21:02] Alex: yeah, i figure i got that part of the class covered and if i bust my ass i might do ok on the other part to

. . . .

[21:02] You: you will do fine

[21:02] Alex: i think so, plus i hear you have to be able to write if your a nurse

[21:03] You: yep, ya do. writing comes into every part of your life whether you want it to or not

[21:03] You: might as well learn to do it well

[21:03] Alex: yeah you cant write a letter home in math equations

[21:03] Alex: thats what i figure

[21:04] You: so you're gonna be an RN??

[21:04] Alex: thats the goal, then Doctors Without Borders

[21:04] You: COOL. I have a lot of friends who are nurses.

[21:05] Alex: really? where are they working?

. . . .

[21:05] You: Well, one works at Vandy when she's not travel nursing and another is an administrator at Vandy and one is at the VA and anotherr is in the prison system

[21:06] Alex: huh. travel nursing?

[21:07] You: oh yea. she's been to Alaska, Houston, San Diego, Boston. Just about anywhere she wants to go. 13 week assignment

[21:08] Alex: yeah one of the nice things about nursing is that they need them everywhere, so it's not hard to find a job

[21:08] You: not hard at all.

[21:08] You: you'll have job security

[21:09] Alex: yeah, but thats not really what i am going for . i want to help, always have

[21:09] You: Which is why I'm a teacher.

[21:10] Alex: that was my second choice, not english though

[21:10] You: LOL I'm sure

[21:10] You: Tell me something if you don't mind.

[21:10] Alex: shoot

[21:10] You: Would you have ever talked with a professor like this the first night
of class??
[21:11] Alex: no, i don't think so
[21:11] Alex: am i going to be a nice paragraph in your study
. . . . ["*Second Life* Chat" 30 Aug. 2007].

This student and I had had little communication during the class period. In
fact, the only reason I knew him/her at all was because she/he had helped a
student from Japan during class with technical issues.

This in-depth conversation with a student on the first day of class is
rarely heard of, and even this student admits that this is not something he/she
would normally do. The same type of behavior was exhibited by the students
who had a less than academic conversation. So what is it about an online virtual presence that allows people to communicate in different ways and how
should we prepare students for this?

Outward Identity, Persona and Core Identity in Virtual Environments

When considering student preparation, one of the most important things
to consider is that of identity. Our outward identity, persona, and core identity
(the three main areas that make up our overall identity) are topics of much
discussion in virtuality, and are areas that any teacher wanting to use these
worlds should be aware of and be prepared to discuss with their students as
preparation for a virtual environment like *SL*. For the sake of this article, I
will define them as follows:

Outward identity means the way we are recognized by others — what do
we look like, body type, hair color, weight, and so on.
Persona means the way we perform our identity — how we present our outward appearance and how we outwardly act.
Core identity includes the values that are often a part of who we are — how
we were raised and the things we believe we would never change.

With those definitions in mind, we will look at how both play out in virtual
spaces and places in general, and in my classroom in particular.

Our outward identities in RL change, but perhaps not as drastically as
one might wish. We can change our hair color, add piercings and/or tattoos,
and lose weight (with enough will power or medical help). With enough money
we can even reconstruct our entire faces and become, outwardly at least, someone else. But these types of modifications to our outward appearance require
a degree of commitment or disposal income, and often both, that most of us

do not have. For many of us, our outward identities only change with the passage of time.

This, however, is not the case in MMORPGs or MUVEs. In these virtual spaces, as Au points out, we are "freed from the accidents of birth that define who we are, to ourselves and the people around us..." (71). In other words, in these worlds, we can choose who we want to be outwardly. At first, I do not believe my students truly appreciated this concept, but after the Kool-Aid man assignment, they soon began to understand the importance of outward appearance.

In this assignment, the students became the easily recognizable Kool-Aid man, complete with pitcher filled to the brim with red Kool-Aid and ice cubes. It is important to keep in mind that they were not "dressed" as Kool-Aid men; they did not put on some type of costume where they kept their body and heads. In fact, the only thing human about them were the big red arms and legs of the Kool-Aid man. Donning this outward appearance, they went into the world of *SL* and attempted to communicate with other residents.

This assignment helped the students understand what it felt like to be an Other: someone marginalized for the way they look outwardly. They experienced reactions from *SL* residents ranging from friendly laughter, to ridicule, to discrimination, being asked to leave establishments due to their size. The students discovered what it felt like, to a degree, to be someone marginalized by the culture in which they live. They began to understand, if only on a lower level, what it means to be an "Other." One student writes in his/her essay that "I, for the sake of our experiment, cannot control my Kool-Aid-Ness, and now understand how frustrating it is to be denied rights simply because of physical appearance" ("Otherness" 1). Similar sentiments are seen in many of the students' essays from this assignment.

Assignments like this one can help students understand how others perceive and react to outward appearances/identity. If a student enters *SL* as a furry or robotic alien without first considering how others might react to that appearance, he/she may not be prepared for those reactions or understand them. I believe it is important for students to play and experiment with their outward identity in *SL*, but some discussion about the possibilities of how *SL* residents might react will help them be prepared.

Another area of identity is that of persona, or how we perform our identity. Unlike our outward appearance, which we can only change to a certain degree, how we perform our identity for others is something that can change on a whim. Refer back to the discussion that occurred during that first night of class, and it is apparent that most of these students are performing an identity: the macho male and the sought after female. Even though the students were in class, they performed these identities as if they were in their own dorms or hang outs with no one else around but their peers.

One way in which some residents of virtual worlds perform identity is that of gender or race swapping by creating an avatar that is, on the outside, the opposite sex or race of their RL self. The performance begins with the choice of an avatar. One resident tells Tom Boellstorff, author of *Coming of Age in* Second Life, that he/she had "'come to observe that the outward appearance really does communicate a lot about who you are, because it's made up of conscious choices about how you want to present yourself'" (130). Whether or not one can actually pull off the performance is another matter. One of my male students chose to represent himself as a Japanese androgynous samurai warrior. However, he never performed this identity in any way other than his outward appearance. Unlike the students who were performing the "macho male" and "sought after female," this student's performance closely resembled his RL persona. His only comment, during the first conversation above, "and so the internet in effect destroys the english language" (qtd. in Baldwin 115), was decidedly not what I expected from a Japanese androgynous samurai warrior, but who is to say what that performance would look like. In many other ways, however, I believe he very much resembled the persona he attempted to embody. He made his sense of honor and duty apparent in his actions, not succumbing to the juvenile conversations in which his peers took part.

Others in class struggled with their sense of persona, trying to make connections between their RL and *SL* embodiments. One student, an African American, writes, "in the virtual world I'm white. I see every different color but mine" ("Student Quick Write" #2). The embodiment of a Caucasian did not feel natural or right for this student, and she/he experienced feelings of not belonging and of not being able to perform the expected persona his/her outside appearance. As T.L. Taylor argues, "avatars are central to both immersion and the construction of community in virtual spaces. They are mediators between personal identity and social life" (110). Being forced to embody an avatar that is non-representative of one's own identity will likely prevent that person from feeling a sense of belonging or socializing in this environment.

Many factors complicate the performance of a new identity, but one stands out above others. Regardless of how hard we try, we cannot escape our RL selves completely.

We are all made up of core identities: the things that make us act in certain ways. So why would students behave in a way completely outside of the social norms? As many scholars have noted, online spaces are renowned for allowing people to ... well, be different. And it's not just virtual worlds either. Turkle argues that the "anonymity of MUDs [multi user domains] ... provides ample room for individuals to express unexplored parts of themselves" (xii).

It also occurs in environments like online chat programs such as MSN or Yahoo. People who might never be confrontational in real life, for example, may find that in an online chat not only can they be, but they may even have a propensity to be. Walt Turner claims that "online personas become freed as some rules of social interaction become suspended" ("Out of the Ghetto").

When students first enter a virtual space, they often act differently or outside of the social norm without understanding exactly why. Most students in first-year-composition classes are between 17 and 19 years old and come to college with the notion that their identities are set. One student even commented during a discussion on identity that by the time you reach college "your identity should already be shaped" ("*Second Life* Chat" 08 Nov. 2007). Other students were not as sure, however, and one comments that he/she has "no clue what or [how] to define me. I'm only 18!" ("*Second Life* Chat" 08 Nov. 2007). This revelation, though, came after a lengthy discussion on what identity is, how it's formed, and its fluidity.

Identity is fluid, but one's core identity is much slower to change, and for some, much of that identity never does. So how does this core identity play out in virtuality? While virtual and actual selfhood vary, one resident tells Boellstorff "'I don't think ultimately anyone succeeds in concealing who they are'" (121). I believe hiding our core identity in *SL* is not likely, but I do believe that *SL* can and is used to actually figure out who we are, that core identity. FYC students enter college with ideas instilled in them by their family and friends. Some begin challenging these core ideals while still in high school, but many do not begin this journey until they enter college, if then. Online spaces can actually help this process. As Turkle notes, "when identity was defined as unitary and solid [which it has been for many of our students in FYC], it was relatively easy to recognize and censure deviation from a norm. A more fluid sense of self [which online spaces often give people] allows a greater capacity for acknowledging diversity" (xvi). Beth Kolko argues that "the fact remains that sooner or later participants in a text-based virtual world come to recognize that their sense of self, of identity, is slippery" (254). Students participating in virtual environments have the opportunity to explore their sense of core identity/values and recognize the fluidity of their own identities.

It's this suspension of social norms and cultural practices that allow many who enter into online environments in general and virtual ones in particular to "act" differently both outwardly and inwardly than they would in everyday RL. Rymaszewski et al. believe that "*Second Life* is often held up as the perfect place to get your fantasy on — and yes, there's no other place like it for becoming something you aren't, or even for working out just what it is you want to be" (301).

The formation of this online identity begins when one first enters a virtual environment and chooses an avatar to represent them in this new world. In *SL*, that avatar can now represent a wide variety: anything from humanoids to furry creatures to robotic looking machines driven by aliens. What surprises most is the very real connection they feel with this pixilated being from the moment they immerse themselves into the *SL*. They likewise find a freedom in this second life that they cannot experience in real life. The combination of immersion and freedom often leads to questions concerning not only their outward identity and persona, but also the values and social norms — core identity — they thought were ingrained and unchanging. Virtual environments such as *SL* can induce self-discovery in students.

The End of the Story

The more I typed the IM to the griefer, the more my frustration and anger grew. I mean really, how dare someone, a complete stranger be so disruptive in what was clearly a class environment. They knew it was a class because anyone who crossed the borders of our land received a message to that affect, which also stated that by remaining there they understood they were agreeing to participate in the research project. They knew, and yet they proceeded.

I typed, I erased, and I typed again. Finally, after much angst, I simply typed "Are you the one responsible for disturbing my class on hale ukana tonight?" ("Second Life Chat" 13 Sep. 2007). *I did not really believe I would ever hear a reply from the woman, so I tried to put the incident out of my mind and work on the lesson plan for the next virtual class. It was more than a little surprising, then, when half an hour later I heard the familiar "ding" of someone IMing me in SL, and it was her.*

What I expected out of our conversation was anything other than what I got. She denied being the one who griefed the class, as I expected. She also appeared agitated, which I also expected, but what I was not prepared for were the reasons she related for being upset. She fired back, "I was in the area shopping, and was attacked by three of your students, so if anyone is responsible for anything, it's yourself ... for not keeping track of them and explaing [sic] to them that foul language, and harrasment [sic] are unacceptable behavior" ("Second Life Chat" 13 Sep. 2007). *My only thoughts were "what have my students gotten themselves into?"*

On that night, while I attempted to get the class settled and ready for discussion, three of my students wandered into the shopping district next to our parcel of land and happened upon this young woman. According to her, she was "attacked by three ... students" who surrounded her and continually bumped into her avatar, saying things like "hey baby, come over here with me" (*"Second Life* Chat" 13 Sep. 2007). She asked them to stop bumping her and then tried ignoring them, at which point one of the students said she was "probably a fat ugly old woman anyways" (*"Second Life* Chat" 13 Sep. 2007).

I continued to chat with the young woman and assured her that the students would be reprimanded. I explained that without her chat logs I would not likely be able to take official action against them, but that she could expect an apology from each of the students.

My students and I had discussed things like sexual harassment on the first night of class, but another conversation on the topic seemed warranted. We started class with a conversation on appropriate behavior and how people could feel threatened in virtual environments, but I could tell by the reactions of several students that they weren't buying it. After class, I asked to speak with the students the young woman had named. The students admitted that they had met her during class time, but were shocked when I informed them she was accusing them of sexual harassment by repeatedly bumping into her and using offensive language.

This sense of shock, however, was nothing compared to what they felt when I told them I took these things very seriously and that they would be reported to judicial affairs. Frankly, universities are not prepared for dealing with this type of situation. After sending a memo to a representative in judicial affairs, the outcome was that the students were in violation of Code 33E: Abuse of Computer Resources and Computers and were warned that further "abuse" could lead to a more severe punishment, up to and including expulsion. While the outcome did not surprise me, I did wonder how the actual problem of "sexual harassment" had somehow become buried in phrases like "abuse of computer resources," which makes the offense sound like no other humans were involved. I believe the victim says it best when she writes that "people on the internet are animals, they sit safely behind computer screens and figure ... the only confrontation [repercussion] for outrageous behavior on here [*SL*] will be a few typed words ... that's the worst that can happen which is easy to stop at a simple command" ("*Second Life* Chat" 13 Sep. 2007). She argues the worst that can happen to someone who acts out is that someone might type a message which they can close without even reading.

My students, however, did not get off quite so lightly. As I promised the young woman the night I chatted with her, I required each of the students write and send her an apology for what they had done. I never got the sense, however, that the students understood the gravity of what they had done. They had treated an avatar as an object for their own pleasure and entertainment, not considering the person behind that avatar, and they did not seem to comprehend that. As Ferganchick-Neufang relates, "feminist scholars of virtual spaces argue that the Internet is, like real life, a very sexist and hostile environment" ("Harassment On-Line"), and the incident in my class confirms it. Women in virtual environments must remain cautious and diligent about their safety.

Changes and Renovations

Zoe's Law for *SL* was in full play with my class; however, many of the problems have pretty simple solutions. Others, though, are much more complicated. While I'll discuss the changes I made to avoid repeats of the same incidents, I want to stress the need to be *prepared* for the worst to happen and know, it's an opportunity for a learning experience for both instructors and students.

Keeping our class area open for people to come and go became impossible after that first night of class. One of the decisions made to ensure there would be no more naked women scrolling across my students' screens was to block the Island from anyone not a part of our class. This was easily accomplished by using the group that I had set up for the class. Anyone not a member of this group was banned from entering the parcel. This small change ensured that no outsider could place an object on our parcel at any time.

Another change to the class was that every student had to go into their "friend" settings and give me permission to know exactly where they were in world. This allowed be to teleport to their in-world location whenever I wanted. I made this decision hesitantly. Unlike locking down the parcel where we held class (which I paid for monthly), this change directly impacted the students' privacy, as I could see where they were any time they logged into *SL*, regardless of whether or not we were in class. I stressed to the students that they could change this setting when not in class, but to my knowledge, no one ever did. I never "spied" on students outside of class, but it still felt "wrong" to have this power. Ethically, I'm not confident I would ever insist on this again. However, for this class, I could and often did teleport to their locations to see if they had any questions and to make sure students were actually doing the assignment and not harassing residents.

These were the two main changes that I made inworld to both keep my students safe and to ensure they were focusing on class content during class. These changes, however, are not the things I would consider most valuable. I learned that students entering *SL* for the first time need permission to play and to experiment with online identities. This needs to be built into any class syllabus for *SL*. Even if it is just one night, students need to know that they can go into *SL* and play. This play can be either organized, left completely up to students, or some combination of both. Following are a few suggestions:

1. Create boxes of clothing, skins, and hair to help introduce students to *SL* and let them begin to explore their online outward identity and persona. Core identities will be challenged throughout their *SL* experiences.

2. Create a list of places for students to visit their first few times in. Be

sure to include some good locations to get free things, as well as live music venues, museums, art exhibits, etc.

3. Create a list of things to avoid in *SL*, like accepting friend requests, group requests, and anything offered by a stranger.

4. Allow students the freedom to go exploring on their own, but warn them repeatedly that sexual harassment is real and that visiting mature sites with explicit sexual content is out.

Conclusion

Second Life offers a wealth of opportunity for educational experiences. It gives students the ability to go beyond the classroom, beyond the town in which many of them grew up, and beyond their own identity. And they can do so without many of the dangers of real life. If they find themselves feeling threatened or unsure, they can immediately log off.

Virtual environments have a lot to offer. With that, however, comes a plethora of opportunities for things to go horribly wrong. When things do go bad, as they will sooner or later (even if it's technical difficulty), it's up to the instructor to know how to handle the situation and avoid over reacting. It would be easier to walk away from a space like *SL* when things do not go as expected, but that would not only be sending the students the wrong message of "quit if things don't go like you want," but it would also perpetuate the idea that these places are somehow bad as educational tools, when in reality, they can be life changing for some students.

Notes

1. A term I will use to distinguish *Second Life* from other online environments like *World of Warcraft*, which is a MMORPG or massively multi-user online role-playing game. *Second Life* is not a game.

2. See Charles Wanket and Jan Kingsley book entitled *Higher Education in Virtual Worlds: Teaching and Learning in* Second Life and Judith Molka-Danielsen and Mats Deutschmann's *Learning and Teaching in the Virtual World of* Second Life for articles that discuss the pros and challenges of using *SL* in classrooms.

3. Rez is a term used in *Second Life* to indicate virtual objects becoming visible to the user. This can take varying degrees of time, depending on ones' internet connection and bandwidth.

4. In *Second Life*, there are many shops that offer residents free virtual goods. Much of these goods are very amateurish, but some are very good.

5. Griefing is a term used in *Second Life* to describe someone who wishes to disrupt the experience for others.

6. I refused to allow voice communication during class time for numerous reasons, but the primary one is that this was a writing class. Typos and mistakes are neither corrected or acknowledged in this exchange, as it is a part of text chat.

7. Lag is the delay between two computers and causes slow and/or jerky movements in a

3D virtual world. This can be caused by bandwidth clutter, video card, or hard drive (Ryma-szewski et al. 328).

8. Typos and mistakes are neither corrected or acknowledged in this exchange, as it is a part of text chat.

9. Typos and mistakes are neither corrected or acknowledged in this exchange, as it is a part of text chat.

Works Cited

Anderson, Traci L. "Online Instructor Immediacy and Instructor-Student Relationships in Second Life." *Higher Education in Virtual Worlds: Teaching and Learning in Second Life.* Ed. Charles Wankel and Jan Kingsley. Bingley, UK: Emerald, 2009.

Au, Wagner James. *The Making of Second Life: Notes from the New World.* New York: Harper-Collins e-books, 2008. Kindle e-book.

Baldwin, Dianna. *Everyone's a Kool-Aid Man Today: Pedagogical Implications of Teaching First-Year Composition in Second Life.* Saarbrücken, Germany: Lambert Academic, 2010.

Ball, Simon, and Rob Pearce. "Inclusion Benefits and Barriers of 'Once-Removed' Participation." *Higher Education in Virtual Worlds: Teaching and Learning in Second Life.* Ed. Charles Wankel and Jan Kingsley. Bingley, UK: Emerald, 2009.

Boellstorff, Tom. *Coming of Age in Second Life: An Anthropologist Explores the Virtually Human.* Princeton, NJ: Princeton UP, 2008.

Carter, Bryan W. "Enhancing Virtual Environments." *Learning and Teaching in the Virtual World of Second Life.* Ed. Judith Molka-Danielsen and Mats Deutschmann. Trondheim, Norway: Tapir AP, 2009.

Ferganchick-Neufang, Julia. "Harassment On-Line: Considerations for Women & Webbed Pedagogies." *Karios* 2.2 (1997). 15 Aug. 2008 http://english.ttu.edu/kairos/2.2/binder2.html?coverweb/julia/honline.html.

Jæger, Bjørn, and Berit Helgheim. "Role Play Study in a Purchase Management Class." *Learning and Teaching in the Virtual World of Second Life.* Ed. Judith Molka-Danielsen and Mats Deutschmann. Trondheim, Norway: Tapir AP, 2009.

Kolko, Beth. "Bodies in Place: Real Politics, Real Pedagogy, and Virtual Space." *High Wired: On the Design, Use, and Theory of Educational MOOs.* Ed. Cynthia Haynes and Jan Rune Holmevik. Ann Arbor: U of Michigan P, 1998. 253–65.

Meadows, Mark Stephen. *I, Avatar: The Culture and Consequences of Having a Second Life.* New Riders: Berkeley, CA, 2008.

"Otherness" 1. Unpublished essay, 2007.

Rymaszewski, Michael, et al. *Second Life: The Official Guide.* Indianapolis: Wiley, 2007.

"Second Life Chat." 30 Aug. 2007,

"Second Life Chat." 13 Sep. 2007.

"Second Life Chat." 08 Nov. 2007.

Student Quick Write #2. Unpublished, 23 Oct. 2007.

Taylor, T. L. *Play Between Worlds: Exploring Online Game Culture.* Cambridge: MIT P, 2006.

Turkle, Sherry. "All MOOs are Educational — the Experience of 'Walking through the Self.'" Foreword. *High Wired: On the Design, Use, and Theory of Educational MOOs.* Ed. Cythia Haynes and Jan Rune Holmevik. Ann Arbor: U of Michigan P, 1998. ix–xix.

Turner, Walt. "Out of the Ghetto and onto the Net — Queer and Loathing in Cyberspace." *Kairos* 5.2 (2000). 16 Aug. 2008 http://english.ttu.edu/KAIROS/5.2/binder.html?coverweb/overview.html.

Exploring the Virtual World of *Second Life* to Help Bring Human Rights to Health Care

KARA BENNETT, PH.D., *and*
SUSAN PATRICE, M.D.

Introduction

Imagine you have a life threatening illness and don't know what to do. The journey to find the knowledge you need to survive may have many obstacles besides the difficulty in discovering what actions to take. For example, how people decide the best way to diagnose and treat illness can involve many choices of knowing how to fit the ideal goal of health to the actual situation. They include both beneficial problem-solving strategies, and those that are not helpful, such as prejudice, discrimination, the need to control others, and/or conformity without reason. In other words, ignoring the human rights of the person who needs health care can hurt the discovery of life saving truth and lead to health care abuse.

The United Nations adopted the Universal Declaration of Human Rights in 1948 to try and prevent the kind of atrocities that occurred in World War II. The declaration contains the right to health care that respects both the person and community. However, there is little education about how to bring the intellectual understanding of these rights into the daily life situation of the individual. There is even controversy as to whether health care is a human right, which has left millions of people without care. Consequently, when someone is injured, it is essential for them to have their own guidelines and make their search for answers a personal journey of discovery, besides engaging professionals in their care.

Previous research by the first author explored how mental representations of health information could be designed in ways that fit the concerns of the individual person. Her research used a new approach for studying problem-solving strategies in real life situations. Adapted from previous research by Herbert Simon and Alan Newell, the methods involve documenting the actions and statements made by a person as they are engaged in solving a problem. The description of their own journey as they try to reach a particular goal can help to better understand the strategies they are using, and other ways they might try. For example, one of Bennett's studies used actors to play patients to offer physicians a chance to explore different ways of making a diagnosis. Video and audio records of their actions and comments were analyzed for their problem-solving strategies. The physicians could talk aloud and discuss their strategies without the concerns or time limit of the real patient. Then their best strategies could be applied to an actual patient. The research suggested the need for better understanding of the important role that the dynamical qualities (stability and change) of mental images play in making the adjustment between the abstract medical knowledge and the person directly experiencing the illness.

Could this kind of research methodology be used for studying how a person thinks about human rights and health care to learn how to bring the knowledge necessary for survival into one's daily life experience?

The authors believe this is possible and decided to explore these research methods in the virtual world of *Second Life* (*SL*). The rich imagery and immersive environs offer a chance to create a place where a person can try out different ideas and images to help construct guidelines for health that respect the rights of the person and community. We want to share what we have discovered in trying to build this place in *SL*.

Our Adventures in Second Life (SL)

Second Life is a software program that uses avatars to represent a person in 3D interactive environments (*Second Life*, 2012). This makes it possible to express a person's ideas with text, voice, images, gestures, animations and videos, while interacting with people from anywhere in the world, represented by their avatars. *Second Life* can be accessed using any computer with suitable hardware and a high speed internet connection.

The authors joined *SL* in 2007 and for the first year tried different activities to learn how to use the program. Our avatars are Dancers Yao and Kasuku Magic. Because we were familiar with The Tech Museum in San Jose, California, and often checked on their events, we decided to attempt designing a museum exhibit at The Tech Virtual when they invited the general public to build exhibits for their 2008 Tech laureates.

The laureates included the Witness organization which is concerned with documenting and bringing awareness to violations in human rights. Designing an exhibit for the Witness organization offered an opportunity to learn how we might offer some of our ideas about *SL* education in human rights and health care. For example, we could present information that might normally be seen in two dimensions on a web site or textbook as part of a 3D virtual museum exhibit where people from around the world could meet as Avatars and talk about human rights.

Our exhibit was called "Create a Universal Language." We used a virtual circular drum with a fire burning in the center that displayed images and ideas about human rights. Over the fire was a video screen showing advocates of human rights, like Nelson Mandela. The exhibit encouraged people to suggest their own images of a universal language, and learn different ways of knowing about this subject, like through science, art, common sense, and spiritual beliefs.

For instance, they could learn how static images that allow a person to be viewed as acceptable only if they have one example of a human characteristic, such as their type of skin color, could result in treating a person with prejudice. They could also view images that are more dynamic, as they include ways that different types of people and cultures can work together. (http://url.com/secondlife/The%20Tech/38/165/38)

(Table 1 on the next page is an example of information shown on the drum.)

We learned during the process of creating the exhibit that *Second Life* offered an environment where our interest in new ways of doing research about problem-solving in health care could be applied. For instance, people could document their strategies for achieving their desired goals by being able to have a log of their conversation, usually given in text. The *SL* log is like a transcript of a real life conversation when it is recorded as it happens.

An example of this kind of transcript is from The Virtual Tech meeting when we were starting to build our exhibit. The log shows how people can share their ideas with each other through their Avatars as they collaborate on a project. The log is edited to give an overall idea of the process. (see the complete log at http://thetechopensource.thetech.org/forums/ucantu-20080624).

CHAT LOG FROM THE TECH VIRTUAL MUSEUM, 2008

[11:02] Dancers Yao: the interaction with the touch screen drum top will give a chance for people to create their own images of how an individual can be part of a community and still respect their human rights.
[11:04] Dancers Yao: It is played in the sense of moving the images around - e.g.

LINKAGES BETWEEN HEALTH AND HUMAN RIGHTS

Promoting and protecting health and respecting, protecting and fulfilling human rights are inextricably linked:

- Violations or lack of attention to human rights can have serious health consequences (e.g. harmful traditional practices, slavery, torture and inhuman and degrading treatment, violence against women and children).

- Health policies and programmes can promote or violate human rights in their design or implementation (e.g. freedom from discrimination, individual autonomy, rights to participation, privacy and information).

- Vulnerability to ill-health can be reduced by taking steps to respect, protect and fulfil human rights (e.g. freedom from discrimination on account of race, sex and gender roles, rights to health, food and nutrition, education, housing).

Examples of the linkages between health and human rights:

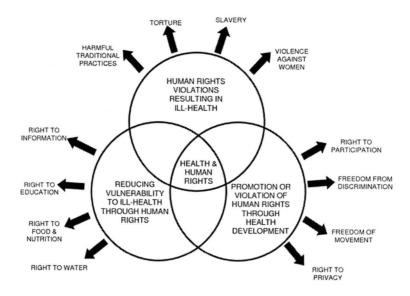

An example of information shown on the drum (reprinted with permission from the World Health Organization, "Linkages Between Health and Human Rights," http://www.who.int/hhr/HHR%20linkages.pdf).

skin color – should not affect a person's Human Rights – one would be "playing" with their images and concepts of what human rights mean to them
[11:05] Garvie: drum is a good metaphor for universal speech too
[11:05] Shakini : universal everything
[11:05] Orcaman : the drum is also very unifying for me

[11:05] Dancers Yao: so they would see how something can be changed - keeping the diversity but also keeping our common humanity

[11:06] Orcaman : it's the soul of music and the driving force behind it

[11:06] Shakini: agreed!

[11:06] Dancers Yao: Yes - thanks - the video on one wall screen will show Nelson Mandela speaking about human rights with drum music in the background-

[11:07] Shakini: nice

[11:12] Dancers Yao: I hope the energy will be used to create something wonderful together

[11:26] Shakini : maybe there could also be a way to trigger voices of civil rights leaders - i.e. snippets of Nelson Mandela's speech as people play the drum

11:29] Shakini : i think its really great that we're having this discussion about racism — this is exactly what the exhibit is supposed to elicit for people and its not even built yet!

[11:31] Dancers Yao: Orcaman - thanks for your comments - am adding new things almost each day to the project website

[11:31] Shakini: we should probably wrap up soon..or you are all welcome to hang-out, i have a mtg in rl on this end thanks for coming everyone!

Besides learning that we could obtain a record of the virtual experience as it happened, we wanted to find whether these transcripts could offer people a place to better understand their ways of thinking, just as the use of a simulated or theater space might do in real life. We decided to first look at our own methods for building our exhibit. To help define them, we used the criteria for a general set of mental processes Bennett investigated in her research about mental imagery and problem-solving. These processes involve defining the goal, finding the distance between the goal and where one is at the moment, imagining a way to cross this distance, trying out this idea, then comparing the result to the desired goal. Then the same processes are repeated if necessary to continue to change the present experience to fit their chosen destination, or one can celebrate being where they want to be!

Our goal was to show how the museum exhibit we were building offered some of our educational material in a virtual world. Sometimes we were successful in building what we imagined, and other experiences, like in the real world, did not match what we hoped. Like finding we could not get the video to play very well on *SL*. Our strategies were a combination of science and art, with a major need for perseverance and hope. We found people very helpful in offering their skills on *SL*, and the opportunity to collaborate with others we had never met in real life gave exciting new ways to learn and share information.

We were grateful to win an award for presenting the most inspiring exhibit, which encouraged us to keep learning how *SL* might help people discover ways to bring the ideals of human rights into daily life health care. Next we decided to join other nonprofit organizations at the Nonprofit Commons (NPC) and build a virtual office for Elder Voices where people could go on journeys to learn how to create their own health care guides: guidelines for their survival, not only physical survival, but to find personal meaning and humanitarian values. Our current adventure is called *A Human Rights Health Care Journey* and is happening at: (http://slurl.com/secondlife/nonprofitcom mons/243/93/22)

On this journey, we offer examples of problem-solving strategies for people to try out in *SL* that could transfer to their real life health care. Discovering the guides that can save your life and others is an adventure story, a mythic journey, where you have the chance to be the hero. Here is what you might experience on your journey if you visit us at Elder Voices on *SL*.

At the beginning is a volcanic crater surrounded by a pond. The crater represents the start of a new quest, offering information about billions of years of life forms, such as how each has their own ways to survive. The crater is a place to wonder about the nature of life and what we need to sustain it. To ask questions like how do we live with meaning and purpose? How do we find ways to respect the individual life and the global community?

To search for possible answers, the person can visit a cavern inside water-falls where resources are displayed on the walls, like the Universal Declaration of Human Rights from the United Nations, and how these affect health care. To suggest guides for health, there is information about The World Health Organization. They define health as "a state of complete physical, mental and social well-being and not merely the absence of disease or infirmity." How do you define health? These questions and examples offer an opportunity for the person to record and document their ideas, so they can examine their own problem-solving strategies, try out new ones, and decide what the guidelines are for their health.

One of our favorite educational materials displayed in the cavern is from the celebration of the Tenth Anniversary of the Universal Declaration of Human Rights, where Eleanor Roosevelt asked: Where after all do human rights begin? Her answer was given in a community guide for action entitled *In Your Hands*:

> In small places, close to home — so close and so small that they cannot be seen on any map of the world. Yet they are the world of the individual person, the neighborhood he lives in, the school or college he attends, the factory, farm or office where he works. Such are the places where every man, woman, and child seeks equal justice, equal opportunity, equal dignity without discrimination. Unless these rights have meaning there, they have little meaning anywhere. Without concerted citizen action to uphold them close to home, we shall look in vain for progress in the larger world [udhr.org].

The authors are following her advice.

After visiting the cavern, people can play "Magic Drums" near the water-falls. Each drum presents information about problem-solving processes involved in discovering the best guides for your health care journey. The drums are "played" with your imagination as you explore ways of defining and expressing what you believe to be necessary for your survival.

The first drum helps define your health goals. The drum displays an image of the sun shining through the trees as it breaks into the color spectrum. Touching the top of the drum will link to a story about the inventor of a solar light for people who did not have electricity in their village in Kenya. Many of the steps important for designing your health guidelines are suggested in this story like defining your goals, judging how your present experience compares to what you want, and learning how to cross the distance between where you are and want to be. The story illustrates how inventive the human mind can be in finding ways to survive. Perhaps you can invent guides for other people to use, like Cardio-Pulmonary Resuscitation (CPR), a lifesaving technique most people are able to learn.

To find where you are in relation to where you want to be, the second drum helps locate the immediate sensory experience of your health. The top of the drum shows a shimmering light image that links to information about how to document the personal experience of one's health, like making patient diaries to keep track of the dynamics of your health over a period of time.

In another drum you will find a link to the story about the "Message from Arecibo." This is a message sent from scientists on Earth to try and contact intelligent life in the universe. The message was sent in a binary code like that used in computers, and shows how people can invent abstract symbols to represent their ideas and images.

Underlying each language or code used for health care is the knowledge that the symbols must be capable of being translated into actions that guide us toward survival. For example, learning how to take the immediate experience of our senses, such as the feelings of wellbeing or pain, and place this information into some type of mental representation, such as an image, is a way to hold onto our sensory experiences over a period of time and see their possible connections to each other. It is the beginning of an extraordinary "map" to see how our personal vision fits into a bigger picture, connecting the momentary experience to our health goals and to other people's knowledge of medicine. We might need to guide the journey from where we are to where we want to be.

With images and ideas, one can create anything they want in their mind and invent the guides that might take them to their chosen destination. In a virtual world, you may create images that can be seen outside your imagination and share them with others, before trying them out in real life.

The next drum suggests ways of bringing one's health guides into real life situations. The drum has a picture of Redwood trees that inspire questions about longevity and connections to one another. These trees can live as long as 2,000 years. Standing in one place. They are able to connect their roots to share nutrients and hold each other up during a storm. The drum links to a YouTube video of people singing the song "Stand by Me" that shows how people can also support and inspire each other.

The fifth drum represents the guidelines the person has decided to actually try out in their real life environs. The picture on the drum uses the words, "Learn to save a Life" and refers to the ability to use CPR by linking to a video from the American Heart Association. The person could then practice the same actions seen in the video. CPR can be a guide to help physical survival, while learning ways to care for people offers guides for personal and community health.

The next drum with the picture of a Mermaid represents the person's health guides that were selected after trying them out in real life situations, and finding how well they fit their goals. For example, the Mermaid image can stand for the physical, personal, and humanitarian guides the person has chosen, such as being able to perform CPR to save a life, and sharing music and stories that inspire each other to act in ways that respect life. If however, the guides designed in *SL* need more work, the person could go back to their imagination and the virtual world, to continue exploring their problem-solving strategies.

The last drum, the seventh drum, is a large drum in the center, surrounded by the other drums. It has an image of a galaxy and represents a place to share your ideas about guidelines for survival. For example, a link is given to the story of how Chilean miners applied their mental, physical, and spiritual abilities to survive after being trapped underground. Elder Voices is working on designing a way that the center drum will connect to our web site to create global images and ideas to bring human rights to health care. (www.Elder Voices.net.)

*A Real Life/*Second Life *Example of the Human Rights Health Care Journey*

A personal example of how the virtual world of *Second Life* might assist in finding guidelines for health is using this setting to bring attention to a rare and dangerous form of cancer that does not have a cure. Almost a year ago, the cofounder of Elder Voices and coauthor of this article, Dr. Susan Patrice, aka Kasuku Magic was diagnosed with small cell neuroendocrine carcinoma.

Her avatar on *Second Life* is now a virtual mermaid to help discover a possible treatment. The following is a recent chat log showing how we are exploring problem-solving strategies with the Magic Drums to begin our journey to find a cure for her cancer.

CHAT LOG ELDER VOICES *SL* 2012

[17:22] Kasuku Magic: (dances while playing drums) yo - over here

[17:26] Dancers Yao: what a great dance!

[17:26] Kasuku Magic: ty

[17:27] Dancers Yao: now we can play the drums on *SL*! And Dance!

[17:27] Kasuku Magic: and practice a little martial arts

[17:28] Dancers Yao: and yoga...many ways of moving our Avatars and our minds.....

[17:29] Kasuku Magic: Yes- do Mind Dances too

[17:30] Dancers Yao: we can play the "Magic Drums" to find what we need to know to help search for a cure to your cancer

[17:43] Dancers Yao: like how do we connect the information we imagine to the specific needs that you have...perhaps if we could look at your tumor cells under a microscope, in 3D, and find what would help change them to normal cells, or ones that are not harmful.

SL[17:49] Kasuku Magic: When I'm on *Second Life*, I am transported beyond my own experience, and yet take a new look at it. And I can share this experience with others, to help bring awareness to this rare cancer.

[17:50] Dancers Yao: each of the drums we have here on *SL* represents a problem solving strategy I hope can help us..

[17:51] Kasuku Magic: Remember the dance of cells reproducing — mitosis and meiosis — well maybe we can teach the cancer cells a new dance. And how Kekule imagined the pattern of the benzene ring, then later demonstrated it really could have the pattern he imagined.

[17:53] Dancers Yao:we must imagine a path from the edge of life...to find a way back to health

[17:54] Dancers Yao: it will take everything we know how to do....our work together all these years...to understand how to respect human rights in health care...

SL[17:55] Dancers Yao: you have a right to find a cure....to search .....not to be treated as if you are not equal to others because of illness. Or be denied care in any way because you chose to be a volunteer physician, so you couldn't afford more expensive health insurance.

[17:55] Kasuku Magic: People on the edge of life have much to teach about human rights.

[18:04] Kasuku Magic: There is even prejudice, though not intentional, against a rare cancer as I found by calling the US foundations that offer support for people with cancer. The foundations are mainly donor driven, meaning those with a certain cancer type contribute to a foundation that they or a loved one or friend has endured. Understandable, but it does not address the universal needs.

[18:07] Kasuku Magic: Even the organization for rare disorders hadn't heard of my cancer - , rare unlike in rare books, jewels, or rare human achievement - does not yet generate respect, or much beyond even mild curiosity.

[18:09] Kasuku Magic: When I typed in "Small Cell Neuroendocrine Carcinoma" on Google, I found blogs about people asking if anyone had heard of their cancer. A few people responded. But I didn't find an organized approach to "raising awareness"

[18:17] Dancers Yao: The groups on *SL*, like Virtual Ability, Relay for Life, Faster Cures, there are many people here we can ask.

[18:19] Kasuku Magic: Yes, The American Cancer Society has a beautiful site on *Second Life*.

[18:19] Dancers Yao: I never imagined when we began our work on *SL* it would be you that needed the magic of science, of spirit, of love, because you were so healthy, and strong..

[18:21] Kasuku Magic: Thank you - we are kind of like the Chilean Miners hoping to hold on while we also need others to help with our rescue, but they made it.

[18:21] Kasuku Magic: I know answers are out there in the universe waiting to be found and created. If I don't survive, I hope that by helping people become aware that they can be involved in the search for their health care guides, will help others in the future. I didn't realize when I wrote a poem for a friend who has cancer, that someday it would be about me...it is called ...*Beyond courage.* Beyond courage there is a place.....I have glimpsed its' light through the cleft beneath the door. Beyond courage....there is a feeling, I have knelt beside its' cradle. Beyond courage...there is music, I have heard its' choir. Struggling to survive, a rare few burst into a thousand stars blossoming. The glow warming us standing near. The strength healing us far away. I have witnessed courage and beyond....Grace to share your table. Beyond Courage there stands hope, and hope is my friend.

Conclusion

Virtual environs offer immersive 3D interaction to help discover guidelines for the health care of the individual and community. Guides that respect the unique values of each person, yet share the common theme of discovering how to survive with meaning and purpose in an ever changing world.

We have learned how people from many different cultures can try to create new ways for understanding ancient questions with new media technology. Ultimately the ability of technology to augment our survival depends on the choice to respect human rights. Hopefully, this ongoing challenge will lead to educational materials that encourage the prevention of health care atrocities.

Elder Voices, Inc., a 501(c)(3) nonprofit organization, offers an interactive pilot program for learning problem-solving strategies that help to apply the guidelines offered in the Universal Declaration of Human Rights about health care to real life situations. We are doing this by showing examples of problem solving strategies that can be used to design each step in the process of creating the ideal goal in real life.

Elder Voices is funded by local community and private donations, free services such as space from the nonprofit commons on *Second Life*, (www.tech soup.org) volunteer health care professionals, and Google sites.

Works Cited

Abraham, J. L. "Dynamical Systems Theory: Application to Pedagogy." W. Tschacher and J. P. Dauwalder, eds. *The dynamical systems approach to cognition.* Studies of Nonlinear Phenomena in Life Science vol. 10. New Jersey: World Scientific Publishing, 2003.

Bennett, K. S. "A Construction of a Diagnosis: A Study of Physician's Mental Strategies for Fitting a Patient's Symptoms and Signs to a Disease Category." Doctoral dissertation, U.C.L.A. 300 pages. 1981.

Bennett, K., and H. Barrows. "An Investigation of the Diagnostic Problem-Solving Methods Used by Resident Neurologists." *Mathematical Biosciences* 15 (1972): 63–181.

DeAngelis, T. "Virtual Healing." *Monitor on Psychology* (September 2009): 36–40.

Elder Voices. Web. 2 July 2012

Ericsson, K. A., and H. A. Simon. *Protocol Analysis: Verbal Reports as Data.* Cambridge: MIT Press, 1993.

Gosling, S. D., and J. Johnson. *Advanced Methods for Conducting Online Behavioral Research.* Washington, DC: American Psychological Association. 2010.

The Hub Health Care. Web. 2 July 2012.

Maheu, M. M., M. L. Pulier, F. H. Wilhelm, J. P. McMenamin, and N. E. Brown-Connolly. *The Mental Health Professional and the New Technologies: A Handbook for Practice Today.* New York: Routledge, 2004.

Murray, J. M. *Hamlet on the Holodeck: The Future of Narrative in Cyberspace.* New York: The Free Press, 1997.

Roosevelt, E. IN YOUR HANDS: A Guide for Community Action for the Tenth Anniversary of the Universal Declaration of Human Rights. March 27, 1958 United Nations, New York.

"2010 Copiapó Mining Accident." *Wikipedia.* Web. 2 July 2012.

"Universal Declaration of Human Rights." *United Nations Humans Rights: Office of the High Commissioner Human Rights.* 1948. Web.

Van Orden, G. C. "The Fractal Picture of Health and Wellbeing." *Psychological Science Agenda,* vol. 22, no. 2 (2007) Washington, DC: American Psychological Association.

Virtual Ability. Web. 2 July 2012.

Ward, T. B., and M. S. Sonneborn. "Creative Expression in Virtual Worlds: Imitation, Imagination, and Individualized Collaboration." *Psychology of Aesthetics, Creativity, and the Arts* vol. 3, no. 4 (2009): 211–221. doi: 10.1037/a0016297

"WHO Linkages Between Health and Human Rights." *World Health Organization.* 2 July 2012.

The Virtual Sky Is the Limit:
Women's Journalism
Experiences in *Second Life*

PHYLIS JOHNSON

There is a more level playing field for women in SL *than there is in* RL. *No glass ceiling in here. There is no virtual glass ceiling. Women can do anything in* SL *the same as men.*—Persia Bravin, Interview with author, 2011

In May 2010, a number of *Second Life* media moguls and reporters gathered to celebrate the 5th Rez Day party for one of the leading *SL* newspaper entrepreneurs. *Second Life Enquirer* Founder and CEO Lanai Jarrico was celebrating her *SL* birthday. Those who attended the event were a virtual "who's who" among the media, business, and entertainment" sects including longtime friend Frolic Mills, CEO of *Best of Second Life Magazine* (BOSL). I was on assignment to report on the event for *BOSL*. When news breaks out across the grid, the *Second Life* media arrives quickly on the spot to cover those issues and events that impact residents. The media often reports on its own events, for there is an impressive community of journalists and media makers in *Second Life*—many of whom are women.

Second Life offers a variety of news media; some present high glossy photos and spectacular interviews on leading women news makers of virtual life. Among those women is one well-known on the grid: Persia Bravin, editor for *Best of Second Life Magazine*, a European journalist, who keeps her identities separate between *Second Life* and real life. In *Second Life*, she has established herself as an entertainment reporter and event publicist. She has a long list of writing credentials in *SL* at various journalistic posts. In real life, she covers "hard" news on a daily basis. Bravin is featured on glitzy *SL* magazine covers. Her avatar is sleek, beautiful, and classy. She is written about in the media, nearly as much as she reports on others. She is a celebrity television host and is involved in a number of *SL* not-for profit events. She is one of the many women journalists of *Second Life*. She is a key person in the success of Pop Art Lab, a Northern European based international entertainment arts venue that has hosted virtual and mixed reality cultural events. In Spring 2010, PAL hosted some activities related to the internationally acclaimed "Through the Virtual Looking Glass" exhibition. Part of that exhibition involved a mixed reality showing of virtual world art in conjunction with the real world Harbor Gallery of the University of Massachusetts at Boston. Her real life journalistic experience, combined with her virtual world savvy, has actually made her a credible voice in the *SL* news media. She started her virtual career writing for Jarrico, now a close friend.

A brief overview of the journalistic history of *Second Life* will be presented in this essay, particularly how it relates to women, and some roadblocks in the professional practice of journalism will be shared in an effort to suggest why this virtual world has become an attractive option or an extension to a media career for many women, some of whom are expanding their reporting specialties beyond their real life beats. For others, it is an opportunity to fulfill a dream of being a journalist in another life. Bravin and Jarrico represent two groups of women with interest in virtual journalism — those entering as seasoned professionals like Bravin and those following through on a dream like Jarrico. The heart of this chapter focuses on those two options, as expressed through the words of virtual journalists Bravin and Jarrico. I interviewed both women at length regarding their motivations for this virtual path and asked them what they had hoped to gain from these experiences. I begin with my personal experience as a virtual journalist. I consider myself a seasoned media maker, who felt compelled to return to my "dream" (and roots), having graduated with a Bachelors of Arts in Journalism only several years after the Watergate era and inspired toward investigative reporting years after. Alas, I would eventually become entrenched in the academic world, as I followed a somewhat family-friendly career route.

A Personal Lens

Women are involved at every level of the news world in *Second Life*, from television anchors, documentary producers, blog writers to beat reporters, columnists, and editors and publishers of newspapers and magazines. Look at the credits in any number of virtual magazines or media productions and see how many women are involved in the creation process. Of course, in newspapers, magazines, and production credits, it is difficult to identify gender unless you speak to the person in voice chat or on the phone. Yet, from my personal dealings with women media makers, from conferences to cocktail parties, it is proportionally a woman's voice heard across the virtual globe. I entered this second world of journalism several months prior to the launch of my book, *Second Life, Media and the Other Society* (Peter Lang Publishing) in June 2010. I had been a business woman, researcher, and educator in *Second Life* before engaging in my virtual journalism career, arriving on the grid in 2007. During my investigation for the book, I had met and interviewed so many media people that I had become enamored by the significant role of journalism inside *Second Life* and in the larger gaming world as well. It was time for me to return to my journalist roots, although this time with a bit of twist. I would assume the role of Sonicity Fitzroy, an attractive thirty-something, slender on-the-go, feature journalist (in contrast to my older, thicker self), and join the ranks of women like Bravin and Jarrico who proceeded me.

In 2011, I created the real me, which perhaps reflects my comfort within *Second Life* now among those I have met along the way. As time progressed, my experiences in the virtual world would become part of who I am in real life, as a professional and as a person. I would enter *Second Life* no longer through the lens of a character comprised of parts of me. Consequently, the only difference between my virtual and real self would be that I needed to log-in to report on this world. But there was even more than that. I began to write features for a magazine called *Retropolitan*, a monthly publication focusing on those *SL* residents role-playing the Victorian era to the 1950s. In *Second Life*, you can look toward the future, as well as relive the past — and with that, reporters have an opportunity to reconsider what it might have been like to cover such time periods, from daily life to historical events. Some of these communities that I reported on had their own community and/or metropolitan newspapers. Your mind begins to wander, contemplating the role of a journalist back then. You begin to sense what it felt like to walk in those shoes, although generations apart from your predecessors. For women journalists, who were few back then, it becomes a way to gain insight into the past and consider how those times have played upon our present. It became, for me, a path to connect to other women journalists and media makers from around the world in the here and now. I would learn from my virtual lens, a woman's perspective, not only through the making of my media works, but reviewing those of my *Second Life* colleagues. The pioneering spirit connects us all, and my story is no more special than theirs, but rather contributes to a greater sense that women have grabbed a hold of the future and claimed it. In the beginning, I was merely curious about what it would be like to be a journalist in a new world, and soon I found myself a part of a maturing community of media professionals that keeps the buzz going with regards to a plethora of in-world events, regularly engaging *SL* citizens and touching upon their real lives. Many media companies within *Second Life* provide publicity and even host relief efforts for natural disasters that might happen anywhere globally and help to promote fund raising for non-profit health campaigns, such as supporting breast cancer awareness and research. *Second Life*, in particular, offers many journalists opportunities in reporting within a convergent media market. Moreover, through their contacts across the grid these women gain international perspective, being that its residents represent many countries. They can easily compare notes with other women in *SL*, working otherwise under various journalist constraints in real life.

Through the lens of "virtual" women behind the bylines and in front of the camera, and that includes me now, one begins to understand the significance of mediated communication in *Second Life*. Print media, notably newspapers and magazines, consume the largest segment of in-world journalism.

Second Life *Newspapers and Magazines*

If *Second Life* is considered mainly a game, it is then comparable to the game of life. Daily life exists of attending events, making friends, and even working to buy homes, nice clothes, and customized avatars to create your fantasy. Linden Lab policies, *SL* economy, corporate news, major art exhibits or celebrations, or any number of events can make news. Some communities have their own village press and radio stations that announce local events and small town celebrities. The media in all these cases become an important voice, and many of the media people are critical to maintaining the community's visibility and economic health. Increasingly, those owning and working these enterprises are more often than not — women.

It may have started out with a few more men in the driver's seat, but that has shifted as women have found their way to *Second Life*; many had been members of the game *The Sims*. But in *Second Life*, you create your own life — and that means, career too. The incentive is professional experience that carries over into the real world, as well as celebrity status and possibly financial reward for some. The latter — the money issue — is not what typically motivates the journalist in any life. What appears to drive the virtual journalist is a love for media and its significance in fostering a community spirit among members. When the media shows up, that means your event is real — right? When you see your event published in the local press, that is a big deal for you, as a citizen, and you have become part of something much bigger than yourself.

In the past decade, the number of virtual journalists has been on the rise, as news media organizations in *Second Life* continue to be established, and some from the mainstream are moving inward (and some are moving out, typically because of economic or real life issues, or both). Yet, consider this: the journalist is an avatar reporting for a virtual audience. Wagner James Au was hired by Linden Lab as an embedded journalist to report on the activities and events across the grid. It culminated in his book, *The Making of Second Life*. He hired virtual stringers to cover events with Linden dollars, the game currency. Salon.com archived his stories. He was interviewed by mainstream media outlets. His observations were printed in *Wired* and other tech press. He now watches trends as an independent journalist inside *SL*, and also covers virtual worlds for real world media. His observations have been consistently reported by other media outlets in *SL* and RL. Au has promoted women's efforts in *Second Life* on a regular basis, and it does seem at times like a woman's world in nearly every aspect from the arts to the media and business. A good bulk of press, however, centers on the entertainment side of virtual life.

In some *SL* papers, and during slow news times, you might anticipate headlines like *Interview with an SL vampire* or *SL Supermodel Debuts Spring Fashion*. Space might be allotted to feature the *Resident of the Month* and *Business of the Week*. But when big news breaks out across the grid, the *SL* media arrive quickly on the spot to cover those issues and events that impact the residents. *Second Life Herald* was one of the earliest newspapers launched, with that happening on October 23, 2003, by philosophy professor Peter Ludlow. Ludlow was one of the first to document virtual life, and he covered *The Sims* initially. In its earlier form, it became known for its virtual muckraking, particularly its investigation into gambling and prostitution. Its coverage was hard-hitting, yet sensational.

Other newspapers soon followed. *The Metaverse Messenger—A Real Newspaper for a Virtual World* was a weekly newspaper that began in 2005, and ran regularly through 2010. It had an online presentation style that was similar to a traditional newspaper. Its readership was measured through its more than 100,000 hits on its Web site, with some of its content making its way to mainstream newspapers in the USA. It was established by RL journalist Katt Kongo, who also had provided specialized training to *SL* journalists. Her news philosophy was simple and rooted in community journalism; she states, "A newspaper helps residents function by providing a tool which they can then use to make decisions with — where to buy the best clothing, what to do on a Friday night, how to use new *SL* features and more" (Zimmer). *The Metaverse Messenger* may have continued in another form, but its last publication online appears to be in late 2010. Its staff was primarily comprised of women.

Another long-time newspaper, *SL-Newspaper,* included a staff mix of seasoned real life journalists and *Second Life* writers. The newspaper's content was fairly typical, with a mix of *SL* news, art, music, fashion, business and other lifestyle topics. After a four-year run, its editor Dana Vanmoer shut down the paper, announcing on the company web site her desire to shift her goals to real life, noting she was frustrated with Linden Lab policies and other issues as well.

Real life is a factor in some of the women's decisions to launch a virtual career in journalism; take for example the staff profiles of *Second Style*. All of the primary magazine positions there were held by women, many of whom mentioned the need to balance family and career in their biographies. Some brought real life media experience; for others they developed a career in virtual journalism over the past several years. The publisher and editor-in-chief of *Second Style*, Heather Dawn Cohen, became involved in the magazine since its inception, in April 2006, primarily handling layout and design initially. In April 2011, she closed the magazine after a 5-year run, citing the downturn in economy as the reason. When she assumed ownership, she was a single mother and had a full-time job, but for Cohen this publishing opportunity had meant she could also be a business owner (*SecondStyle*). The skills and experience she gained are real, although her work was in the virtual realm.

The myriad of publications over the years has been primarily those dealing with fashion and lifestyle in *Second Life*: *The Best of SL Magazine, Second Style, BeStyle: The Best of Italian Style, Avenue Magazine, Essence of Style, Vain Inc, Retropolitan,* and *ICON Lifestyle.* The majority of such magazines are or have been owned by women, and those publications that are not owned by women tend to have female executives on staff. Often, magazines are delivered in a "prim" version as an object in *Second Life.* The magazine can be opened within *SL* and set on a table in a virtual living room. Certain magazines have large subscriber bases of readers. Often readers can pick up copies of magazines at vendor stands in popular regions of *SL.* Most magazines are available online as well. Some are only presented online. Bottom line is that the top magazines have accumulated a healthy circulation and a strong base of advertisers to support their operations, and that takes quite a lot of time and commitment by those involved in the publishing process.

The Broadcast Media

The broadcast media market in *Second Life* has expanded exponentially in recent years, but was present in some form early on. Over the years, corporate partnerships have been formed between print and broadcast media. Finding leads for events and stories takes someone who can build a network of virtual contacts. The advantage is that a reporter can interview a person across the world in minutes, and this person could share a valuable RL/*SL* perspective from a particular part of the globe. The immediate connection between real and virtual life becomes one that cannot be easily ignored on the grid and is readily available for coverage.

During the 2008 U.S. presidential campaign, *Fox News* and *The BBC* reported that Barack Obama and John McCain supporters had created virtual campaign offices inside *Second Life* (Grimm). On Election Night, people from both camps filled the campaign sims. Some cheered waving banners, others jeered; and others wore virtual T-shirts with political logos. Many *SL*ers participated in-world, while watching events unfold on mainstream media in the real world. I was among those journalists, as I was taking notes for my book in progress. Others tuned into *SL* media for updates.

In 2008, CNN established a citizen journalism program for *SL* residents. Rather than establish reporters inside *Second Life*, they would encourage wannabe reporters to post photos, text, audio and video to iReport. The stories would be curated on its Web site, with the idea being to encourage a grass roots perspective (Wagner). CNN's move into *SL* was an extension of its citizen reporting efforts. It has collapsed its involvement in the virtual world into its broader iReport Assignment Desk blog, with a specific category for *Second Life* reports. The iReport news staff is mainly comprised of females, including its editorial leader, according to its web site.

There have been somewhat comparable efforts by other real life news organizations, such as Reuters, and successes have varied. *Second Life* also seems to offer interesting possibilities to journalism schools considering innovative ways to train future journalists. In fact, journalism programs from universities across the world are increasingly using *Second Life* as a means for vetting issues and giving students practical experience in interviewing and reporting. The London School of Journalism (Morgan) and the Edward R. Murrow College of Communication in Washington State University (WSU) have actively discussed and explored virtual opportunities in recent years, to varying degrees. A related documentary, *Virtual Journalism: Inside the Virtual Newsroom of the American University in Cairo*, examined these issues as part of the economic and cultural transformation of journalism globally (Dancing Ink).

In-world media caters to a unique audience of avatars. Basically, the news is available online through virtual media websites, as well as Vimeo and YouTube. Metaverse Television, part of Metaverse Broadcasting Company (MBC), is among the leading broadcast networks in *SL*. Long-time virtual television newscaster Dousa Dragonash has worked with rotating teams of anchors. The typical 22 minute news program begins with a newsy music opening and an

MBC News logo keyed to the left of the screen, as professional images of the news team appear one by one on the right. On one particular show in early 2010, Dragonash was joined by anchors Sigmund Leonminster and Malburns Writer. She began with a round-up of real world events—keyed as "In the Real World," which included an update on the Thailand demonstrators calling for the resignation of the nation's prime minister and the release of a report that asked for inquiry into claims of Google's invasion of members' privacy. In between the stories, and during, there was much cross-talk among the anchors. The stories were serious, but the anchors sometimes took a tongue-and-check approach to the delivery. Typically its newscasts deal with trends or information related to *Second Life* and reports on technology and other virtual worlds. This newscast concluded with a review of upcoming public service activities, including an interview with an event organizer. At the end of the newscast, the final shot was of all three anchors in bikinis—including the men (MBC). The news team in this case was European-based.

The diversity among news staff within media companies reflects the global nature of *Second Life* journalism. Some journalists are assigned to certain events or, as in the MBC instance, to work together as a news anchor team due to residing in similar time zones. Yet, many journalists across the world work together and socialize at all hours of the day. There are always events to cover and people to interview, and journalists seem to gravitate toward chatting on virtual news perspectives with each other. The taboos of real life journalism, such as sharing information and sources with competing media outlets, do not always apply (the more virtual press on an event the better; and the general thought is to beat out the mainstream media of real life, not necessarily in-world media although there are exceptions); it is a world of civility and collaboration, presenting opportunities and perspectives for those feeling oppressed by real life constraints to look inward toward *Second Life.*

The Virtual Sky Is the Limit: Lifting the Glass Ceilings

Women are flocking to the virtual world, and some might perceive *Second Life* as a place for media opportunities. There are some roadblocks or requirements to living and working successfully in the virtual world—having some computer savvy, a good computer that quickly processes images in an immersive, graphically rich game like *Second Life* and a good internet connection. Time and money are common issues for many. A talent for social networking and team building help offset some of that. To be a major media player in *Second Life* it does take some investment. Yet, for many women, it does seem worth the effort and they seem to tackle the technology challenges quite well.

Sometimes you hear a dog barking or a child laughing in the background. (I have had both happen during my *Second Life* radio show, and the audience accepts that as merely real life coming through the virtual portal, and that helps further solidify the connection between both realms.)

Besides opportunities for stay-at-home mothers, what might be other factors that influence a woman's decision to build a media career in *Second Life*? Might it be what is going on in the real world that compels women to move inward? In 2010, The Global Media Monitoring Project (GMMP) released the study "Who Makes the News," on women's status at news organizations among 59 nations around the world. The results from this comprehensive report, under the direction of Dr. Carolyn Byerly (2011), indicated nearly 75 percent of the executive management jobs are occupied by men, and generally men hold nearly two-thirds of the jobs. Women, with senior level experience, are moving closer to equity, with more than 40 percent of the news gathering and editing positions (GMMP, vii). In *Second Life*, much of the news caters to entertainment, and there are few that perceive the need for investigative coverage, given the nature of the world as owned by a corporate entity, namely Linden Lab. But *Second Life* does seem inviting to women media makers, from film to print to art and design, and communities seem to develop around these media interest areas (and some of these women meet regularly in specialty groups). It is a particularly interesting space for those women that wish to launch their own projects for minimal investment. And *Second Life*, being an online platform, is positioned for the media convergence happening across the internet in the real world. One woman at the heart of this convergence is Jarrico, a newcomer to the real life profession of journalism but extremely experienced with virtual world platforms and virtual media.

Lanai Jarrico, Virtual Newspaper Entrepreneur

"Got News? Get it Published." That's the motto of *The Second Life Enquirer*, founded and owned by Lanai Jarrico, one of the leading ladies of virtual world journalism. She has paid her virtual dues. Jarrico is a self-made woman. Since her journalistic debut into virtual worlds, there has been a rise of female editors and even publishers, mostly among magazine publications. Jarrico is a newspaper publisher. She was among the first, and to her knowledge and her perspective, she has been fairly much alone at the top of the news game, first reporting on *The Sims Online*, and now several years from inside *Second Life*. "It has been a men's world, from what I saw," she told me. I interviewed her via voice chat on December 9, 2011, inside *Second Life*. She is a tall brunette, long hair, looking perhaps in her late 20s to early 30s, virtually and in real life, as there was a real life photo of her in the news room. On this day, she wore black pin-striped pants, with a matching vest, under which she wore a sleek tie and white blouse. She was professional in every aspect, from appearance to conversation and mannerisms. She represented herself well as a business woman. In her left hand, she carried a rolled up newspaper, *The Wall Street Journal. Second Life* offers her opportunities not easily obtained in real life, at times. Jarrico pointed out, she has been a writer since a child, shaping ideas into stories:

> Writing has actually been a creative outlet for me ever since I was little. I used to write poetry, little stories, and ad libs; it's just something I naturally love to do. So I decided to apply it. Before that I was a sculptor, making my own figurines and selling them at trade shows and over the Internet. I did that for about 6 years. As the paper was growing, I had to make a choice, do I continue to create my art work or do I proceed fully into the paper because both of them were very demanding on me. I also have a family life, children and am married. It was a hard decision to make; both were creative outlets to me. Right now I am a full-time student, and I contribute that to being in *Second Life* and doing what I do because I am studying communications and media [Jarrico].

Jarrico is not new to storytelling but in virtual worlds, she seeks the truth — the reality behind the avatar, you might say, for she likes her readers to "get to know the people behind the headlines." Her spotlight interviews are an important part of *The Second Life Enquirer.* Her journalistic adventure came about from her exploration and game play in *The Sims Online,* starting in 2003: "I had my small circle of friends, and I realized in this virtual world when a lot of personalities come together they clash and provoke drama. There's a lot to write about. It was more of a fluke for me" (Jarrico). Her friends would sit around with her, talking about what was happening, virtually: "There were a lot of things going, and interesting activities. And one day I decided, I'll make a newspaper." In the beginning, she merely intended to entertain her friends. "It pretty much went viral. I started off by myself with only 5 pages and fairly much reported on my own for a year. Then I started getting some writers involved. At first I was reporting on the *SL* Mafia because that was the biggest community in *The Sims Online*," she continued (Jarrico). Her newspaper would be the medium between the warring in-world families, which were role-playing the mafia scene. She would report on the conflicts, "so basically they would use my paper to get across whatever they had to say to the other families, and it would be back and forth. I did that for about a year and a half. It is because of them that my newspaper became viral; there were a lot of people involved in mafia role play. They just flocked to my paper" (Jarrico).

In 2004, she had some amateur filmmakers from *Second Life* approach her in *The Sims*, having heard about her newspaper and wanting to produce a segment for a documentary about virtual worlds and the people who play them. They flew out from Paris to the USA and interviewed her. They encouraged her to set up her newspaper in *Second Life*. When she initially came into *Second Life* and looked around, it was still early in the launch of the game. The graphics, for example, were extremely slow then. She went back to Sims, yet returning to *Second Life* occasionally. It was when *The Sims Online* was about to end, that she seriously began to transition her newspaper's coverage. At first, she published all her articles in *TSO Enquirer* (*The Sims Online*) — that was the original publication. In 2006, she decided to completely cross over, leaving Sims, and the paper has remained solely dedicated to *Second Life* since then:

> My objective with *The Second Life Enquirer* isn't to make money because I have actually not made a living or transferred any Lindens to my personal account. Everything that is generated through the *SL Enquirer* goes back into it like a non-profit. I pay my writers or I buy things to market. As far as my objective, I think it has always been my creative outlet, sharing it with other people who enjoy writing [Jarrico].

Her newspaper has provided opportunities for not only her, but for other writers:

> My writers, and anyone who comes to me, I don't expect them to have a degree or have a writing background; if they love to write and are good at it, then they can join and it is a shared project. I definitely don't have any motives here to become a millionaire. But what it has done is that it has helped me through college. Everything I have applied in the virtual world, as far as doing the media and such, was relevant to my course work in college. I basically flew through many of my courses; moreover, doing what I have done in *Second Life* has given me a real job. I am a (real life) fashion blogger for a company called Melco based in Denver, Colorado, and I write articles along that line every month. I think it has presented doors of opportunity for me, preparing me for the real world. I would like to cross-over into the real world and do media [Jarrico].

Writing is a competitive field in both worlds. She adds, no doubt having already had her fill of conflict since the early days of virtual worlds, "I don't want to write on gossip or politics. More likely I would like to write features about culture" (Jarrico). She sees herself in a man's world, even virtually, given that she is not only a journalist, but a media entrepreneur. Being a woman has its roadblocks and advantages. She has found some men find women approachable and particularly interesting because of their status; other men do not like women in authority. It might become difficult to communicate with them in those situations. Either way, she explains, she prefers not to concentrate on those negative things and chooses to push forward and do her job. Her advice to others is, "Stay true to yourself and do things in a positive way. One thing about women is that we often have a quality that allows people to feel comfortable enough to tell us the stories" (Jarrico). That is what she plans to continue to do, tell stories, and to stick to what she has done — it has worked well and has built her a strong community presence within *Second Life*, establishing her newspaper among readers and businesses. The newspaper reports on headline news and offers the regular features of any community newspaper — culture, music, fashion, art, entertainment, sports, humor, astrology — but Jarrico notes that she likes especially the spotlight features: "Just like any newspaper, you want to share what is going on with the community, and sometimes through spotlight features and interviews you get to know about the people behind the events."

Her focus remains on her newspaper, while her company has expanded somewhat to take *SLE* to the airwaves. Every Tuesday, her staff has a little get together at the Chill Lounge within *Second Life*, with music spun by a radio DJ from the in-world station Black Soul Rhythms. The newspaper business is a stressful operation in any world. I ended my interview with a tour of her publishing facility, a professional headquarters complete with an information desk and assignment board. Jarrico has come a long way since 2004; that is the year she marks as the beginning of her journalism career launched with *The Sims*. She is moving closer to real life media opportunities she would like to pursue in the near future. She was born again on May 9, 2005, into her *Second Life* persona, and that transition was a career move that has served her well in real life, as well as propelled others who have worked alongside her toward virtual paths still unfolding — one of those being Bravin.

Persia Bravin, Born Again as a Virtual Journalist

The names of certain journalists have become household words: Peter Jennings, Cokie Roberts, Katie Couric, Bernard Shaw, Geraldo Rivera, Judy Woodruff, Stone Phillips and the list goes on. Then there are the MTV journalists and entertainment reporters who appeal to a new generation of audiences. In 1997, Alicia Shepard in the *American Journalism Review* questioned how celebrity journalism had impacted the profession. Does the celebrity status of a reporter impact the credibility of what is being presented to audiences? And how so? (Shepard). The rise of journalists as stars or merely as significant icons in virtual worlds is a phenomenon worthy of contemplation. Persia Bravin is not only a serious journalist when it comes to real and *Second Life*, she has also earned a reputation across the grid to the point that she has achieved celebrity status of her own.

Bravin, United Kingdom journalist, has already established her career as a seasoned reporter. She spent more than a decade rising to the top in a predominately male industry — journalism is a business. News is her specialty. I interviewed her via voice chat in *Second Life* on December 3, 2011, but I had conversations with her numerous times before. Over the past two years, as a writer myself for *Best of Second Life Magazine,* I watched Bravin hustle about the grid, covering event to event, some of which she herself had organized to either help others with publicity or because she sought ways to create and/or promote events that would bring both worlds together in an artistic, immersive, and creative way. What became odd to Bravin was how she would feel when she started her new life virtually.

She explained, it felt like being "born again, not in a religious sense, but literally being a baby, learning to walk and talk, learning to communicate" (Bravin). Those early days at *The Second Life Enquirer,* working with Jarrico, "really did feel like my days as a cub reporter in real life when I was 18 or 19 and even before that. I started writing semi-professionally at 16. It kind of felt like that. I look at my time at *SLE* as my teen years" (Bravin). Bravin brought her experience into *Second Life* in 2008, prompted through her role as a member of a real life media research team investigating the future of news reporting. She explains:

> What we were doing is looking at the future of news reporting, and how news will eventually be paperless. The idea is, so you won't be buying *The Washington Post* in paper format. It will be online in a few short years; well, it has already happened when you think about it. The amount of news that we consume online other than via web sites or online papers has exploded in the past three years. But we were looking at different ways too other than that. Among the options were virtual worlds for reporting news in a more immersive way than was presently the case. You can imagine instead of just watching the news, you would almost be part of it. In *Second Life,* for instance imagine walking into a video dome, which would project the news all around you. There were lots of other things we were doing as well, but *Second Life* was mentioned as one such virtual world. And to be honest one night, I thought, I would take a look at that. It sounded interesting [Bravin].

She created the account, logged on, not intending to become involved, and soon would play a major part in helping to build and shape the media world of *Second Life*:

> I remember, after being in *Second Life* for a week, then mentioning it in real life work; it turned out quite a few other people I worked with in real life also have accounts in here. So I said, "Okay I guess I'll see you tonight then." I mused, "Oh what am I going to do?" The people that I knew were in here for fun. But for me, I thought reporting would be a good way to know *Second Life* better, by becoming involved as a journalist or some related work. Being a journalist in real life, I knew it was a fantastic and perfect way of meeting people. And I'm naturally curious any

way. So I thought let's see if I can do a little of the same in *SL* too. I ended up meeting Lanai. *The Second Life Enquirer* was the first newspaper that showed in the *SL* search entries. I contacted her in August 2008. I was about two months old. I ended up working there for about two years [Bravin].

Bravin also began to help write and edit for *Best of Second Life Magazine*. She left *SLE* when Best of *SL*, the company, started up its radio station, and Bravin became the CEO. The radio operation took much time, plus with a demanding real life schedule, and a readiness to advance, she parted ways with *The Second Life Enquirer*, but remained close friends with Jarrico. "I felt ready to progress. It had been a fantastic opportunity" (Bravin). When I asked her to consider how *Second Life* has altered her perceptions of reporting, she readily had an answer, having evidently already contemplated what this new experience has meant to her, perhaps in those moments when deadlines from both worlds come crashing upon her:

> What is quite fascinating are the differences and similarities between real and *SL* media. When you do something in *Second Life* you really put yourself out there even more than real life. You can feel vulnerable sometimes. It's like writing for a very popular local newspaper in a large town. Rather than a large virtual world, *SL* is a large town, not even a city proportionally..." [Bravin].

That is particularly true, she explains, if you think of it in terms of residents that are online at any one time. She continues, "The good news is *SL* media is finally being taken seriously. It isn't just a means of communication within *SL* anymore. So much has changed in three years. The media in here has exploded. I personally think it will continue to gather pace, not only within *SL* but other virtual words definitely" (Bravin).

Although an accomplished journalist, Bravin sees benefits to her media work in *Second Life*, espousing its virtues fairly quickly when asked, and noting that it has helped her in real life substantially:

> I can sum it up quite simply, the biggest way *SL* helps me in real life, is it keeps my real life writing sharp, because I believe if you can write about the virtual, and make it read and feel real, and your reader can connect to it in a real way, then you have done your job. Writing about the virtual takes skill, practice and an awful lot of intuition. In real life, if I interview someone, I tend to do it in person, one-on-one or within a press conference environment; there's eye contact, there's physical and verbal cues, but in *SL* we don't have that. So you develop extra senses as a journalist. *SL* helps me in real life because it keeps my writing skills sharp ... and it has also helped me in real life, for I have almost developed a sixth sense about people and motives. Then of course there are the really obvious ways it helps me in life, like being involved in real life book projects and of course Pop Art Lab has been a big part of my real life too [Bravin].

Pop Art Lab, on hiatus since November 2012, is an international project that intersects the virtual and real worlds of art and entertainment, showcasing talent and creating an immersive space in which they perform, from live concerts to art shows to a variety of entertainment events. Bravin, as the publicity manager, became involved in nearly every aspect of these events. Bravin is royalty among journalists when it comes to social networking, but all that has to do with her willingness to envision and follow-through on a project or an event. Her vibrant personality shines through her voice and hard work, plus her intuitive social skills, and in *Second Life*, she senses no boundaries:

> The immediate thing for me is in *SL* you are not judged on what you look like in real life. For instance, I work in a very male dominated industry, still unfortunately, and I would say that 7 out of every 10 people I work with in real life are men, if not proportionally higher. It is still incredibly male dominated, and along with that, you get all the usual (laughs) so it is nice not to be judged on looks [Bravin].

Bravin is an attractive woman in real life, as well as *Second Life*, slender with blonde hair. For the interview, she was wearing a stunning red evening dress. She had been at a formal reception for the Miss Virtual World competition moments earlier. Bravin elaborates, saying, "I think *SL* judges you on talent rather than gender."

She, like Jarrico, resembles her real self. "I have to mention, I don't think I have a particularly beautiful avatar. I am just me as much as possible in *SL* as I am in real life. There are far more beautiful female avatars but I am more interested in using *SL* for a canvas rather than how I am judged on the perfectness of my prims" (Bravin). Maybe it is the journalist in them, a sense of honesty about who they are in real life and a desire for that to project into *Second Life*—giving credibility to the kind of work they enjoy in-world, reporting on events that are very much real to their virtual readership. It is community journalism, after all, in virtual worlds: a concept that Bravin holds dear in *Second Life*. She is invested in *Second Life*, professionally and personally, and it allows her to extend her talent to the fullest of her abilities and imagination:

> There is a more level playing field for women in *SL* than there is in RL. No glass ceiling in here. There is no virtual glass ceiling. Women can do anything in *SL* the same as men. I have met a significant number of people who have set up themselves from nothing, including women. I think *SL* is a brilliant platform for women in general because it allows women to work for themselves from home, while looking after their kids [Bravin].

Bravin, further, pointed out that a number of women she knows, particularly fashion designers, have earned enough money through *Second Life* to impact their real life in significant ways, like paying their children's way through college. Bravin has worked with and interviewed a number of these leading women of *Second Life.* "It was most obvious to me, going back two years when I was about a year into *SLE,* that female journalists have an ability to connect with other women" (Bravin).

Outside of her usual art and fashion social circle, Bravin decided to investigate the Gorean lifestyle at one point, and why women would get involved in that in *Second Life.* As a female journalist, she had an opportunity to interview the women involved, and found that some of them were career women, who had successful professions in real life. She walked away with a different perspective on the role players and shed some light on stereotypes associated with the in-world communities. To get those interviews she had to build up trust. It is obvious that she is a female journalist because she does quite a bit of public speaking in *Second Life.* Her voice, sultry and definitely charming with her British accent, is a give-away. To Bravin, it is the "trust thing:"

> I think people tend to trust you as a woman maybe more than a male journalist. There are certain aspects of our personality naturally that help our work as journalists in *SL,* such things like we tend to be more patient, more understanding, and empathetic toward people. One of the questions I always ask is, "Please describe yourself in RL in six words." That is someone telling me how they feel about themselves. That does allow me to fill in more blanks to give credence to my intuition. I don't think many male journalists would do that" [Bravin].

As we neared the end of our interview, I asked Bravin to answer that question about herself. The first four adjectives came easily to her ... "relentless, focused, professional, compassionate" (Bravin). Then she paused, and said, "Now I understand why people say 'what a hard question.'" She continued a moment later, saying, "I'm loyal, definitely very loyal like I would never go to another magazine in *Second Life.* I am with *BOSL* until I decide I am not doing this anymore. I am not that ambitious in *SL.*" Then she added, "Perceptive." That was her final descriptor.

In closing she said:

> I believe none of us act in isolation if we are going to achieve something. You know getting the magazine out is like going through childbirth every month. Like some days, until the day it is published nothing is altogether. I often sit at my PC and say, "Nothing is together. It is not going to happen."
> *BOSL* literally comes together the day we publish. It is as stressful as in real life. Often I am at a real life press conference with my laptop open, ready like I am going to write a story, and I am actually editing *BOSL.* I also sent a real life editor an *SL* article by mistake. That was very amusing [Bravin].

Notably, Bravin has interviewed many of the key people on the grid, from the "Lindens" of Linden Lab (*Second Life's* parent company) to artists, fashion designers, and other newsmakers. She keeps a positive attitude, and remains polite, leaning on her real life sense of manners and social etiquette:

I am much more patient in *SL* than in RL, a thousand times more patient. In RL, I have been known to walk out of interviews, with quite famous people, because I don't like their attitude and I don't like being kept waiting. It's rude. But in *SL*, there are so many things to consider, like cultural differences, language barriers, time zones, that you have to give benefit of the doubt [Bravin].

And, beyond that she loves it — it intrigues her curiosity and journalistic spirit of exploration.

Conclusion

Jarrico had provided opportunity for Bravin to report and write for her virtual newspaper, *The Second Life Enquirer*. Bravin has since become Editor of *Best of Second Life Magazine*, and has subsequently inspired me to not let go of my journalistic dreams and to explore them virtually and vigorously to their fullest reach. I have changed somewhat from my original goals in college in that I am not attempting to "investigate" the world as much as to explore it and connect to those who reside in it, be that inside *Second Life* or external to it. My personal lens is a much more cultural one, rooted in a sense of global community, expanding beyond my physical borders, virtually, to connect to others across the world. One of those connections has been with The University of Western Australia. Through reporting on their efforts, I became involved in some of their activities. They have established partnerships with virtual media and the *SL* art community, as well as educational institutions to create a much smaller world that can make a big difference in connecting *SL* to real life and connecting people across the world.

The UWA collaboration, for example with *Best of Second Life Magazine*, launched the building of a massive amphitheater custom designed for educational and not-for-profit events. This space provides an arena for global gatherings and media presentations exemplifying unique and fairly inexpensive possibilities for community partnerships not physically or economically possible in the real world.

News organizations like *Best of Second Life Magazine*, Metaverse Broadcasting and *The Second Life Enquirer*, among others, are thriving, and many of the top media companies in *SL* that once began to expand their coverage to other virtual worlds — or at least had been preparing themselves for the possibility — have found that *Second Life* is where the people are at. It's also where many women find opportunities to build either a virtual or real life career. The other virtual world competitors have failed to build an audience, at least to a point where a significant media presence is justified. For that reason, at the very least, *SL* has become an interesting place to examine media convergence — a bringing together of journalists and the technology that allows them to communicate.

It is a space that is inviting of new voices, particularly of women's voices as expressed through print and broadcast media. Moreover, it is the place for virtual citizens to actively express their voices through the media as community reporters. And according to the GMMP report, women are more likely to deliver gender-balanced perspectives when reporting the news (x). So is *Second Life* a cutting edge opportunity to the burgeoning online expansion of news media, or merely a place for gaining or honing journalistic experience? Perhaps it is both. For so many women, it is a real business and a way around the glass ceiling and traditional roadblocks of an age-old craft dominated by men. Sarah Margaret Fuller challenged the old boys network in the mid 1800s and wrote of the westward expansion of the United States and is considered to be the first international female news correspondent. Now there is a new expansion — online and to virtual realms to be discovered. Women are at the forefront of this new world and its mediated implications.

Amy Spindler, more than a decade ago, wrote an amusing but relevant commentary on celebrity journalism, which in a sense describes a large part of the *Second Life* media culture. She spoke of a friend who had an idea for a screenplay, in which "celebrities become so godlike that they live in a separate world in the clouds, while mere humans toil on the earth below as their servants."

A separate world? *Second Life*, perhaps. That is merely an amusing antidote and not intended to belittle the real value that journalists contribute toward facilitating communication and fostering community among *Second Life's* active users. These residents draw meaning from their creations and relationships formed inside *SL*. Spindler's words regardless can serve as timeless caution to journalists, who might consider looking inward at their own motivations from time to time, and to those who look in-world to *Second Life* for fame and fortune. Most virtual journalists will tell you, as much as they enjoy what they do, it's hard work with minimal financial reward.

When Spindler wrote the article in 1998, Executive Producer Don Hewitt had mentioned adding Candice Bergen, then a journalist on *Murphy Brown*, as a correspondent for *60 Minutes*. The problem, Spindler admits, "We're all down here on the ground, serving the celebrity machine, using it to sell our magazines, movies and fashions." It would seem that *Second Life* merely reflects what is going on in the real world of journalism, lest we forget there is always a sizeable audience waiting for the latest juicy morsel of entertainment news. But there are real voices and issues to represent in both real and *Second Life* — and in the latter case, the voices telling the virtual stories are often those of women like Jarrico and Bravin.

Works Cited

Au, Wagner James. *The Making of Second Life*. New York: Harper Business, 2008. Print.

Best of Second Life Magazine. Web. 2 Feb. 2012.

BBC. "Obama Takes Lead in Virtual World." BBC News. November 12, 2008. Web. 2 Feb. 2012.

Bravin, Persia. 2012, December 3. Voice Chat Interview in *Second Life*.

Byerly, Carolyn M. (2012). *Global Report on the Status of Women in News Media*. Washington, DC: International Women's Media Foundation, 2007. Print.

Dancing Ink Productions. "The Launch of a Journalistic Experiment: The Virtual Newsroom of the American University in Cairo." *The Imagination Age*, April 7, 2009. Web. 2 2012.

GMMP. "Who Makes the News? Global Media Monitoring Project." 2010. Web. 2 Feb. 2012.

Grimm, Kathryn. "Get Real, Virtual Campaign Draws Followers." Fox News.com, October 23, 2008. Web. 2. Feb. 2012.

Jarrico, Lanai. "Lanai's 5Y Rezz Day Party" (Lanai's Diary). *The Second Life Enquirer*, May 17, 2010. Web. 2 Feb. 2012.

_____. December 9, 2012. Voice Chat Interview in *Second Life*.

Ludlow, Peter, and Mark Wallace. *The Second Life Herald: The Virtual Tabloid That Witnessed the Dawn of the Metaverse*. Cambridge, MA: MIT Press, 2007. Print.

MBC News (newscast). *Second Life* Newscast. Metaverse Broadcasting Company, May 23, 2010.

Morgan, Ruth. "London School of Journalism to Offer Lectures in *SL*." *Online Journalism News*, April 23, 2008, Web. 2 Feb. 2012.

Pop Art Lab. Web. 2 Feb. 2012.

The Second Life Enquirer. Web. 2 Feb. 2012.

"SecondStyle Farewell." *Second Style Blog*, April 19, 2011. Web. 2 Feb. 2012.

Shepard, Alicia C. "Celebrity Journalists." *American Journalism Review*, September 1997. Web. 2 Feb. 2012.

Spindler, Amy M. "All You Need Is Celebrity." *New York Times*, August 16, 1998. Web. 2. Feb. 2012.

Vanmoer, Dana. "Goodbye and Thank You." *SL-Newspaper*, June 5, 2010. Web. 2 Feb. 2012.

Wagner, Mitch. "CNN Creates Citizen Journalism Channels on Web in *Second Life*." *InformationWeek.com*, March 24, 2008. Web. 2 Feb. 2012.

Zimmer, Linda. "Real Journalism in a Virtual World: Interview with *Second Life's* Metaverse Messenger Publisher Katt Kongo." *Business Communicators of Second Life*, September 2006. Web. 2 Feb. 2012.

If She Can Build It, She Will

Suzanne Aurilio

This essay is about discovery, the kind that equates with learning for the satisfaction of it. It's also about the narratives rendering women's lives, and the stories we re-render and learn from. It depicts the experiences of seven women, myself included, who built, lived and learned in the virtual world, *Second Life*.

In My Life

In my life, technology has always played an empowering role. It's allowed me to express and create, envision and expand. Aside from the role of computers in my life as a songwriter, composer and musician in the 1980s and 1990s, information and communication technologies (ICTs) enabled my life's work to transition from the performing arts to education. In 1998, as I finished my undergraduate degree using distance education, I instantly saw and embraced their potential to bring learning and education to people who otherwise might not have access to it. For individuals and communities in remote areas of the world, and for women for whom the home is the central to their identities, I saw ICTs as portals to unprecedented opportunities to connect and expand. Fast forward to 2005, when in the context of leading an innovative faculty development program, I created my first avatar and explored a rather empty, albeit intriguing virtual world.

In My Work

Since then, I've spent a lot of time working with and thinking about *Second Life* primarily through the lenses of an educational designer and researcher, and faculty developer working in a large, urban public university.

In the summer of 2007, when educators became interested in *Second Life*, I allocated funds for a research and development initiative, the pICTSL Farm.[1] Its goal was to explore the potential of virtual worlds for teaching and learning. I employed a *Second Life* instructional designer and educator who built out our leased parcel, and with whom I still consult and exchange ideas. She and I have explored ActiveWorlds, OpenSim, Wonderland and Teleplace. Between 2007 and 2008, we introduced faculty, instructional staff and administrators to *Second Life* (Introducing university faculty and instructional staff to second life: A pilot initiative), looked at survey instruments used for assessing learning, conducted reviews of educational uses of the platform, and generally, built a case for why I did not recommend the platform as an educational technology in our institution.

This work was the first of two catalysts for my dissertation study titled *Learning in the Wild of a Virtual World*. The project focused on how everyday Residents learned to create *Second Life* and their motivations for doing so. The second came as an antidote to the frustration I felt learning the platform, observing others learning it, and the opinions I had developed while exploring it professionally. I became discouraged by the cult-like absence of critical discourse and dearth of instructionally sound practices among *Second Life* educators. So in early 2008, I withdrew from the educational community, and in another avatar, I became an everyday Resident. That year I spent the bulk of my social life in-world and, in the process of play, became fascinated by how much my friends knew about this sophisticated platform and how fun and "easy" they made learning look.

In My Fields

In my field, educational technology, we have a saying, "If we build it, will they come?" Engendering American pragmatism, the idea is rooted in the American military industrial complex where the field was conceived and still flourishes. Being a pragmatist myself, and an educator who works primarily with busy faculty, I can't help but embrace the sentiment. Why build something no one will see the value in using?

We have another saying, "It's not about the technology; it's about the learning." When I approach *Second Life* as an educational technology, which I do more often than not, I employ the rhetoric of learning goals, measurable outcomes and marketable skills. I do this because as an educational designer, I see their value. It's also good practice.[2] Teaching will always be first and foremost a human endeavor, however technological systems mediate human experiences, and as yet, we know very little about how this impacts learning.

In my field, education through a critical theory lens, the enterprise of schooling is fraught with incongruities. As a social system, it's historically oppressive and designed to maintain social inequities (Spring 26). It should be no surprise then that women are still marginally represented in STEM (science, technology, engineering and mathematics) fields, although they outnumber men overall in obtaining undergraduate degrees. Between 2000 and 2008, the number of women graduating with computer science undergraduate degrees fell from 20 to 18 percent (National Science Foundation), ICTs exploded, and the Internet became a household word. Female scientists and engineers make up just 26 percent of science and engineering occupations, while women overall make up 50 percent of the U.S. workforce (National Science Foundation).

At the same time, public education is under public assault. Led by neoliberal ideologues, whose claims are neither new nor unexpected (Shiller 55), multinational technology and media conglomerates advocates at the federal, state and local levels of government promote technological solutions for nontechnological problems, most notably in the form of "educationalizing" social problems (Labaree 447). Larry Cuban and Diane Ravitch, two of the most outspoken educators debunking these claims, do so with historical perspective and empirical data. Technology itself does not "fix" schools, nor lead to more effective learning. Poverty is the single most predictive variable in determining a student's, indeed a community's educational success.

As one might suspect, I approach my work with an inherent tension between the immediacy of learning and the politics of education. With this tension I carve out a middle ground. It is the discursive space on the outskirts of these fields, where theory meets the habits of everyday people and their technologies.

Data Collection

I draw data from several sources. The first is from an educational study of *Second Life* Residents informal learning practices. My methodological orientation was a virtual ethnography (Mason). I took online human endeavours as constituting legitimate cultural contexts in themselves (Markham). My avatar studied other avatars, or as I would say in-world, I was a Resident who studied Residents. As a researcher I viewed study participants I interviewed as sources of the questions, answers and hypotheses of my inquiry. In my field notes and subsequent narratives, I prioritized their verbatim language in order to decenter my disciplinary interpretations as an author (Spradley).

I realized early in the course of data collection that my focus on Residents was problematic. The person at the keyboard was present in numerous, influential ways, so I devised several codes to account for this. I also decided to collect basic demographic data of the seven main participants towards the end of the project. I asked about real life gender, age range, marital status, highest educational level achieved, and self-rated comfort levels with computer technology.

In addition to the informal data I had collected preparing for the study in early 2008, formal data collection took place over a six-month period late 2008 through 2009. It consisted of semi-structured and unstructured interviews, observations, journal entries, and gathering artifacts focused on the research question: *How Do Residents Learn to Create Second Life?*

I also draw on data from a university-based research and development project and a review of literature on virtual environments as social and functional locations of human endeavors. The university project generated data between 2007 and 2009. It consisted of impressions of *Second Life* as an educational technology in a large public university. I surveyed faculty, administrators and instructional designers following an introductory workshop to *Second Life*. I also reviewed survey assessment instruments, *Second Life* educators were developing and using to assess learning. In addition, I draw from informal observations and interviews with faculty and instructional designers using the platform.

Theoretical Lenses

Computing is a creative process. It involves emergent and generative acts, which in the case of *Second Life* result in users world-building. In 1991, Seymour Papert and colleagues proposed the notion of *constructionism*, a theoretical lens born of studies of children using a computer program to build computer programs. Grounded in constructivism, the theory holds that building knowledge happen particularly well when one builds something (See for example Harel; Papert). Moreover, one's creations express self in concrete forms, a proposition fitting to *Second Life* with its infinitely malleable space and avatar-based embodiments. As one engraves oneself into the public space she becomes a socially meaningful configuration of lived and living artifacts. For educators and learning scientists, all of this is akin to good learning (See for example, Belenky et al.; Gee; Lave; Lave and Wenger).

World-building in *Second Life* is also a political act; it's empowering. It initiates what Boal (13) describes as an "aesthetic space," a performance-platform that is both a part of, and distinguished from one's (real) life-space. In the aesthetic space, the individual discovers that she can observe herself, and thus perceive what she is, what she is not, and what she could be. By doing so, she opens a conversation with her (real) self, one that requires an "investment in the moral, social and political of what it means to be human" (Boal 13). *Second Life* presented on a computer screen sitting in a room in one's home is this aesthetic space. It is where we perform and simultaneously observe our performance.

When I merge these lenses — constructing technological systems with the politics of the aesthetic space — I envision virtual world-building as a uniquely edifying process. In the remainder of this essay, I describe what that can look like.

Brave New Worlds

Aurora, Celia, Jules, Star, Suz and Kat (pseudonyms) are the Residents I came to perceive as technological trailblazers and pioneer-artisans in a largely brave new world. According to data collected between 2009 and 2011, only 4 percent of American Internet users[3] have visited a virtual world (Pew). In addition, a person with no gaming experience needs about 30 hours just to master the basics[4] of the software. The reasons these women logged into *Second Life* sometimes 40 hours per week were not particularly unusual. They socialized, world-built, conducted businesses, tended their homes, took and taught building classes. I did what I do in real life, explored landscapes and art-scapes for the pure enjoyment of discovering and being in new places. Time and again, I was awestruck by the artistry and imagination of this built environment.

When I met them, the women above did far more world-building than I did. And like me, each expressed wonderment about other Residents' builds. These women were inspired enough to want to emulate them. And this inspiration, I discovered, was empowering. They each expressed the sentiment: *If they can do it, so can I.* And each set out to figure out what that entailed. Self-directed and determined, these women used the platform's 3D modeling tools to create objects based on geometric shapes, called prims (primitives) and the Linden Scripting Language to add functionality to them. They also use external software to manipulate graphics and create more complex 3D objects (sculpted prims or sculpties), textures for objects and animations and gestures.

What became obvious early on was how this inspiration and the creative desire it aroused, grew in organically unpredictable directions. I experienced this myself too with the modest world-building I did. One's virtual existence consisted of an endless stream of absorbing creative projects, one after the other, after the other until suddenly seven hours had passed. Csikszentmihalyi (107) calls this *flow*, an optimal psychological experience. These women all used the word "projects" to talk about their world-building. When I first heard it, I thought it sounded rather serious. I later came to understand projects as connoting commitments to one's virtual life endeavors.

Projects as Commitments

AVATARS AND PROFILES

One's first and perhaps most urgent project was always one's avatar, the most intimate expression of self in the built environment. Creating an avatar reached beyond the psychology of identity construction or identity play. It was part and parcel of devising, acting upon and within one's aesthetic space, and engaging a conversation about the meaning of oneself virtually and materially. Although an avatar could look like anything,[5] these women, aside from Aurora,[6] had created idealized feminine avatars. Suz and Kat were tall, scantily dressed, large-breasted women; Celia and Star were elegantly gowned, delicate fairies, and Jules was often dressed as a stylized,[7] 1940s socialite.

One's profile further expressed self in terms of interests,[8] desires and relationships to people and places. Profiles were revealing and heartfelt. In the 500-character, open-ended *About* field of her profile Jules had written at one point, "~A woman in love can't be reasonable — or she probably wouldn't be in love. ~Mae West." Celia had written, "Like a sprite this butterfly has a bit of curiosity and a tendency to flit about exploring. Sometimes quiet and sometimes exuberant." Star had written, "~ The point of the journey is not to arrive. (Neil Pearl). ~ Your friends will know you better in the first minute you meet than your acquaintances will know you in a thousand years. (Richard Bach)." And Aurora had written, "Just your average Child of the Light, wanting to find something better. If you have are having trouble, just ask me for some help. I do have a few skills. I tend to wear WHITE or shades of Black and White, so don't panic if I rez in a strange way." Finally, Suz and Kat had written their texts similarly. Here is Suz's:

"A kiss is a lovely trick designed by nature to stop speech when words become superfluous."— Ingrid Bergman

Constructing one's self as these women did with their avatar and profile could be an ongoing redecorating project on the one hand, or a birthing process on the other. Jules edited her profile from time to time. As I was getting to know her before the study, I sometimes wondered about her mental health. Did she know this make believe? I had the feeling sometimes that she was so absorbed in her play, she lost touch with reality. Indeed, for Jules this was reality; it was an expression of her ideal self. Celia once said *Second Life* was like playing with dolls. Her avatar and profile were doll-like to me. Suz and Kat were in love, plain and simple. I never questioned their relationship. Experimenting with love, sex and romance was a common occurrence in *Second Life*. In comparison, Star and Aurora each seemed to be on a leg of a personal growth journey. Their play was a deliberate strategy for dealing with challenging real life situations. I experienced each of them as using *Second Life* for reflection and distraction. Aurora said in *Second Life* she felt normal. In hindsight, I came to see these women's avatars and profiles as the self-discovery process itself. Self and others perform and observe avatars and profiles. They are part and parcel of our personal, and the collective aesthetic space.

Objects, Places and People

Projects were large and small. Aurora and Star learned how to build things like birdhouses and Chinese New Years' Lanterns so they could teach others how to build them. Celia often participated in building contests. Lasting an hour or several months, contests were thematically-driven, project-based building opportunities. Suz, Kat, and Jules built spaces: projects that carried a much deeper commitment of time and money. Leasing space in-world usually involved a monthly fee. Suz and Kat had an island together. In addition they had a separate shop, where they sold greeting cards, music boxes and tattoos they made. Jules leased an 8192 square meter grassy island parcel, which cost $33 per month, and which she transformed into an island oasis. A 38-year-old, single mother who worked in retail full-time in real life, she was frank about wanting to get her money's worth out of her investment. She often spent more than 40 hours a week in-world she told me. Over the course of the study, she had had several large spaces.

Jules' world-building served to manifest her idealized world, she said, and thus it emulated aspects of her real life. Her island had a quiet sandy beach and tall grassy mountains, resembling real life landscapes she enjoyed. In real life she was an amateur burlesque dancer.

After she gave up her island, a friend let her use his parcels where she created and managed several jazz clubs, complete with burlesque dancers, an

MC, bartender and bouncer. As the club-owner and hostess, she would glide across the club in some of the most stunning outfits I had seen in *Second Life*. Her clientele were international she told me. When Jules' talked about the club, her language and tone sounded experienced and again, serious. In one session she talked about having a "staff meeting." She had eight staff including herself. She wanted to pay them (in Linden dollars) because her clientele rarely had a lot of money for tips, she said. Jules was committed to her staff and clientele. Her world-building, she told me, was about creating an experience. It wasn't about making objects per se, but about acquiring and modifying them to fit into her world. She prided herself on the quality look of her avatar and wardrobe, and was not shy about prioritizing the visual beauty around her.

Celia had the same high-quality aesthetic orientation to world-building, however she was far more moderate in her play time than Jules. A stay-at-home, married mother in her mid 40s, she was a seasoned virtual world user. She spent on average 20 hours a week in-world. For her, *Second Life* was about playing a character, as she did in the role-playing MUDs she participated in.[9] She had designed almost her entire avatar, including creating her own shape. Her creative endeavors included making a little bit of everything, from animals to furniture to clothing. A friend had let her use a shop in a Victorian village to display and sell elegant hats she made. She had also played a shopkeeper character in a MUD. I thought Celia was an extraordinary craftsperson. Like her avatar, her builds with exquisitely detailed and visually refined and she was often complimented on them. She told me that in real life she had similar types of creative hobbies.

Suz and Kat were officially partnered. Suz was in her early 50s and a married grandmother, who did not work outside of the home. Kat was 33 years old and single. She had been unemployed for several months. Suz lived in the northeast U.S., Kat in Australia. To catch them together, I logged in at seven in the morning. They spent most mornings together from six to noon, eastern standard time. That was eight in the evening until two in the morning for Kat. Their leased island parcel was twice the size of Jules; their shop was located on another parcel. Their creative endeavors revolved around their island and shop. Of the two of them, Kat was particularly adept at making small objects such as greeting cards which when opened would "explode" with sparkles. She worked with Photoshop, editing layers on images, as well as with the scripts[10] used to create the exploding sparkles.

Star was an active member of a building school and sandbox, Serenity, where she regularly taught building classes and participated in contests along with Celia. She built objects such as snow globes, Chinese lanterns, and small scenes for contests. She enjoyed *Second Life* for the social connections, saying that her *SL* friendships were as important as her real life friendship. She said she was very committed to Serenity and spent on average 40 hours a week there, where she also volunteered. In addition to teaching, she helped with community events and had shifts overseeing the sandbox. She was 44 years old, unemployed and going through a difficult divorce. She and her two children were living with her parents while she regrouped.

I met Aurora first as an avatar named Mica, an androgynous looking male with long straight, silver white hair and iridescent eyes. Aurora had a similar otherworldly look. Like Star, Aurora focused on learning how to build small objects in order to teach others. And like Star and Celia, she also participated in building contests. She was 44 years old, single and lived in a remote area in the northeastern U.S. She spent on average 30 hours per week inworld. She also had a chronic illness, which prevented her from working. She said that *Second Life* made her feel normal.

What made *Second Life* a culture also made it a wonderfully motivating learning space for these women. It had a lively economy, which in turn encouraged Residents to sell their builds. Celia, Suz and Kat all said that it wasn't the money but the respect earned, when someone bought their wares. *Second Life* was also a social space. Relationships of every conceivable kind sprouted and flourished. All these women indicated the importance of friendships in motivating them to build. Jules, Suz and Kat built spaces friends would want to spend time in. Star and Aurora were community-oriented and saw their world-building as giving to the community. Both of them belonged to building groups. Celia was the least socially oriented of the six, describing herself as a play-by-herself builder. Still, she did most of her building in public sandboxes and, in particular, at Serenity where she was considered a regular. Building contests were also a key motivator for Star and Celia, who participated in them weekly at Serenity. Contests were social, playfully competitive opportunities to practice world-building. I enjoyed them immensely and observed them as being one of the most effective ways to learn to build. They had all the ingredients of a well-designed learning experience: an interesting project to complete in a manageable timeframe, explicit instructions and guidelines, incentives and rewards, and social support.

To summarize, this is a brave new *learning* world. Committed to construction projects embedded in personally and socially rich experiences, these women have thrived here. They have also amassed expertise not only in worldbuild, but in learning itself. They have defied stereotypes too. With a can-do attitude to high tech play, they make technology look easy and fun. Finally, whether consciously or unconsciously, they use *Second Life* as an aesthetic space. In doing so, they are empowered to discover what it means to be human and virtual.

Brave New Worlds Unpacked

Creating lives and communities, and constructing technologically sophisticated things, large and small, are the stuff of good learning. Moreover they encourage commitments to the kind learning women don't often get to make — concentrated play: playing characters, playing an idealized self, playing to heal and to distract. Learning is the *raison d'être* of *Second Life*, because world-building is. This was evident in the endeavors of these women and in my own endeavors and reflections. World-building is also synonymous with deep learning because constructing an aesthetic space within a socio-technological system is fundamentally educative (Dewey, 10). How could it not be?

First, one's virtual life is a computationally-derived experience. To be human virtually requires a woman to engage existentially with technology. If she does not, she does not exist. To put it another way, she must engage with the mechanics of the platform as she would with real life food and water. There is no avoiding the fact that her virtual life is comprised of complex of computations, she must wrap her mind around. Moreover, a white male likely conceived of and programmed these computations. To be female virtually, then, means she must engage with a world designed and rendered by a male culture. She must be cognitively flexible and culturally competent. These are good things for women to be, however these observations bring to the fore why women must gain entry into and influence the fields and industries creating virtual experiences. These observations also bring to the fore the question of women's overall lack of deep engagement with technology. It's not theirs, in mind, body nor in spirit.

Second, to world-build is to understand and manipulate layered arrangements of computer hardware and software. It requires a woman to engage with technology conceptually and materially. If she cannot wrap her head and heart around its concepts and mechanics, again she does not exist. Computing with ICTs is also a generative and interactive endeavor. It invites her to explore, create and share. She cannot reject this invitation.

Third, for the majority of adults, living an avatarized self is unfamiliar, if not altogether outlandish. It therefore involves risk, stepping out of one's comfort zone to imagine and explore the unorthodox, and to be seen as someone who does so. At the very least, it involves a capacity to suspend disbelief, to handle ambiguity and to comprehend things as they appear. It also reveals an individual to herself. In a world where she can be whatever she wants to be, what will she choose? And what does her choice say about her? Moreover, what will she say about herself, in her profile? These might seem like trivial decisions, but they can become transformative experiences for the woman who risks them. They are the stuff of the aesthetic space.

With these points in mind, where does world-building fit into the larger picture of learning and education for women? As I mentioned earlier in this essay, there exists a discursive space on the outskirts of learning and education narratives, and it's here I believe world-building lives. The theoretical lenses of constructionism and the aesthetic space live there too; neither has gained much mainstream recognition.

Within contemporary learning and education narratives, world-building is an impractical ideal. As an approach to learning or teaching, it's complex, messy, and time intensive at a time when learning and education are focused on simplicity and rationalization. Simplicity, or specificity, has usually been the aim of the learning adults do. Adults learn with a clear and immediately valued purpose in mind. One that's usually related to the responsibilities of adulthood such as career, home, health or family. Adults also tend to take the quickest and sometimes easiest path to get there. Moreover, the technologies of our lives are becoming simpler to understand and use. Consider Facebook, Twitter and Yelp; each has a narrowly defined purpose that fills a broadly-shared need.

Rationalization is happening across institutions from kindergarten to higher education, in the public and private sectors. It is reductions in resources, instructional staff and increases in the number and size of large classes, and spate of online classes. It is also about seeing education primarily in terms of its value in getting into a good college or decently-paying job. With a focus on simplicity, rationalization and value-driven learning, it's challenging to make a case for world-building.

To this end, I believe the potential of world-building lies in its recreational character. Rather than conforming it to formalized learning and education contexts, I suggest exploiting its non-conformist appeal. One of the tenets of Dewey's notion of educative experiences is learning by doing. Dewey's ideas influenced but were not widely adopted in formal education. The same has been true for Papert and Boal's ideas of constructionism and the aesthetic space, respectively. Good ideas about learning don't necessarily have mass appeal, or the interest of policy makers. Moreover, what we *do* in schools does not necessarily translate into educative experiences. A reasonable goal might then be to communicate to the larger community what world-builders, particularly women world-builders *actually do*, what they learn and what this says about learning for the satisfaction of it.

My World-Building

The year after I had finished the study, I had an opportunity to really world-build. The *Second Life* initiative I had been leading at the university, the pICTSL Farm lost its leased property. I also had no more funding for the initiative. We were at a crossroad. The university's chief information officer was genuinely interested in *Second Life*. He had attended our kick-off luncheon and workshops, and stopped by my office now and then to talk about it. I told him about the situation. He offered to buy an island. That August, I created the initiative and built *Aztlan Island: SDSU in Second Life*.[11] It was a direct result of my study, and influenced by an institutional theme I had become involved with, "High Impact Practices," (Kuh), educational experiences such as study abroad, service learning, capstone projects and internships. I was delighted to be able to apply my findings in an institutional context in a meaningful way. We launched the project with great fanfare that included a video infomercial of the university President as an avatar endorsing the initiative's goals, and welcoming the campus to the island.

Aztlan Island's goals were, broadly stated, to create opportunities for students to world-build in personally and academically meaningful ways, whether that was to create a virtual presence for their club or organization, or to do a capstone project. I envisioned these opportunities first and foremost as student-focused collaborations involving supervising faculty or staff that helped them identify opportunities and create meaningful contexts to realize their goals. I first solicited faculty in the design fields (e.g., set design, graphic design, interior design). An art professor of an undergraduate art-gallery design class was interested. In her class, the capstone project, a model of an exhibition was typically constructed with matt board. She was intrigued by the notion that students could use *Second Life* for their projects. She was also adamant about not wanting to have to learn the technology. I presented the opportunity to her class of approximately eight students, all of whom were young women. Two women were interested. Our collaboration turned out as I had hoped it would. I met with the students weekly to help them with the mechanics of *Second Life* building. They used the island resources and wiki to learn how to build. Their instructor guided them on the conceptual and principled elements of exhibition-design. It was truly an educative experience for each of us in that we each explored an utterly new type of project in a new role. We were very pleased with the process and the outcome.[12]

Closing Thoughts

After completing my study and then building Aztlan, I rarely logged in to *Second Life*. I am Facebook friends with three of the study participants, Suz, Jules and Arieaa, a man in real life. Kat and Suz broke up, and Suz has another partner. She hasn't heard from Kat in over a year. Kat's profile is as it was when I last saw it. Star has written on her profile, "I don't know when I will be back to *SL* if you want to get in touch with me send me an offline IM; it will go to my email. If you want to stay in touch I might just give you my email or befriend you on Facebook ;)." Celia last logged into *Second Life* at the beginning of December 2011. I'm uncertain when Aurora last logged in, but her profile is still available. She had written, "I am cleaning out my overflowing Inventory. If you are new or fairly new and need something, PLEASE let me know. I am giving away a lot of stuff I no longer need."

There is still so much to understand about virtual worlds. *Embodiment* and *authenticity* are two themes I'd like to explore in more depth. As much as I see the potential of virtual worlds to connect and expand us, I'm also concerned about the physical and psychosocial effects of life in front of and behind a screen. During the extended time and long hours I spent in *Second Life*, I noticed how motionless and sensory deprived I became. And although I pursued meaningful friendships, I was unwilling to make them as meaningful as those I pursued in real life. For me, the virtual was "almost real." These experiences led me to reflect on the meaning of authenticity in a virtual world, where authentic denotes actual as compared with a copy or representation, genuine as compared with fake, and legitimate as compared with fabricated. We've only scratched the surface of authenticity in virtual worlds,[13] yet it is a critical element in learning. In fact, learning by doing is nothing more than learning to do the real thing in context, isn't it.

Notes

1. http://pictsl.edublogs.org/
2. By good practice I mean that well-designed learning is informed by research in fields such as cognitive science, educational psychology and instructional systems design.
3. Seventy-eight percent of Americans use the Internet.
4. The interface, including communicating, moving and dressing one's avatar and managing one's inventory.
5. An avatar could be a stone, a bug, an animal or a fantasy creature, as examples. Also, I have no data to support my observation that most avatars were humanoid-based.
6. I had initially met Aurora, as Mica, a male avatar with a similar ageless, other-worldly, androgynous look.
7. Jules changed clothes often. Her large wardrobe was part and parcel of her idealized virtual life.
8. A profile contained of 7 Tabs (2nd Life, Web, Interests, Classified, 1st Life, My Notes) which consisted of 27 pre-defined and open ended fields to input text, images and links.
9. Multi-user domain is a text-based virtual environment.
10. Scripts are programs embedded in objects. They generate interactive elements. In this case, the script generated the exploding sparkles.
11. http://sdsu-aztlan.wikispaces.com/.
12. http://sdsu-aztlan.wikispaces.com/art_exhibits.
13. Virtual worlds are used to create simulations of actual phenomena.

Works Cited

Aurilio, Suzanne. "Introducing University Faculty and Instructional Staff to *Second Life*: A Pilot Initiative." *Educause Learning Initiative Annual Meeting.* San Antonio, Texas. (2008).

_____. "Learning in the Wild of a Virtual World." Diss., Claremont Graduate University and San Diego State University, 2010. Web.

Belenky, Mary Field, et al. *Women's Ways of Knowing: The Development of Self, Voice, and Mind (10th Anniversary Edition ed.).* New York: Basic Books, 1997. Print.

Boal, Augusto. *The Rainbow of Desire: The Boal Method of Theatre and Therapy.* Trans A. Jackson. London: Routledge, 1995. Print.

Csikszentmihalyi, Mihaly. *Creativity: Flow and the Psychology of Discovery and Invention.* New York: HarperCollins, 1996. Print.

Cuban, Larry. *Larry Cuban on School Reform and Classroom Practice. Tag Archives: Technology.* Web. Jan. 14, 2012.

Dewey, John. *Experience and Education.* New York: Touchstone. (1938). Print.

Gee, James, Paul. *What Video Games Have to Teach Us About Learning and Literacy.* New York: Palgrove Macmillan, 2003. Print.

Harel, Idit. "Children as Software Designers: A Constructionist Approach for Learning Mathematics." *The Journal of Mathematical Behavior* 9:1 (1990). Print.

Kuh, George. *High-impact Educational Practices: What They Are, Who Has Access to Them, and Why They Matter.* Washington, DC: AAC&U Publications, 2008. Print.

Labaree, David F. "The Winning Ways of a Losing Strategy: Educationalizing Social Problems in the United States." *Educational Theory* 58:4 (2008): 447–460. Web. 2 Jan. 2012.

Lave, Jean. *Cognition in Practice: Mind, Mathematics, and Culture in Everyday Life.* Cambridge: Cambridge University Press, 1988. Print.

_____, and Etienne Wenger. *Situated Learning, Legitimate Peripheral Participation.* Cambridge: Cambridge University Press, 1991. Print.

Markham, Annette. *Life Online Researching Real Experience in Virtual Space.* Walnut Creek, CA: AltaMira Press, 1998. Print.

Mason, Bruce. "Issues in Virtual Ethnography. Ethnographic Studies in Real and Virtual Environments: Inhabited Information Spaces and Connected Communities." *Proceedings of Esprit i3 Workshop on Ethnographic Studies.* Ed. K. Buckner, 1999. Web.

Papert, Seymore. "Situated Constructionism." *Constructionism: Research Reports and Essays, 1985–1990.* Eds. Edit Harel and Seymore Papert. Norwood, NJ: Ablex, 1991. 1–10. Print.

Pew. *Trend Data.* (2011). Web. 14 Jan. 2012.

Ravitch, Diane. *Bridging Differences. Poverty Category.* Web 14 Jan. 2012.

Shiller, Jessica. "Marketing New Schools for a New Century: An Examination of Neoliberal School Reform in New York City." *The Gates Foundation and the Future of U.S. "Public" Schools.* Ed. Philip E. Kovacs. New York: Routledge, 2011. 53–79. Print.

Spradley, James P. *The Ethnographic Interview.* Fort Worth, TX: Hartcourt Brace Jovanovich, 1979. Print.

Spring, Joel. *Deculturalization and the Struggle for Equality.* 3d ed. New York: McGraw-Hill, 2001. Print.

"Women, Minorities, and Persons with Disabilities in Science and Engineering." *National Science Foundation.* Web. 2 Jan. 2012.

Adventures in Fiberspace:
Quilts and Quilting in *Second Life*
Through the Virtual Eyes
of Ione Tigerpaw

AMANDA GRACE SIKARSKIE

Techne is not episteme, but the ability to craft. — Tom Boellstorff

Ione Tigerpaw is an avatar in the virtual world *Second Life*. She has existed since February 2008, though she has existed much longer in the sense that she represents certain facets of my own personality. She can fly, but then again, so can all avatars in *Second Life*. Also like many avatars in *SL*, Ione's identity, in terms of appearance, is often in a state of flux. Ione sometimes appears in the guise of a woman in her sixties, slender, gray hair, capri-length blue jeans, and a green or orange or rose cardigan. At other times Ione looks very similar to the way I do in real life, about 30, dishwater blond hair, with big hips and thighs. In this case, she is clad in capri length blue jeans and a t-shirt and wears no make-up. Often, Ione appears in the guise of a young female, about 20 years old, thin, with long auburn hair, bright t-shirt that exposes her mid-riff, dark fitted pants, and bright lipstick and heavy eye make-up. No matter how she looks, however, her identity as Ione Tigerpaw remains fixed, and through all these guises, her chief interest is the quilts and other textiles produced within her world, and she spends her time in *Second Life* primarily as a virtual cultural tourist, visiting the shops, galleries and museums that display these digital quilts.

Just as there has been a dearth of focus in academic literature on quilts and quilters in the digital age and upon digital material culture produced in game environments such as *World of Warcraft*, so have academics been slow to document and interpret material culture in *Second Life*. For example, in

his cyberethnography, *Coming of Age in Second Life*, anthropologist Tom Boellstorff focuses primarily upon the self, specifically the avatarizing of the self,
and the meaning of being human in a virtual world, rather than upon the
objects crafted within the virtual world. Though *Coming of Age in Second Life*
is a groundbreaking work in many respects, more ground now needs to be
covered. This chapter sets out to explore some of this new territory, this Fiberspace at the intersection of real and virtual, quilter and computer, fuzzy and
non-tactile. I begin with an autoethnography of my own (a textile historian's)
cultural experiences of quilts and quilting in *Second Life*, including visiting
virtual quilt shops and galleries. Then, I explain some of the mechanics of
how quilts are made and look in *Second Life*, including a case study of a collection of quilts in *Second Life*, that of the real life quilts of the Fenimore Art
Museum collection in their *SL* home in the Folk Art New England Museum.
Finally, I explore the experiences of real world quilter Lidlfish and her avatar
Audrey Fotherington, as described in Lidlfish's out-of-world blog. At the end
of this chapter, I use this data to explore the ramifications of this Fiberspace
within *Second Life* for museum practice and the study of material culture.

Second Life* is a massively multi-user online virtual world in which one
creates one or more avatars and uses them to make and maintain friendships
and romantic relationships, attend events from pub crawls to museum exhibits,
explore hobbies, and engage in free choice learning. The architecture of *Second
Life* allows for a great deal of social interaction and for the creation of material
culture, known as builds, including digital homes, furniture, clothing, and
even sewing machines and quilts. Every interest and pursuit that exists in real
life exists in *Second Life*, and *SL* is a popular forum in which people make
and share information about quilting and the other fabric arts. As Tom Boellstorff wrote, "That's the dirty secret of virtual worlds; all people end up doing
is replicating their real lives" (239). This is perhaps especially true of quilters.
For online quilters, social interaction sometimes centers on the exhibition,
sale, or exchange of these digital artifacts in *Second Life*. One such event is
called "Free Quilt of the Week." Every Thursday afternoon in *Second Life*, an
avatar called Lady Dawn Starbrook hosts this event in the area known as Ned-
ben. A must attend for quilters in *Second Life*, this exhibition allows any avatar
to take home a digital copy of the "quilt of the week." For example, a blog
post advertising the quilt for June 11, 2009, featured a blue and white cor-
nerstones quilt, the design of which "suits both modern and Victorian [virtual]
homes." The weekly event, which Ione Tigerpaw has attended many times,
is sponsored in part by Becky's Quilts, whose slogan is "low prim, low price,
big impact (*Second Life*)."

It is here at Becky's Quilts where Ione Tigerpaw's story begins. This is
because she is a virtual squatter. Ione does not own or rent land upon which

she can set a home, so she "lives" at Becky's Quilts, logging in and out from that location. Ione *could* build herself a house, but without land, she would have to put the house back in her inventory, almost as if stuffing her residence in her pocket each time I logged out. She is in the homeless state because of Lindens. Lindens, the currency of *Second Life*, are required to buy or rent land, and the two ways by which one can acquire Lindens are to purchase them with real world money from Linden Lab, the creators of the virtual world, or to receive Lindens from other avatars in exchange for goods or services. Finding neither of these options particularly appealing, Ione lives at a quilt shop, Becky's Quilts. While there are certainly many quilt shops in this world (and I have attempted to visit them all), Becky's is one of the oldest and most established, its share and share alike ethic of giving away free quilts each week appeals to me. There is simply something genuine about the place, a quality that is definitely lacking in much one finds in a virtual world, where so much of the activity involves trying on personas apart from one's own.

Users find places, such as Becky's, for their avatars to visit either by the recommendations of friends or by searching for a word or phrase such as "quilt." In these search results, each listed location provides a short description to let the user know information such as what their place is like, for example, if it has a particular theme, and what one can buy or do there. The description for Becky's Quilts reads: "Quilts, quilts, quilts! Becky's is one of the first quilt stores in *SL*. There is always a free quilt out and a small yard sale on the patio. Closed Sabbaths [Saturdays]." Typically, one can find out a great deal of cultural information from these short owner-submitted descriptions. We know that "Becky" has been in *Second Life* for a relatively long time and that she is a religious-minded avatar in *SL,* and quite possibly a religious person in real life as well, closing her shop and potentially losing out on some virtual customers in order to keep the Sabbath. The interior of Becky's shop also features signs advertising in-world group Bible study, which corroborates these assumptions.

ZhuQuilts is another shop in *Second Life*. The shop's description reads, "RL quilts come to *SL*! Bedquilts, comforters, wall hangings, flexiquilts, all based on RL quilts. Custom quilts available for you [*sic*] *SL* (or RL!) home. Conveniently located on Route 8" (*Second Life*). This statement from Zhu Quilts slips effortlessly from the "real" to the virtual and back again, touting the fact that their digital quilts are modeled on real world examples. We can infer that ZhuQuilts is a maker of both real world and virtual world quilts and believes that an analog in the real world gives digital objects added credibility and value. The name Zhu suggests that the avatar might be of Chinese descent, and indeed the real world user might be as well (though many people come into *Second Life* to be someone completely different than who they are

in real life), while the use of a location called "Route 8," which is not an official area within *Second Life*, but rather a place name of the user's invention,
recalls Route 66 and conjures images of the heyday of the blue highway in
the United States.

The description of Granny Gruppman's Quilt Boutique, a small shop
on Red Rock Mesa, a community for "Native American Indian and Southwest
Arts," perhaps reveals the most ethnographic data of any shop in *Second Life*.
"Granny Gruppman told Grandson, Boon, to make her a shop so the neighborhood Ladies' Quilting Bee could sell their beautiful handiwork. Full perm
textures to make yer own quilts too" (*Second Life*). While this quilt shop is
located in an American Indian–themed community within *Second Life*, we
can infer from the language use (Boon, yer, etc.) that Granny Gruppman has
chosen to take on the persona of an aging Appalachian woman and to cultivate
an image of what eminent material culture scholar Henry Glassie called "old-
timey stuff." Whether Granny Gruppman is indeed a grandmother, or Appalachian, or even female, is impossible to tell, but the persona that she has
chosen to fashion is quite clear. Though her shop description seems on the
one hand very explicit and direct, it raises more questions than it answers
about the participants in Fiberspace. Why did she choose this Appalachian
persona? Is that where she lives in real life, or does she simply think that such
characterization will help her to sell more virtual quilts, or does she enjoy trying on the persona of the Appalachian just as I sometimes enjoy appearing in
the guise of a woman in her sixties?

This description also muddies the distinction between the real and the
virtual in a fascinating way. Is there even a neighborhood Ladies' Quilting
Bee? If there is, are these women her neighbors in real life, or are these female
avatars her neighbors in Red Rock Mesa in *Second Life*? Merely calling the
output of the Ladies' Quilting Bee, (which must necessarily be digital in
nature, made of prims rather than fabric), *handiwork* suggests that Granny
Gruppman believes at some level that these virtual quilts are indeed material
culture in the old sense of the word, a statement that has far-reaching consequences for the study of material culture. Finally, Gruppman's statement seems
contradictory in her level of technical mastery of *Second Life's* software and
user tools. One the one hand, she volunteers the information (which may well
simply be part of the persona) that her grandson had to help her create the
shop within *Second Life*. This could be rooted in many people's assumptions
that older people are not as capable with technology as younger people. However, she closes her description by advertising her "full perm textures." Clearly,
this person knows the language of the technical building blocks of *Second
Life*. In the twenty-first century, the average person in the developed world
has multiple cultural affiliations in the *real world*. These cultural affiliations

are made much more complex in the virtual world, where cultural identity is totally self-determined, yet mediated by real world expectations and stereo-types and the retention of cultural baggage from the real world.

Despite the fact that I have participated in multiple online virtual envi-ronments for some time, despite being a textile historian and having much first-hand knowledge of quilts and quilting, and despite crafting my avatar to look like a woman in late middle age or early old age, I cannot help feeling somehow that I am the Other in this world (Boellstorff 157). This is, I should mention, in direct contrast to my experience in real life, in which, as a Cau-casian woman living in the Great Lakes region of the United States, I cannot really say that I have ever felt like an outsider in the place where I live. Perhaps I have perceived this Othering to occur in *Second Life* because there is no established norm or power structure. People try on and take off political and cultural affiliations, genders, races, and even species at will, often living in themed communities with like-minded avatars. No one is the Other in this world, and yet, simultaneously everyone is the Other. This detached feeling may also stem from the way in which I relate to the virtual world. While I have participated in, even thrived in, virtual environments such as *World of Warcraft* and *Second Life*, environments predicated upon their high degree of sociability, I choose in these worlds to very much be the "loner." I have attended "Free Quilt of the Week" gatherings and other informal gatherings if great quilts were involved, and joined Quilters in *SL* and Art New England, a *Second Life* group dedicated to New England folk art and artists, but making friendships with others through the virtual world has not been my own per-sonal interest; the quilts themselves have been my interest. The loner may be the true Other in virtual environments, the loner, the solo player. In *Coming of Age in* Second Life, Tom Boellstorff did find some people who preferred a solo experience in the virtual world:

> Some residents did not seek friendship online; their sociality was oriented around what they saw as superficial shopping or entertainment, meaningful but solitary creative activities like building or designing clothes, saying things like "I've been trying to keep 'knowing someone' down to a minimum here." For most residents that I encountered during my fieldwork, however, friendships were a primary reason for their participation [157].

The loner or solo player has been under examined in the literature on virtual worlds and massively multiplayer online games to date. Thus far, the discussion has focused mainly upon these places and cultures in which one can find quilts in *Second Life*. Now, I shift from where and in what circum-stances they can be found and bought to how they look, how they refer to and rebel against quilts in the real world, and how these digital quilts are made. As Rebecca Tapley writes in *Designing Your* Second Life, "Let's take virtual scissors, needle and thread (64)," and now explore quiltmaking itself.

Quiltmaking in the real world could be said to begin when one turns on the sewing machine or takes up a needle. Quiltmaking in *SL* begins when one clicks the "build" button at the bottom of the user interface (as does every other conceivable craft in this virtual world). Once in "create" mode on the "object" tab, quiltmakers create a prim, short for primitive. Prims are the basic matter of *Second Life*, the stuff of which most things within the world are made. The quiltmaker then switches to "edit" mode, the mode in which prims can be changed by the maker into any shape or size imaginable. To make a quilt, logically, the prim is made to be rectangular and flat and sized to fit well on the average avatar's bed.

All prims begin with the approximate look and texture of a honey oak wood panel. So, thus far, the quiltmaker has made something more akin to a large piece of plywood than a quilt. Whereas fabric in real world quilting has its color, texture and pattern before ever coming together into a whole, color, texture and pattern can be applied to a quilt in *Second Life* only after the quilt has essentially been made. Another key difference between the processes of the quiltmaker in the two worlds is that in the real world, quilts may be wholecloth (one piece of cloth decorated with quilted or appliquéd designs) or pieced (several pieces of fabric sewn together to comprise a patchwork top and then quilted). In *Second Life*, almost all quilts are by necessity wholecloth. One large rectangular prim is made. Theoretically, quiltmakers could make several small square or rectangular prims and arrange them side by side, but each *Second Life* region is, as of 2011, only allowed 15,000 prims (Weber 22, *Second Life*), leaving individual prims at quite a premium. This is because each of the small squares would equal one prim, increasing the prim count of the whole quilt. This problem of the prim count explains the motto of Becky's Quilts, "Low prim. Low price. Big impact." While almost all quilts in *SL* therefore begin their lives as "wholecloth" prims, just as texture and color are used to change the look of the prim from wood to cloth, texture, color and pattern are used to give the illusion of a pieced quilt when that is what the maker desires.

Prims in *Second Life* are virtually endlessly customizable, and may be given a wide variety of textures, colors, levels of transparency or opacity, brightness or darkness, shininess, bumpiness, etc. Colors are chosen with a color picker that allows for precise RGB values and hue, saturation and luminosity values, permitting the maker to replicate with precision the color of any real life object. Textures generally already have colors attached to them and may be derived from digital photographs taken in the real world or hand-drawings. A quiltmaker desiring to make a vintage, Depression-era quilt in *Second Life* could, for example, scour real world fabric stores and antique shops for real examples of fabrics from the period, photograph them at high resolution on their digital camera, and then import those fabrics as textures into the virtual world. Another type of texture, procedural texture, is created by an object's maker within *Second Life* using a mathematical algorithm (Weber 61). All of these textures can be enhanced by visual light and shadow effects. Shadows built into the texture itself are said to be "baked" into the texture. Advanced programming, known as scripting, can be used to animate quilts in *Second Life*, though this is not commonly seen. This scripting can be used for various operations, such as causing rhinestones, beads or other attachments to sparkle or twinkle, appearing to catch the virtual light. Obviously, quiltmaking in *SL* requires a rather different skill set from quiltmaking in the brick and mortar world. However, there are many quiltmakers who have mastered both skill sets and excel in quilting in both worlds. And while the skills and processes used in making quilts in the two worlds may differ dramatically, ideas about quality and craftsmanship have remarkable similarities.

The lines between quilting in the brick and mortar world and *Second Life* are further blurred by the desire of many *SL* quilters to buy and sell virtual goods and services relating to the skills, materials and processes of real world quilting. Caravane City Quilt Village is a kind of virtual mega-mall for quilters interested in creating a virtual quilting experience more attuned to analog quilting. Retail shops in the outdoor mall include a longarm quilting service — curiously named "Manquilter's" — and Quilt Country, a fabric store. Also in Caravane City Quilt Village is the *Second Life* headquarters of Quilter's News Network, or QNN-TV, a real life quilter's Internet media network.

As with all material culture that has not been mass-produced, individual objects, such as quilts, can be judged by the quality of their craftsmanship in *Second Life*. "Hand-drawn stitching," "realistically draped or folded swathes of cloth," and "highlights shadows and wrinkles in the cloth that 'catch the light'" are some common standards of quality for digital fabric objects such as clothing and quilts (Tapley 60). Some of the "best" quilts that I have seen in *Second Life* based on this set of values were modeled on real life quilts held in the collection of the Fenimore Art Museum of Cooperstown, New York. A comparison of the Lone Star quilt from *Second Life* with a photograph of the actual Star of Bethlehem quilt upon which the *Second Life* example was modeled gives a more concrete idea of the extraordinary quality of these reproductions. The avatar maker(s) of these quilts (I use the phrase "avatar maker" to avoid confusion with the real world quiltmaker) are curatorial staff at the Fenimore Art Museum in the brick and mortar world. From within *Second Life*, what we can learn about the quilts beyond the visual, is provided by the avatar maker(s) on the "notecards" for each quilt, which contain the museum description and accession number for each quilt.

These quilts are housed in *Second Life* at Folk Art New England, which is the virtual home of the highlights of the real life collection of the Fenimore Art Museum. Ann G. Older, Chairperson of the New York State Historical Association, noted that the Fenimore Art Museum in *Second Life* project allowed the museum to connect with new — and younger — audiences:

> This new web is very different from the one we are used to; it is social and encourages contributions from many different users to create a vibrant online community. Social networking sites such as Facebook and MySpace offer museums the opportunity to create and foster communities of interested people and get them involved in the activities of their institution. There are also many other new technologies that make websites more interactive and attractive to younger audiences. Over the course of the past several months, we at NYSHA [New York State Historical Association] have been exploring the new web to find opportunities to connect with more people. Two specific initiatives are underway: we are planning to institute cell phone tours at the Fenimore Art Museum in 2009; and we have a significant presence in the popular virtual world *Second Life*. *Second Life* is a 3D virtual world with more than 13 million registered users worldwide, each represented by individual "avatars" that walk, fly, or teleport through a digital environment created by its residents. Our Curatorial staff has built a museum and installed several virtual exhibitions on this site, and these efforts are connecting us with a whole new audience.

Digital quilting in virtual worlds is not the exclusive preserve of Generation X and Millennial quilters, however. Older quilters, too, are using Web 2.0 applications such as *Second Life* for artistic and social purposes. Cathy Stevenson is a quilter of about 50 who maintains a blog about her health, her family, and her experiences with quilting in this world and in the virtual world of *SL*. In her blog, Stevenson, known as Audrey Fotherington in *Second Life*, negotiates quilting in these two worlds:

> To square off the photos I have cropped it, but I promise there are a few more inches worth of border and the quilt is square in real life. On the other hand, in *Second Life* I can force my quilts to be square! LOL Audrey has been building a treadle sewing machine and she attended a quilters meeting. At her very first meeting, she won the draw and is being sent 48 reels of Aurifil!!!!!!!! Real Life ones! [*Lidlfish's Quilting Days*].

Stevenson notes that the challenges of quilting in the brick and mortar world and quilting in a virtual world are in many ways different. For example, one can more easily make a quilt perfectly square in *Second Life* than in the real world, even if one is an experienced quilter. Some of the things that Stevenson does in *SL* as Audrey, such as attending meetings of fellow quilters, can be done in both worlds, but some other activities, such as building a sewing machine from scratch, while difficult, if not impossible, for quilters in the real world, are easy enough for quilters in a virtual world. Further, Stevenson not insignificantly refers to Audrey in the third person, talking about her avatar's life in terms of "she attended" rather than "I attended." This language suggests that Stevenson views her avatar as a different individual, separate from herself. This is further complicated by the fact that when writing as "Lidlfish," the username of her blog, she seamlessly switches back and forth between blogging about Stevenson's life and blogging about Audrey's life. In the diegetic environment, who is Stevenson? (When is she Cathy Stevenson or Audrey Fotherington of Lidlfish?) (Rehak 112). Rather than a *double* life that one might live in the real world, for example having a secret family in Cleveland while living with one's wife in Battle Creek, the use of the third person suggests a truly second life.

While Cathy Stevenson is still far from elderly, one senses in her online writing that participation within a community of quilters on *Second Life* greatly enhances her quality of life and sense of self-actualization. In her blog posts, she is quite proud of the accomplishments of her avatar, Audrey, reflecting upon them perhaps as a proud mother might speak of their child's accomplishments.

> She [Audrey] entered her treadle in the Newbie Show and Tell at NCI (New Citizens Inc) where she mostly hangs out learning how to build in graphics. She got third place but I personally feel she was ripped off! LOL Here are some piccies of Aud's Gorgeous house that she has built herself. She doesn't have any land, so when she building, she has to pack it back into her inventory and save for another day.
>
> She has a cutting table with mat, ruler and Olfa cutter. A small stash of bolts. What you don't see is all the mess I am sure she would make if I let her make a quilt from scratch! See the fire place? The flame in the fire flickers semi realistically. And the treadle foot plate and needle go up and down in time with each other when you touch the machine!!! Ok ... if you don't know *Second Life*, this may not seem amazing ... but to an old chook it is very exciting to be learning so many new things! [*Lidlfish's Quilting Days*].

There is a sense of pride in ownership and in manufacture — the house is gorgeous and she built it herself. The use of the permissive language, "if I let her make a quilt from scratch," again suggests this parental approach to her avatar. However, it is clear that Audrey is not the child of Stevenson because Audrey shares all of Stevenson's passions and pursuits. Most precisely, Audrey represents Stevenson in an ideal world of her own making. In this virtual world, Stevenson is a buxom teenager, or perhaps in her early twenties. She goes to holiday parties as well as sewing circles. She has her own darling little house complete with fireplace, where she quilts and displays her work, stores her tools and bolts of digital calico.

The division between the physical, or analog, material culture and digital material culture worlds is a much smaller gulf than one might presume. For example, a quilter can win a drawing for a brick and mortar prize, the 48 reels of Aurifil, at a meeting in a virtual world, but then claim that prize in the real world. Certainly, in real life, quilters use fabric, batting and thread to make quilts, and in *Second Life* quilters use code, but in both media and both worlds, they are quilters. One could argue that a fundamental difference between quilting and quilters in the two worlds is that there are some quilters in *SL* who have never made quilts in real life. Granted, it is highly likely that several people who have made quilts out of code with digital menus in *Second Life* cannot even sew in real life. However, an exhibition in *Second Life* answers this question about the importance of sewing as the hallmark of the quilter and the differences between quilting in brick and mortar and virtual worlds.

In the brick and mortar world, people personally touched by HIV-AIDS sometimes make quilts for the NAMES project to honor a loved one who has battled the disease. Usually, these are people who have never quilted before. They become quilters for a specific purpose, to make work to honor a specific person and raise awareness about a specific issue. This does not only apply to the NAMES project. There are people who use quilting as a form of expressive activism to speak out on other issues. For example, volunteers with the Ugly Quilt Project make quilts and quilted sleeping bags for the homeless, often with no prior knowledge of quilting, let alone sewing. Avatars volunteering at the *Second Life* HIV Prevention & Education Center and avatars with the Chilbo Community Building Project have organized the making of several digital quilts by avatars throughout the virtual realm of *Second Life* to commemorate lives (and avatars) lost to AIDS, both in real life and in *SL*. In terms of both creativity and poignant expression, these digital quilts equal those real, tactile quilts made for the NAMES Project. At this virtual exhibition, the liminal gap between real life and *Second Life* closes before one's eyes. Clearly, the demographics and motivations of quilters online are strikingly similar to those of people who make quilts in real life. The question remains, though: What is the true difference between the code (architecture) of quilting on a sewing machine (or a sewing computer) and the code of quilting in a virtual world such as *Second Life*?

As Tom Boellstorff wrote in *Coming of Age in Second Life*, "Culture is our killer app; we are virtually human" (5). Traveling to new worlds, new places, even virtual ones, broadens a person's world view through the introduction to new ways of life and new ways of doing and making things. This statement is just as valid for journeys through *Second Life* as it is for a journey through an unfamiliar country in the brick and mortar world. The virtual world allows one to look at human culture and cultures with fresh eyes.

Quilt-oriented virtual tourism in *Second Life* has, besides giving me hours of personal enjoyment, allowed me, through the eyes of my avatar Ione Tigerpaw, to see many different kinds of virtual quilts in many settings and has ultimately given me a new perspective on quilts created in "real life." These cultural experiences have been invaluable to me, the textile historian. A quilt manipulated from a prim is, to me, as much a quilt as one pieced from calico. It is my hope that academics especially will pay a visit to *Second Life* and explore their field of study — be it quilts or chemistry education or musical theatre or museums or whatever. Looking through the eyes of an avatar allows us to see that which we think we know very well in a new light.

Works Cited

Alfoldy, Sandra, ed. *NeoCraft: Modernity and the Crafts.* Halifax: The Press of the Nova Scotia College of Art and Design, 2007. Print.

Blank, Trevor J., ed. *Folklore and the Internet: Vernacular Expression in a Digital World.* Logan: Utah State University Press, 2009. Print.

Boellstorff, Tom. *Coming of Age in* Second Life. Princeton, NJ: Princeton University Press, 2008. Print.

Brackman, Barbara. *Patterns of Progress: Quilts in the Machine Age.* Los Angeles: Autry Museum of Western Heritage, 1997. Print.

Fotherington, Audrey. "Audslife." Web. 31 Dec. 2009.

Glassie, Henry. "Meaningful Things and Appropriate Myths: The Artifact's Place in American Studies." *Prospects* 3 (1977): 1–49. Print.

Kramarae, Cheris. *Technology and Women's Voices: Keeping in Touch.* New York: Routledge, 1988. Print.

Older, Anne G. "Letter from the Chairman." *The Headwaters: News and Events from the New York State Historical Association, Fenimore Art Museum, and Research Library.* Fall 2008. Print.

Paasonen, Susanna. *Figures of Fantasy: Internet, Women, & Cyberdiscourse.* New York: Peter Lang, 2005. Print.

Rehak, Bob. "Playing at Being: Psychoanalysis and the Avatar." In Wolf, Mark J. P. and Bernard Perron, *The Video Game Theory Reader.* New York: Routledge, 2003. Print.

Stevenson, Cathy. *Lidlfish's Quilting Days.* Web. 31 Dec. 2009.

Tapley, Rebecca. *Designing Your* Second Life. Indianapolis: New Riders Press, 2007. Print.

Weber, Aimee, Kimberly Rufer-Bach, and Richard Platel. *Creating Your World: The Official Guide to Advanced Content Creation for Second Life.* Sybex, 2007. Print.

Wolf, Mark J. P., and Bernard Perron. *The Video Game Theory Reader.* New York: Routledge, 2003. Print.

Creative Immersion and Inspiration in *Second Life*'s Virtual Landscapes

PATRICIA A. FACCIPONTI

I may never know what sparked the explosive energy that touched off a torch under my muse and unleashed in the spring of 2009 what was for me an unprecedented flash-fire of creativity. Maybe it was that our five offspring were finally on their own, forging careers, finding love, spawning children. Except for a puzzled but tolerant husband and an equally acquiescent dog, our quiet house freed my mind during off-work hours to ruminate, uninterrupted, upon whatever it wished.

Then again, this newfound creative urge could have been triggered by my discovery of an online virtual universe called *Second Life*. It teemed with affordable yet powerful possibilities for exposing students and faculty to unexplored horizons, methods, viewpoints, and ways of interacting and collaborating with others. I saw the potential for learning a whole new set of skills and exploring fascinating terrains constantly evolving or even yet to be dreamed and developed.

At the same time, I was beginning to realize that after a lifetime of teaching and occupational wordsmithing I also had within me words that might reach deep inside others to mirror their own pains and joys. When giving readings I could see in the faces of listeners that my poems were increasingly received as gifts to the heart. Their tears and laughter were telling me, as had the trusted few with whom I'd shared my work, that it may be worth a wider audience.

But I was also beginning to realize that if I were going to get serious about my creative writing, it would have to be sooner, because there may not be much later. I had a recurring vision of my family someday sorting through a lifetime's accumulation of lines scribbled on envelopes and grocery lists, trying to make sense of a woman they never really knew. Then, too, I think the words and feelings of a lifetime were simply and resolutely gnawing their way out of my innards and bursting to the light.

But maybe, just maybe, the tumultuous burst of creative energy that I experienced that spring also came about because, along with my exploration of *Second Life*'s educational possibilities, I tumbled into the very personal opportunity to live a virtual second life freed from the bonds of the expected and the conventional.

First Steps into Virtual Adventure

It took months to choose a name for the avatar that would represent me in this new world. Franchella Milena took shape January 29, 2008, as a younger, slimmer me. Like me, she is not particularly courageous, but quiet, observant, curious, studious. Like me, she wears comfortable, casual, modest clothing, and although she has hundreds of costumes to wear, she prefers slipping out of her shoes and into well-worn jeans and a familiar hand-crafted top. Like me, she is more comfortable in the classroom than skirting the wild side. But a major advantage in sharing my life with Franchella is that she is not really me. Although we mirror interests and attitudes, Franchella's words and actions are not likely to discomfit my family, my co-workers, nor the college where I worked as an instructional technologist. Moreover, as a lithesome 30-something, Franchella is accepted in some virtual settings and situations where the real-life me might seem out of place.

Of course, *Second Life* is only one online virtual world within a rapidly expanding universe filled with similar and very different three-dimensional opportunities to explore and interact. However, the majority of my virtual experience has been within *Second Life*.

One of the many things I appreciate about *Second Life* is the wealth of opportunities to travel and explore, easily and safely, over a broad, seemingly limitless, universe of cultures; *Second Life* provides places where I can open my mind to making acquaintance with the most bizarre-looking avatars and the often anonymous real-life people they represent. Franchella is fearless even in the most challenging situations because her Teleport Home button is always at the ready. She can defy gravity, build the impossible, move earth, hoist and transport virtual objects with nary a pulled muscle.

Age, gender, varying strength, agility, or physical inabilities do not mar the *Second Life* experience. In real life I walk with a bit of a wobble and look forward to receiving senior citizen discounts. Franchella is ageless and agile. She has several alternate body options and can instantly assume the muscular frame of a sword-wielding knight or the persona of a fire-breathing dragon. Unlimitedly powerful, she can move multi-storied buildings with the flick of my mouse. Delightfully flexible, she can cavort, tumble, dance or fly for hours with never a shortened breath.

She can also change her *Second Life* environment, call up a sunset, design clothing, transform her appearance to represent the real or the fancied, the male or female, human or animal. She can whisk into being an animated vision of technical wizardry or build a virtual skyscraper. If you can envision it, it can be built in *Second Life*.

Learning to Teach in a Virtual World

As an educator I have found members of *Second Life*'s educational, literary, and artistic communities to be generous with ideas, training, and support. Free and low cost classes in building, scripting, animation, and creating art in *Second Life* are readily accessible around the clock. *Second Life* runs 24/7, for the sun is always rising and setting somewhere across and around both the real and virtual worlds. *Second Life* classes and workshops, lectures and meetings on writing, storytelling, health issues, science, economics, and myriad other topics can broaden and deepen almost any field of knowledge and abilities.

A four-day Construction Junction Workshop on Educational Design & Building Skills in *Second Life* included generous building privileges on a plot of *Second Life* land. Offered by Mali Young (aka Lisa Dawley, Ph.D.) through Boise State University,[1,2] the workshop helped me gain confidence as I learned to manage and reshape land, design plazas and paths, houses and towers, create villages on platforms far up in the clouds. I even tunneled deep below the Island's surface to create a watery cave and populated it with an avatar masked as a snake-headed Medusa.

An extensive series of free beginning, intermediate, and advanced scripting workshops hosted by the International Cooperative Education (ICE) group and taught by Kelly Young set me on the road to *Second Life* scripting competence. Numerous virtual professional conferences, held in *Second Life*, made it possible to share ideas and learn from other writers, educators, and artists.

The Challenge: 30 Poems in 30 Days

It was a posting early in 2009 on SLED, the *Second Life* Educators e-mail list,[3] that swept me into a whirlwind of new adventures in poetry. Storybook Island was to host a Poetry Quest that April in celebration of National Poetry Month.[4] It posed a daunting challenge: write 30 poems in 30 days. I'd been writing poetry since I was a child, but never on 24-hour demand. But why not give it a try?

A former teacher of writing and at that time an educator working as an instructional technologist on the college level, I considered that by taking part in the quest, I could learn more about how to use *Second Life* to enliven the teaching of a broad range of subjects, including writing. I'd often provided technical support for classes that employed video-conferencing to join distant groups of students with their faculty instructors. So I could appreciate how *Second Life* could offer to teach, simultaneously and inexpensively, students in widely dispersed geographical locations.

A minor but enticing incentive to participate in the Poetry Quest was a $1,000 Linden prize. Lindens, purchased online, are the currency of *Second Life*. Its economy flexes and flows very much like any real life country's economic health. At that time, $10 could buy about 1,000 Lindens. Although joining *Second Life* and installing its software are free,[5] you can drop a lot of Lindens clothing your avatar in designer clothes, hair, skin, and jewelry as well as purchasing land, buildings and furnishings. But, since I was most interested in using *Second Life* to enrich teaching, I wanted Franchella to function on a student's low or non-existent budget. She quickly collected a vast inventory of free items, but still needed Lindens for instructors' tips as well as fees for uploading textures for designing clothing and constructions. Franchella was then earning her meager Lindens by camp dancing in the Welfare Island streets (no longer existent). In an effort to populate landscapes and dance halls, some landowners then paid avatars to "camp," or hang out, on their property. You could pop your avatar on a placeholder and allow the script to move her through a repeated series of animations. Camp dancing paid in the neighborhood of $2L per 15 minutes. At that rate a $1000L prize was a fortune.

But I soon discovered that this Poetry Quest was not "just" turning out 30 poems in 30 days, it involved visiting each day a specific location in *Second Life* and writing a poem in response to detailed specifications. Jenaia Morane (aka Jena Ball), our guide and taskmaster, primed the pump just past 12 A.M. each morning with a notecard listing a destination SLurl (link to a *Second Life* location), what to observe, and the form of poem the judges were expecting. We were to deposit each day's poem by midnight in the Storybook Island mailbox!

The Writing Begins

So it began. Pick up a Quest notecard in the very early A.M. Pay a quick visit to the designated *Second Life* destination, or sim, and start the thinking process churning under the shower spray. I'd jot notes at breakfast, mouth lines to the steering wheel on the drive to work where the task would simmer all day on my mental back burner. Left-handing lunch at my office computer, I'd revisit the site, perch Franchella in its midst to absorb the atmosphere while I played with lines on another screen. Homeward, I'd gnaw words, shove them around in my head. After dinner, I'd retreat to shape and hone. Just before midnight, I'd pop a notecard with the results into the Quest's virtual mailbox. After midnight, I'd start again: visit, decide, consider, research, write, rewrite, re-rewrite, and drop!

The hardest part for me was dropping the results, irretrievably, into that box! I am a pondering poet and may ponder a single word for years! I visit and revisit each poem, tweak it until it is untweakable. I have not yet decided if this is a virtue or a vice. But rules were rules. I wrote on and on each day — and dropped each night.

Floating on Water on Air

For the first assignment, Franchella danced in the cooling mists of a Storybook Island fountain sculpture. Suspended above a lake in a picturesque, natural setting, it consisted of multicolored, swirling translucent bands lit from within and without. We were instructed to set our time of day to midnight and allow a related script to animate our avatar. Thus possessed, Franchella soared into the fountain and danced and twirled and tumbled up and down within it.[6] Mesmerized, I watched for hours and attempted to turn the experience into words. If it were my own body softly gyrating above cascading waters within that feast of colors, how would the moonlit mist feel upon my skin? What would the experience bring to mind? Just before midnight, I popped my first *Second Life*–inspired poem, "Dream Dancing," into the Quest mailbox:

> The fountain's buoyant dance is like slipping
> Surfacebound into through the eyes of gigantic, golden squid
> Gleaming deflected sunset as they yearn dank primeval depths.
> Or, could I, as new-hatched sperm, spawned with swirling tail
> Vault upward downward flowing inward outward
> In blissful ignorance of life's vital mission, intended goal.
> Rather, I float through the sparkling night
> Cool mist upon my skin as I rise and fall again again
> For no reason whatsoever than pure joy.

For 30 days, I responded to *Second Life* environments, experiences, even fears. More than one task involved interaction with water. Because the *Second Life* landscape is built and frequently rebuilt by its participants, it is a world in constant flux, and change is not the exception but often the order of the day. The fascinatingly surreal sim Immersiva was then flooded ankle deep in water.[7] The Island's surface was dotted with metallic flotsam and oddly futuristic sculptures. A pair of figures intrigued me. One, indubitably male, had a light bulb head and lounged on a bench in his boxer shorts. The other, very female, wearing a mini-skirt that showed off her wire legs, stood before him.[8] Their environment and body language, coupled with my own electrifying experiences with technical equipment, inspired me in "Current Events" to try to capture her side of what I imagined would have been an almost — but not quite — love story:

> You see, it was like this.
> I'd reached the end of the line.
> There was no spark whatsoever.
> Everything, everyday was dim going on deep dark.
> Every night, switch on. Every morning, switch off.
> So, like, predictable. But no electromotive force.
>
> One day, though, I was, like, making my circuit
> Around and around, ebb and flow, line after line,
> You know, trying to make a connection.
> Not looking, mind you, but a little spark or two
> Might brighten up my life.
>
> Then I saw him.
> He had a sort of glow about him,
> Tungsten tough, you know.
> Always did go for those big blue-white incandescents.
> No fickle flickering fluorescents for me.
> So there he was, practically unpackaged, stretched out
> In the middle of that sort of Wal-Mart wasteland,
> Dozing on a bench, looking totally disconnected,
> Way out on the checkerboard grid,
>
> Something deep inside me began to crackle
> Spitting sparks, sort of arcing between us. Pulsing.
> As if I had generated some kind of back flow
> Into his line. You could tell he was hard-wired,
> Smooth-turned, easy on the socket.
> He sputtered and jump-started to life,
> Picked up that big superwatt head, and
> Smirked when he spotted my bright red, standby button.
> He must have thought I was one of those quick-start types.
>
> There was this magical humming sound.
> Like the wind whistling the lines just before the storm.
> My multimeter was flipping, my amperes ramping.
> I could tell he was hot to close the circuit.
> But nobody's going to flip my switch just like that.

He may be dealing with a high-voltage line,
But I've got my insulators, resistors, thick rubber gloves.
I may have skinny prongs and a kinda weathered screw-top bulb,
But I'm made of tougher filament than he must think.
This babe is no flash in the night.

Besides, I wouldn't touch him unless he produced
A certified, properly installed Underwriters GFI.
Mix with hot juice? You gotta have protection.
If he thinks I'd let him push my buttons out in this soupland and
Leave me zapped in a lightning puddle, he has popped a fuse.
He's not the only generator in town.

Yeh, it was a megawatt moment,
But he and I were so completely polarized,
Better to light a candle than blindly lose my way.
The LCD on my control box began to flicker.
Ohms sweet ohms, I had to get out of there.
Alarm bells went off, sirens blew.
Static, nothing but static. Flatline.
Time to power down.

But throwing that switch was
No easy click in the night.
When I left him behind on that watersoaked bench,
Went on down my oh-so-lonely path,
Short-circuited, unplugged,
It was over. It never even began.
Burned out. No ground. No more hum.
Totally dark again.

In Karuna's stone-walled cavern Franchella slipped in among rushing waters, abandoning herself to the sounds, sensations and her own "Waters Within."[9] Franchella floated, perfectly relaxed, arms stretched. I led her to the edge where the flow tumbled over a lofty cliff and dropped into a chasm beyond sight. I considered the power such a cascade could wield, how it might feel to be carried out upon that surge, over the rocks, and down to where?

The waters churn, carving currents new and strange,
Spit froth against the walls, roar their triumph,
Propel clouds of vapor to mist cathedral domes above.
Earth-bound stars kiss the surface like snowflakes on the wind.

Today the waters are swift, channels strong. There is danger here.
The waters rush to escape the cave, cascade down falls.
They want me to follow, dissolve myself into and within them,
Tumble down the cliff, crash against boulders.

But for the waters' mutterings, the cave is silent.
Condensation drips from the upper rocks.

Its echoes slip and tap, rebound wall to wall.
But no foot falls across the rocky ledges. No voice tugs my ear.

I am blissfully alone.
Spring-fed, sun-sheltered, the pool is liquid ice.
My fingers, toes, and lips are no longer there.
I hear my heart beat. Blood flows. I am alive.

Buoyant, oh so relaxed, I lie back upon the surface,
Crosslike, arms outstretched, I surrender to the waters and my self.
I close my eyes in peace, prepared to drift
Wherever the waters choose to take me.

Walking the Dark Side

The path to Alchemy Immortalis' forbidding fortress wandered over dark uneven ground long claimed by tangled vines. As Franchella passed what looked like a bottomless pit,[10] I wondered what or who might be hidden in its depths. Later, inside the castle,[11] I invoked its imaginary resident and considered how he might ravage his women as he would likely torment the delicate harpsichords that filled the manor's hall. I learned that the action of the harpsichord, at least historically, depended upon the flexibility of the quills of ravens' feathers to strike its notes. So I dubbed the castle's master "Lord of the Raven's Quill":

Lord Elfwinder, the house staff say,
Has a heart like a black velvet rose.
Couched in thorns, bound in wire ivy,
Encased in a trellis of tempered steel,
It lies in matted moss at the base of his spine.

No winsome maid would willing wander
To and through those murky depths
In search of tenderness, for
Like all Muircastle men,
He reaches but will not touch,
Grasps but cannot hold,
Breeds but does not love.

The castle reeks of the rotting locks of long lost pilgrims
Who, lured by ice-blue eyes, heedless stumbled into terror.
Now these many years they, their sisters, mothers, lie
Secreted deep in the meadow's long dry, blackened well.
Silent guardians of the castle gate, they've long putrefied the water.

Alone, for now, at night, he moves from board to board.
He skims across the keys, commands without a stroke.
Each key thus bidden lifts its jack and with its tongue
Gently lofts a pick to pluck a string. Then like its master

Brushes past the string without a touch yet makes it sing.
Notes so commanded, as his women, dance to their macabre end.
Their cries swirl upward like thunderclouds of ravens' wings.
They rebound galleries, roost the ramparts, perch upon the towers' bells.

They rain down silver excrement that dries, suspended in the shifting mist.
The dust sifts between, upon the keys, drinks the essence of each dying note,
Seals the board and traps each grounded raven quill to squelch its tongue.
As did each past Muircastle lady, the harpsichord screams its final rondo
Whilst the castle's lord moves on to the next virgin Empress Eros.

Our tasks prodded me to explore poetic forms I hadn't used since college.
I delved into my literary past to refresh memory on rhyming couplets, iambic
pentameter, poetic wordplay, acrostics, and limericks. Upon visiting the ornate
Avilion Grove Ballroom,[12] we were to produce a ballad. I dressed Franchella
in a diaphanous floor-sweeping gown, but found the ballroom devoid of
dancers. Partnerless, I swayed instead to rhythm and rhyme in "Waiting for
You":

> I was dancing tonight with my arms full of air
> Because, oh my dearest, because you weren't there.
> The band it played beautifully, the dancers entwined,
> But your face, my darling, I was unable to find.
> My eyes they were glued to the bright golden door.
> Waiting for you to set foot on the floor!

> I sought in the shadows, peeked into the damps,
> Looked under the tables and 'round past the lamps.
> I poked my nose over like a bitchy bloodhound,
> But nowhere, but nowhere, were you to be found.
> My eyes they were glued to that stubborn closed door.
> Waiting for you to set foot on that floor!

> The stags they were leaping, but I held my ground,
> Waiting for you, jerk, in my loveliest gown!
> So I paced on the sidelines an hour or more
> For the man that I used to completely adore.
> If you're wise, you'll not darken that damnable door
> While I'm waiting, just waiting, for you on this floor!

On Japan's Tempura Island,[13] we were to consider "what it means to be
found within nature." As Franchella strolled through the radiant colors of
Tempura's fall-kissed forests, I was called back to a time when nothing was
more urgent than the moment and myself. A shy and lonely youngster living
on a remote farm, I would seek solace in a clump of trees on the pasture's
edge. Years later, I rediscovered that sense of retreat on Tempura. Reveling
in nature's dual complexity and deceptive simplicity, I recalled the forms and
feelings of childhood within the rhyming couplets of "The Twilight Woods."

In the woods alone am I at total peace.
I love the smell of dampening earth, the honking of the geese.
I trust the creatures that surround me as I nestle in the leaves.
Shade wraps itself around me and feathers me with breeze.
The slanting sun with rainbow fingers soothes the ragged week away.
I nestle in the fragrant moss and doze afternoon's sweet day.
A cooling gust awakes me, dewdrops kiss my skin.
Soon 'twill be the time for me to stir and go within.
Yet I linger till the dusk to greet the rising moon
That peeks above horizon's line to sail across the dune.
In these woods I can believe that life will land aright.
I roll and rise and stretch my arms, prepare to greet the night.

In yet another sylvan setting, the mystical, mythical Chakryn Forest,[14] the woodland was populated with surprising sculptures, unexpected sounds, lights, messages. I was confused by what I saw, didn't see, couldn't quite understand. In response to that complex environment, I engaged in some wordplay. "Magical Forestry + You," an acrostic of sorts, explores how landscape, unearthly creatures, and magic might intertwine and impact one another:

In the magic forest any thing can happen.
The thing in forest can happen any magic
Magic can happen the thing in any forest.
Forest you the magic any happen can thing.
Any forest in magic can happen to thing you.
Thing magic, any you can happen in the forest.
Can you in the forest happen any magic thing?
Happen you in any forest can be the magic.

Technological Inspirations/Frustrations

Even *Second Life*'s technical mires worked their way into my poems. We were to go to the extraordinary (now extinct) AM Radio sim "The Space Between These Trees." The place was filled with hidden surprises. A visitor wandering that sim might suddenly be transported to a road to nowhere or dropped onto a dusty rural landscape. Our instructions were to start and end the day's poem with the same word or phrase. But the second time it was to mean something different from the first time. A case of intense lag inspired a heightened appreciation of the disabled when poor Franchella became "Immobile":

Immobile.
Young and strong,
I am accustomed to move at will.
Up down over beyond, I have been ever free for motion.

Now in this strange unfathomed landscape
I am frozen, locked to a resting place
From which I cannot alone break free.

Beyond, blithe fairies flit from dune to dune.
They ask not, care not that I cannot move.
They are like me, as I was just before today,
Unthinking, unseeing, unwilling to even lend an arm.
They dribble on as sparkling droplets skip across the pond.
To them I am just scenery, shackled to the ground.
Immobile.

Multiple crashes experienced while exploring the intricacies of the fascinating multileveled Chouchou Chouchou, also no longer part of the *Second Life* grid, became the plot line for that day's poem. Chouchou then opened onto a flooded plain speckled with random objects.[15] A star offered guidance but was powerless and uncommunicative. Instead, curiosity enticed Franchella to follow a rugged ladder into the air, with jolting results. Eventually, she came upon a sparkling, but silent, musical paradise hidden within a skybox. But, alas, return to earth became yet another challenge documented in "When No Star Shines the Way":

Days stretch ahead, bland, seamless,
One smooth rippleless puddle after another,
The endless flatlands barely punctuated with events
Like pinfeathers on a badly plucked Thanksgiving turkey.
I wander through mist seeking only purpose,
Having long lost sight of bright rewards.
I feel leaden, yearn for the migratory sun.
Like a silvery earthworm cast up in rainstorm,
I can barely lift myself to plod across the sodden sand.
Couples, bodies intertwined, writhe the shallow pools
As the soft darkness, waveless waters, caress their skins.
Others, solitary, who stand, eyes fixed to distance,
When I approach, evaporate in flurries of smoke.
I call to the star for guidance but none comes.
In this bleak world of scattered people I am alone.

I sit, waves lapping ankles, at a soundless piano and am not surprised.
I have long lost my music, my tongue consumed by frogs.
With the music fled the joy. Now even fickle hands defect.
In the distance, a jagged ladder lifts upward out of sight
Toward clouds. I pick my way across the spikes.
Scramble past debris transmigrants left behind.
Seeking escape from nothing, upward, out, I grasp a rung.
It erupts in an electric fog, a golden fury of light.
The flatland disappears.

I awake, I think, in a midnight chamber.
Through the blackness, a pinprick calls me.
Like a fetus tunneling to infancy
I emerge bathed in color, sparkling shapes, vibrant hues,
Rippling mist-clouded pools, magically petaled then unpetaled trees.
I think it heaven nestled in the clouds.
I drift through soundless waters, shimmering silence. No voice calls.
Though music-making tools abound, none plays.
At the sky piano, my hands rolling over keys,
My head teems with forgotten Piano II.
But no dreams play, no Miss Mae Ruhe by my side,
No tap across my knuckles, sweet penance for a sour note.
No drums play, no xylophone cajoles, no voices sing.

The eye soon tires of kaleidoscopic brightness.
Yearning return to languid peace below.
I sway through waters toward where the tunnel spat me out,
Following blackness, seeking the familiar.
But the wall through which I'd lightly flowed on entrance
Now stands firm, impervious to cries and poundings.
From the bricks, shines an ancient loadstone.
Its signet: "To the Ground." I reach for my salvation.
Once again, reality's vision explodes to nothing,
But it is a nothing of no return,
I am at last truly, irrevocably, gone.

Within the "Foul Whisperings and Strange Matters" sim,[16] Macbeth's dank castle swirled with ghostly figures chanting evil. Narrow passageways led to its depths where a carpet of snakes slithered warnings of that world and this. Escape opened onto a parapet where a giant black bird offered flight to the unknown. The real and technical nightmares encountered in that adventure evoked past challenges to my concept of self in "Whispers from the Not Forgotten Dark":

Bid by poetic spirits, I funnel down a vagina mist into a pit of voices:
"Fair is foul" ... "unsex me" ... "out out" ... "make thick my blood."
Ah, they know me! Even in this land beyond all earth-mapped lands.
I wander through a dark and timeless, sculpted, tumbled, forest,
It and I both petrified, encased forever, individual crevasses of time.
Framed by shadow trees, wild waters, stony almost Irish cliffs.
Stairs long feathered into stone and dust and gravel
Lead upward to a faceless nowhere's path, tomorrow's journey.
Another pilgrim ghosts past thus pointed, puffs, and disappears.
Conversely, I follow the crown ravenward to "Nevermore!"

Down down I spiral, past memory's dust-filled, almost forgotten, tracks.
Deep deep I go, then am caught suspended, motionless, cannot continue.

Returning to today's me I try again. Again I stall third level down.
Not good. Not a place for life's returning. I know it well and rightly fear it.
Beneath me phantoms parade my past. In them I hear my mother's voice.
I stop my ears, but its insistence leaps all bounds to flaunt my faults.
It drowns two-thirds' a lifetime's voices, sweeps aside success,
As Ireland's windswept Boireann reveals the base rock,
Deeply fissured stone beneath.

At the castle's depth an arbor leads me, I hope, to blossoming and joy.
Alas, the garden crawls with serpents murmuring my mother's words,
Slinking into every corner of my life. I may climb toward joy, but her fangs
Puncture each balloon, send slippery, rubbery shards to the slime below.
Beyond the arbor waits a raven poised to lift me from this voice-filled world.
We fly through dark but land where more mysteries tinge the view,
Where nothing is so certain but is chance.

I sweep through a crystal moor of frozen, feathery chill.
Icy strands claw my skirts, molten comets cascade.
Mists spiral moss-clad arches, rigid lifeless towers.
Winds rattle windows that gaze, sightless,
Out upon stillborn starlit waters.
A bare and blackened tree clings to its rocky cliff,
Reaching over emptiness to sapphire foam-kissed waters far below.
Therein lies peace. Its pristine depths flood toxic words too often told,
Pulsing waves croon to my aged but still so troubled mind:
Twas tales "told by an idiot, full of sound and fury, signifying nothing."

At Quest's end, much to my surprise and delight, I was named a Poetry
Quest co-winner, sharing honors with Lizzie Gudkov, a poet who teaches
English in Lisbon, Portugal. Franchella now had a $1,000-Linden dowry. I
gave my first *Second Life* poetry reading. From the 30 Quest poems I chose
to read "Current Events" and "Roses and Remembrance," a love story inspired
by a rustic rose-covered garden constructed high above *Second Life*'s cloud
line.[17] Quest organizers posted a video of Franchella's reading to YouTube.
They also displayed three of my poems, including "Waters Within," in
Karuna's Poetry Garden in *Second Life*.[18] "Dragon Small," the result of an evening spent by a virtual campfire communing with a young dragon, pays hom-
age to William Blake's "The Lamb." "Equal Punportunity," a pair of limericks,
imagines possible outcomes from trips through a futuristic transformation
machine then on the Alien Isles sim, alas no longer in this universe.

Two quest poems, "Waters Within" and "Tai Chi at the Dawning of My
Time," were published online in Rez Libris: The Magazine for Librarians.[19]
"Tai Chi at the Dawning of My Time," appears at the end of this essay.

I was beginning to feel comfortable in my own words and had discovered
that I could slip into situations, environments, and perspectives completely
foreign to me and craft lines reflecting what I saw and felt there.

Envisioning Paths to Better Health and Understanding

A Vision Quest, also organized by Jenaia Morane, followed. Its goal was to draw attention to and welcome Max, a free virtual guide dog, to *Second Life*. The result of collaboration of builders, script writers, and visually challenged *Second Life* participants, Max provides audible commentary to enable those with vision problems to navigate the *Second Life* landscape, locate items, recognize avatars, read live chat, and otherwise fully participate in most *Second Life* experiences.

This month-long quest introduced participants to the challenges the visually impaired face in real life, as well as *Second Life*. Each received a panting, barking, mobile voice-enabled Max. At times I traveled *Second Life* blindfolded (myself, not Franchella), fully dependent upon Max's guidance.[20] As part of the quest requirements, we could choose to share our experiences by writing a story or poem from the dog's point of view or that of his visually challenged human partner. I decided to do both. On one of many suggested web sites, I found a video of a guide dog leading a blind woman in a wheel chair past several garbage cans that blocked the sidewalk. Inspired by that vision, I imagined the separate journeys of a visually and physically disabled woman, the training of a golden retriever puppy, and their final joyous meeting at Seeing Eye school. Their stories, "Journeys and Intersections," are posted on the Res Libris website.[21] I was greatly honored when asked to share my vision quest poems at a *Second Life* gathering in recognition of Helen Keller Day. One of those Vision Quest poems, "In Sights on Sight," dealt with the miracle of vision itself:

> Vision is that magical ability to activate
> Two small, slippery spheres within the skull.
> They can automatically adjust their shapes,
> Adapt to miniscule shifts of light, distance, movement, angle.
> Together they produce stereoscopic images of curves, distance, depth.
> Then assemble, instantly transmit living data
> About countless colors, shapes and forms, speed, porosity,
> So the brain with lightning swiftness can analyze and act on we see.
> Eyes plus brain can record each subtle nuance on a face,
> Help decide if its owner is friend or foe or lover — or all of the above.
> These wondrous eyes update this input 24/7–365,
> Each waking microsecond throughout our every day.
> So, lucky us, we travel with these birthright-issued,
> Pre-installed optic miracles within our heads.
> We need not calculate, script, or program these delicate devices.
> We need only open them and aim.
> They make it so easy to move, to read, to choose a likely mate.
> They help us create art, compose music, notate dance.
> With them we can see dirt, stairs, stars, and children's faces.

All the beauty and mysteries of life are ours
At the flick of an eyelash.
Our eyes work every waking hour for us.
What do we do for them?
We rub them with filthy fingers.
We stare hours at flickering screens.
We fog them in tobacco smoke.
We insert unclean contact lenses.
We fry them in the blazing sun.
We poison them with toxic sprays.
We do 15-inch work on two-inch screens.
We dye their rims and lashes, wonder why they itch.
We ignore the call for safety glasses.
We laugh at the eyes-friendly diets.
We postpone checkups as long as we still see.
We ignore too long their silent cries for help.

No wonder eyes grow tired, sore, and cranky.
No wonder they feel scratchy, rasped, or dry.
No wonder some become infected, give up, power down.
Then, sometimes only then, we learn
How wonderful they were.

Both quests resulted in intense immersive and emotional experiences.
But a Healing Quest that followed both energized and enervated me. This
month-long multi-platform adventure delved into the need for HIV/AIDS
testing and responses to the challenges and fear of serious disease. As directed,
I researched web sites, tweeted daily messages on Twitter, delved into the
myths and facts surrounding HIV/AIDS, and wrote four AIDS-related poems.

Our first challenge was to think back and mark the times we had been
tested by misfortune or difficulty. A visit in *Second Life* to a dismal rocky
mountain landscape brought me once more to the dark side and impelled me
to deal,[22] hopefully for the last time, with shadowed memories of the past.
"Dragon's Blood," transcended the virtual and burrowed into the early years
of my real life. The results, excerpted below, wrapped in the mythical hide
of the fearsome, led me to a bright new valley of understanding:

I hatched one summer's eve in a cave
On the cold dark side of the mountain.
Within its depths reverberated
Fierce frightening shrieks and wails.
Claws raked the earth and shattered stone.
Streams of flame blistered slime-soaked walls.
The dank air reeked of smoke,
The rotting entrails of defeated prey.
In the shadows cowered my half-grown sibling.

Beyond the entrance paced the dragon's mate,
A spineless warm-blood given to dancing in the moonlight,
Crooning mystic magic tongues.
Before long, she drove him down the mountain.
To disappear into the valley below.
My sister escaped one moonlit night
To distant foothills and did not return.
Left behind, forsaken, half-blood, I felt split in two.
I could feel my father's warmth
Seeping through soft channels beneath my hide.
But when I peered into reflecting ponds,
I saw the dragon's face....

... For years I battled demons of the past,
Turned over memories like long untilled earth,
Wavered between crushing loss and deep relief.
How could I begin to love myself
If I could not freely love this dragon
That I had so justly learned to fear?
Who was she who gave me life?
And who of her am I?...

Yes, she guarded me from wolves.
I, too, have tasted wolves' blood
When such have stalked my young.
True, she'd pluck her spines, send dragonsong
Rebounding mountains wall to wall.
I, too, give voice to strumming rhythms.
She scorched many a deserving scoundrel.
I, too, breathe fire when there is a need.
She gave me shining scales, her glowing hide.
Ever curious, she'd sail the clouds, search strange and new.
I, too, seek and ponder, gather, store.
Bits and pieces of her song and story
Still fall daily from my dragon's mouth.
Best of all, she gave me dragon power,
But my warm blood tempers it in use.
Who was she who gave me life?
And who of her am I? Are we?
The mirror knows, my quarter-dragon darlings,
We need honor her dragoness — and ours.
From its depths well strength and song and story,
Fire, steam, and quests for knowledge
To steel our warm-blood spines.

"The Letter" was conjured from inside the mind of a woman who might fear she had received an official HIV notification sent on behalf of a former intimate, now anonymous, lover from the past:

The letter lay on the table for three dark days.
She'd lift it, turn it over, read, reread its official address,
Flip it, still sealed, top down to join piles of bills and papers
Atop a stack she'd inwardly tagged: later, maybe, maybe never ever.
Its feared message gnawed her loins,
But she could no more have slit that envelope than
She could have sliced her belly navel down,
Poured herself onto the public road.

Inside, she knew, lay death, as certainly as if it contained
A spring-loaded bullet trained up her insides to her heart.
She riffled through the years, pondered the few
Who'd showered promises between her legs then disapparated into fog.
She knew not the who that he might be, but she knew the man he was:

> He did not love me, or
> He would have ensured he could not infect me.
> Had he loved me, truly loved me,
> He would have tested before he ever touched me.
> He did not love me, or he would have told me
> That he could not with surety promise that
> His past would not endanger me and ours.
> He could not have wanted our future or
> He would not have so jeopardized the present.
> He could not have wanted children,
> Or he would not have knowingly sentenced them
> To lifelong struggle with a disease
> That slowly, almost surely, leads to accelerated death.

But there the letter lay
Burning itself into the oak of Nana's table.
Why or who or what did she need to know?
"Sealed things are best left unopened,"
Whispered Pandora in her ear: "Why unleash
That stream of words to further complicate your life?
Done is done, and if it is to be, lie down with grace and die."

On the fourth day, the unspoken answer came
On the winds of future's voice:

> If you love me, you would make sure you could not infect me.
> If you love me, you would know before you touch me.
> If you love me, you would know before you birth me.
> If you love me, you would tell me.
> If you love me...
> You would...

And so she did.

Another Healing Quest poem, "Healing Begins with the Courage to Know,"
urges those unwilling to consider even the possibility of illness to test for it, face
the results, and take proactive measures that might help begin the healing process:

Every day is a test of our willingness to live.
Open your eyes or slink back to slumber?
Brave the day or shrink from its challenge?
Burst out the door or take cover behind it?
Walk a steady path or prowl on the wild side?
Attack the mountain or skid the crevasse?
Dare to love or forever feel unlovable?
Seek the truth or cower from the unknown?

We willingly confine ourselves in walls of ignorance,
Obscure discomforting realities around us.
What we will not see we cannot fear.
But danger incognito stalks us from within.
The undetected enemy, be it disease, dementia, instability,
A virus hitch-hiking on a T cell, a minute cancer lurking in the womb,
Unchallenged, these invaders burst into rampant growth
To easily win the battle never fought.

If you would seek the face of HIV
It may await you in the mirror,
Hide behind your sister, brother, your beloved.
It might bask on the sunlit porch next door,
Smile back at you from the pulpit, desk, or counter,
Rest on the pillow beside your head,
Sleep peacefully in your daughter's crib.
HIV does not flash a neon sign across the forehead.
It may lie in wait a decade before you know it's there,
Unless you hunt it down and rend its covert mask.

Testing can bring relief, but also release.
Relief exhales deeply on a negative result.
Release, rebounding from now knowing the unknown,
Can finally pack away uncertainty, gird for action and direction.
Knowledge is the beacon that can light the path to health.
Like a crusty scab, denial only shields the suppurating wound.
If we reach down into ourselves, emancipate our doubts, our fears,
True healing will blossom from within.

The Changing Landscape of the Quest

This Healing Quest drew few participants, perhaps because of its subject matter, perhaps because of its rigor, and no winner was declared. But I was invited to read my Healing Quest poems as part of a World AIDS Day 2009 commemoration in *Second Life*. The audience gathered under giant trees in a setting representing New York's Battery Park and, sprawled on replicas of AIDS Memorial Quilts, listened to stories and poems of courage and hope.[23] The Healing Quest concept evolved into a non-competitive Uncle D Story

Quest, a project of Karuna and The Virtual Worlds Story Project. It was designed to encourage individuals and groups to learn about the life and challenges faced by a person with HIV. As of this writing participants were still able to explore the life of Uncle D by setting off on the quest from Story Quest Island.[24] "One of the interesting and powerful things about a Quest," says Jenaia Morane in Uncle D's opening clue, "is how it encourages you to see, think and feel differently about not only a particular subject, but yourself as well." The quest is one of Karuna's numerous health-related educational projects designed,[25] says Morane, who directs the Island's activities, to "use the power of immersive stories to educate, create empathy and empower others to make a difference in the fight against AIDS."

Elsewhere in *Second Life*, a poetry competition sponsored by the now defunct The Learning Experience (TLE) to mark VE Day gave me a valid excuse to interview a relative about his memories of World War II. "A Child's Wartime in Coal Town PA," excerpted below,[26] uncovered and preserved a family memory and was included in an e-book of contest entries.

> When the sirens wailed
> Dad would drop the blackout curtains.
> We'd crawl beneath the kitchen table,
> Listen for the drone of approaching planes.
> Some claimed they could distinguish
> The groan of German engines from the purr of Allied craft,
> But to my sisters and to me, it all sounded like trouble on the wing...
>
> ...The war came and went. Each battle's tidal surge,
> Flowed over us buffered children as ripples, puffs of foam.
> Oh, there were furtive whispers of atrocities, of millions,
> Mothers, children tortured, killed, and even skinned.
> But it was then unthinkable that humans could treat other humans so.
>
> Our family fortress seemed, to this small child,
> To float, secure and dry, across the tumbling waves.
> The storms might swirl around us, crackle lightning,
> But bound by common caring, together we were to
> Brave and breast the winds of World War II
> Until the final joyful soundings of "All clear!"

Envisioning the Visual

I was becoming more adventurous. If I could create and share poetry, could I also use my new building skills to create and display art in *Second Life*? I joined a free TLE workshop, "Art in *Second Life*," that was to mark yet another turning point in my virtual cultural adventures. Dan Yapungku (aka Daniël Vandersmissen, a real life painter based in Belgium), was our instructor.

Over several months he led our group on tours of *Second Life* builds, galleries and exhibitions. We met artists working in both real life and *Second Life*, explored their *Second Life* builds, discussed how the pieces were constructed.[27] Dan gently prodded us to build artwork of our own. He and his *Second Life* artist friends became our mentors as the projects began to take shape. AuraKyo Insoo, an Argentinian artist and art teacher, was particularly generous with her time, suggestions, scripts, and hints on technique.

Aura organized an exhibit to honor Dan, celebrate the vitality of his real life, his *Second Life* artistic achievements, and the opportunities he provided for budding *Second Life* artists on his Virtual Holland lands. She invited Dan's *Second Life* students to take part in an exhibit in his honor and designated a lofty exhibition space for each. I worried if my work could measure up to that of my more experienced and talented neighbors.

But when designing structures in *Second Life*, it is easy to think high and wide. My "Heart of the Universe" sculpture examined life forms and concepts of fertility.[28] The design employed scripted water features, swirling figures, and glowing, pulsing translucent egg shapes floating high above in an animated solar-patterned sphere. Visitors to the exhibit were warm and encouraging, and I was beginning to believe I could do almost anything!

The Virtual Holland exhibit grew into the *Dreams, Nightmares & Memories Art Festival* as Aura encouraged other *Second Life* artists to join us in what soon grew to a multi-level art park showcasing the works of more than three dozen artists. Everything came together as I combined what I had learned through the quests, *Second Life* poetry, building, scripting, and art into a broad wall of imagery and words. "Dream Dancing," my first *Second Life*–inspired poem, became the basis for a series of photographs of Franchella slipping, sliding up, down, through the Storybook Island fountain sculpture.[29]

The exhibit remained on view for months. I often visited the site, studied my new colleagues' works, discussed pieces with artists and visitors. Sometimes, I would set the *Second Life* light to midnight and enjoyed watching the glowing, shifting sparkle of what we had built. My pieces may not have been great art, but it was my art, created not with brush, chisel, or knife, but out of my own imagination with my own hand. So, too, my *Second Life*-inspired poems surely constitute no threat to the masters, but they are my own poems, crafted of bits and pieces of myself and what I observed and experienced while traveling the *Second Life* grid.

Putting Second Life *Knowledge and Experiences to Work*

If experiences in this single virtual world could engender in me such a new sense of confidence and capability, what might immersion in *Second Life*, or any of a growing number of other virtual settings, offer our students? Educators around the world are using *Second Life* to help students experience the ocean's depths, dive into a single cell, crawl over reconstructions of geological faults, transport themselves into periods of history, trace Darwin's travels, walk the streets of Shakespeare's time, visit the Harlem of its heyday, and more. These settings are made possible through the monumental efforts of dedicated *Second Life* citizens reconstructing realistic, three-dimensional environments. But creative, adventurous educators go beyond casual immersion and encourage students to cross over to imagination.

Consider how an educator-led *Second Life* experience might inspire students to write. One of the challenges facing those of us who try to inspire students to write is helping them break out of what may have been a rather limited life experience and then challenge them to expand their outer universe, encourage them to react to a totally different landscape and its society.

As co-founder and facilitator of a college poetry workshop, I spent many a cozy evening listening to and fully enjoying poems of love and loss, angst and insecurity, childhood memories, fears and dreams of the future. Some of the more cosmopolitan or well-traveled students voiced echoes of their more varied lives, but sophomoric themes tended to dominate the offerings.

Yes, we might take student writers into the inner city to absorb its atmosphere and interact with local inhabitants. We could organize field trips to a mountain lake, deep into a coal mine, to the seaside. But suppose we could drop them instantly, quickly, safely, and at little or no cost, into unique and challenging landscapes, let them interact with an unpredictably varied citizenry, enjoy earthly and unearthly beauty, experience obstacles and perceived dangers? How would our students react to landing in a virtual version of any of the settings described above? Or, say they take a stroll atop China's Great Wall, wander Moscow's Red Square? What might they experience? Whom might they meet? How might their reactions to a multitude of possible very different environments enhance their writing?

It wasn't until our college poetry workshop had run its course and reconstituted itself into a new student club that I discovered *Second Life* and began to explore its potential for creative inspiration. Our residential liberal arts college had little need to make use of *Second Life*'s capabilities for distance learning. Instead, as instructional technologist and manager of the college's *Second Life* Island, I set out to show faculty how *Second Life* might add new dimensions to the on campus classroom experience.

I scattered breadcrumbs, did demos and workshops, more often to faculty sneers and fears than expressions of possible interest and the courage to give it a try. But eventually, a professor of acting and speech asked to build an information center on our Island, including a performance space for Shakespearean drama. Faculty teaching foreign languages and international culture brought students into *Second Life* to visit German, Spanish and Russian builds and interact through text and voice with native speakers. We set larger-than life poster displays detailing the results of student research in biology, geology, and the sociology of dog/human relationships. Incoming first-year students whose summer readings focused on Darwin's works discovered on our *Second Life* Island a multimedia garden highlighting Darwin's life and achievements. We invited art students to display their work. The *Second Life* exhibits enabled international and family and friends of other far flung students to share in their college achievements. Our Island's World Walkway featured flags of the more than 40 countries then represented by the student body. We encouraged members of our International Student Association to post information about their countries. International music streamed on the walkway and dance balls enticed and enabled visiting avatars to dance.

Based upon what I have learned in pursuing my own adventures as an explorer, creator, and student of and in *Second Life* as well as our institution's immersive experiences in using *Second Life* to enrich teaching and learning, I urge interested teachers and college faculty seeking to employ the learning power of virtual worlds to:

- Think before you click. Clearly define your objectives and hoped-for outcomes in introducing a virtual world experience.
- Before introducing others to *Second Life* or any virtual world, spend enough time in world to become comfortable in the environment and reach a level of competence where you are able to confidently assist newcomers in navigating its three-dimensional terrain.
- Bring, do not send, students into an online virtual environment! Organize a tour with clearly defined objectives, informative notecards, and detailed directions to each destination. Expect that they will get lost, confused, and distracted in their initial visits to a new virtual environment. For example, bring them in through a gentle, focused entryway, such as *Second Life*'s Virtual Ability Island.[30] Take time to help students master the basic skills of communication and motion. Before they can begin to fully experience the offerings of an online virtual world, they must feel comfortable moving from place to place, navigating the maps, interacting with residents they encounter.
- Discuss the usually unwritten rules that govern behavior within that particular culture.
- Prepare a gift bag of free essentials, basic clothing, flight feathers and other useful navigational or environmental tools. Show them how to

open it, save the contents to their inventory, and put the new tools and materials to use.

- When taking neophytes on tour in world, enlist the help of at least one world-savvy assistant who is comfortable in that environment and able to round up stragglers and teleport the lost.
- Give tour participants a written notecard list of specific destinations (with addresses/SLurls and directions) and tasks to accomplish during the tour. If possible, also give them a printable version of the instructions beforehand in addition to those delivered within the virtual environment.
- Explain ahead of time problems that may come up: lag, griefers, getting lost or stuck in place. Discuss and demonstrate how to avoid or get out of those situations.
- During and after the group tour, allow sufficient in-class or online time to discuss reactions, problems, discoveries, and suggestions. They are pioneers and their feedback can help you smooth the way for others.
- Repeat the tour process, with new destinations and goals, as needed.
- When making the first solo assignment, be very clear on where to go, how to get there, what to look for, and what results you expect. If possible, set a specific time frame for the first unaccompanied visit and arrange to be available inworld to answer questions and/or come to the aid of the confused.
- Be realistic in your expectations. Would I send students out to create 30 poems in 30 days? No way! That kind of sustained effort does not fit into a student's experience, demanding schedule, sustainability, and other obligations. Instead, design a writing assignment that requires immersion in a particular virtual environment. Let them choose from a small selection of sites and options. Give them a week or more to experience, write, deliver and post the results. Mid-week, require a draft or at least a statement of purpose or other evidence of engagement and offer lots of help and encouragement. Encourage students to share results on the course web site or course management center. Have a live reading in class. Ask the students to reflect upon the experience and how it did or did not incite creativity. Invite the class to comment on results. Then do it again with a fresh set of options. The virtual universe is wide and they will not be bored. Nor are the less inclined likely to find pre-cooked research papers ripe for plucking from the Internet!
- Provide positive feedback and recognition for any and all positive outcomes. Entering a virtual world is a lot like being born. Everything is different; some things are vaguely familiar; everything is wondrous and frightening at the same time. The newborn has years to become comfort-

able in the postnatal environment. Without lots of support and encouragement, your students may give their transition to a virtual world only a few hours before giving up in confusion and defeat!

- Yes, it is work! Ah, but the results can be well worth it! Set your students down in a magical forest and magic may indeed happen! Send them to Russia's virtual Red Square or China's Great Wall,[31,32] down into a virtual mine, deep into The Abyss, and see what happens.

- Be open-minded on their interpretations of *Second Life* sims and scenes. You may see a gentle sun-kissed meadow. They may imagine a grass-covered pit of quicksand. Sent to a sim full of roses, I saw a wounded relationship studded with thorns. "Roses and Remembrance" was a love story,[33] but not an easy one.

- Don't be shy about asking for advice and help. Members of the *Second Life* community, particularly those involved in education, are often very willing to answer questions, suggest solutions for technical problems. They may invite you to bring your students to their builds or even offer the use of a bit of temporarily vacant land on which to construct your own. As you travel the grid, you will meet many other inhabitants and will develop a list of contacts. The *Second Life* Educators listserve is an excellent resource for meeting experienced kindred spirits. If you particularly appreciate or admire a particular project or build, try contacting the owner of the item or manager of the land or group for more information. Contact information is easily available on an item's Profile or the location's About Land file.

- Be prepared for the unexpected. Anything you see in a virtual world can disappear in the time it takes some distant designer to click a mouse. Island owners lose funding, the level of support can change with the flick of the controller's budget. Permissions and privileges might be adjusted, the old build evaporates and the new is installed. If you are creating a lesson around one or more specific sims, here are some ways to help insure that a rebuild on the morning of your class will not wreak total disaster.
  - Choose popular sims that have been there for a long time and appear to have been built with considerable effort and with a solid purpose in mind.
  - Even then, it is wise to contact the owner and/or manager of the sim to tell them how much you appreciate their work and that you would like to send your students there. Tell them when the students may be visiting and ask if they might have any objections or suggestions. Also ask if they have any major changes planned that might make your plan difficult or impossible.

    o Build your own backup. As with any technology-based lesson, we are
at the mercy of Murphy's Law as well as imps who plague the power
lines and gremlins that infect the Internet. Immersion in the environment is, of course, the most desired outcome. But some pictures
gathered ahead of time can help prime the creative pump with visuals
to generate discussion. When you visit sims that you are considering
using in a lesson, take lots of screenshots, or digital snapshots. You'd
pay a fee to save them to your *Second Life* inventory, but these same
pictures saved to your disk cost nothing more than drive space. I
have amassed a collection of thousands of such images; many of them
document builds that no longer exist.

- Be exacting on your expectations but accepting and appreciative of the
results. Then sit back and watch the learning bloom!

Today I am a different person from the *Second Life* neophyte who in January 2008 followed Franchella Milena into *Second Life*'s brave new three-
dimensional international world. One morning during the Poetry Quest, as
I watched my avatar follow age-old steps across a sunlit granite outcrop, my
mind was on task translating setting and motion into words. But in the process
I also discovered hidden bedrock within myself in "Tai Chi at the Dawning
of My Time."

The tree behind me may seem solid.
It must be, for those above depend upon it for support.
Yet not a leaf rustles in the ocean breeze that surely blows
If not from one direction, the next moment from the other.
How strong can a living being be if it cannot flex with the wind?
Surely, life's gusts and storms destroy if one cannot bend to meet them.
The rock below me, though it too a shell of make believe,
Looks a crushing landing for one who, heedless, walks
The lofty gangplank overhead. But this all-too-solid rock,
So fixed, seems a ready victim to a hard, well-chiseled blow.
But not today, for my shoeless footfalls shatter not the silence of the dawn
When even the music of this timeless dance rings only in my mind.
A granite mausoleum, the eternal cage, is embedded in the rock below
Between me and cool blue, endless waters just beyond.
As solid and lifeless as the desiccated corpse
That might before long lie within, I doubt that it would hold me long.

For on this glowing morning I feel like the sky itself.
Clean, flowing, unfettered, light, pain-free,
I move this way and that, tracing ancient patterns,
Yet knowing that within this enduring ritual
Lies freedom to paint my own shifting colors, storm and rain.
Snowflakes dust my hair, birdsong piques my ears,

Far above, a quarreling squirrel chatters me: be gone.
So I will move on, but yet one more pirouette in this glorious dawn of me.
For I know this morning, finally, that I am I and I am beautiful and I am strong.
I have braved the winds, carried those I love to safety.
I have etched my words upon time's passing scrolls,
Brought sunlight to darkened minds, warmth to chilled and hollowed hearts.
I am the one I this universe has ever and will ever know.
I am here. I am now. There has been no I before me.
Though my seeds are sown, resown, and I can see bits of myself reborn,
There will never be another I, wholly I, from my time on.

Thus inspired by these creative adventures in *Second Life*, the following summer I dedicated my vacation to collecting and editing my pre–*Second Life* poems. I sifted through a lifetime of scribbles and trawled 30 years of digital storage. Freed from my home office/closet by a newly installed wireless router and a borrowed laptop, fed by a still-baffled, but always supportive husband/ retired chef, I worked outdoors on a breezy sunlit patio to corral and tame decades of poems, foal new ones, and gently herd 60 of what I hoped were the best into *The Keeping Places*, my first full-length book of poetry. Will it become a classic? I have no doubt that it will not, but I do not care. It is mine. My words, conceived and nurtured within myself, are at last free to gallop wherever they may, propelled by my buoyant rambles through *Second Life*.

Notes

1. Photos of the Conjunction Junction workshop and some of Franchella's early constructions can be viewed at: http://www.flickr.com/photos/34068607@N05/sets/72157613008816411/.)

2. To learn more about Lisa Dawley and her work in education and virtual worlds, go to: http://edtech.boisestate.edu/ldawley/web/lisa_dawley_vitae.htm.

3. For more information on the *Second Life* Educators listserve and to join the list: https://lists.secondlife.com/cgi-bin/mailman/listinfo/educators.

4. Storybook Island no longer exists. Its organizers became more focused on Karuna's HIV/AIDS education program and quests on Story Quest Island, both now defunct.

5. To join *Second Life*, select your avatar, and download the free software, start at http://secondlife.com/.

6. A photo of Franchella dancing in the fountain can be seen at: http://www.flickr.com/photos/34068607@N05/6332386783/.

7. http://slurl.com/secondlife/Immersiva/39/109/30.

8. A photo of the electrifying couple can be seen at: http://www.flickr.com/photos/34068607@N05/6332288487/.

9. A photo of Franchella floating in the cave's pool can be seen found at: http://www.flickr.com/photos/34068607@N05/6332397811/.

10. A photo of part of the castle grounds is posted at: http://www.flickr.com/photos/34068607@N05/6333136058/.

11. A photo of the interior of the castle can be viewed at: http://www.flickr.com/photos/34068607@N05/6332879345/.

12. Visit the Avilion Ballroom at: http://slurl.com/secondlife/Avilion%20Grove/136/126/53. A photo of Franchella in her "most beautiful gown" is posted at: http://www.flickr.com/photos/34068607@N05/6332392947/.

13. Visit Tempura Island at: http://slurl.com/secondlife/tempura%20island/125/42/33. View a photo of Tempura's woods at: http://www.flickr.com/photos/34068607@N05/6333159648/.

14. Visit Chakyrn forest at: http://slurl.com/secondlife/Chakryn/119/70/54. View a photo of Franchella in Chakryn's magic forest at: http://www.flickr.com/photos/34068607@N05/6473467829/.

15. A photo of the Chouchou landscape as first seen on landing at that time is posted at: http://www.flickr.com/photos/34068607@N05/6333114590/. For Franchella's first view of Chouchou's skybox see: http://www.flickr.com/photos/34068607@N05/6332369083/. A photo of Franchella playing the piano in the midst of a sparkling pool in Chouchou's fabulous build is posted at: http://www.flickr.com/photos/34068607@N05/6332372859/.

16. Visit this very literate multi-storied build at http://slurl.com/secondlife/Macbeth/46/51/54. For images of some of the settings Franchella encountered here, see her encountering a swirl of snake-like phrases in the castle's depths at: http://www.flickr.com/photos/34068607@N05/6332416307/ and Franchella's escape from the castle on the back of a giant raven at: http://www.flickr.com/photos/34068607@N05/6332419889/.

17. A video of Franchella's reading of "Roses and Remembrance" (not included in this paper) and poems by Lizzie Gudkov is posted on YouTube at: http://www.youtube.com/watch?v=GB6MNrESJ2g. On the same page is a link to readings by other participants in the Poetry Quest.

18. Originally constructed on Storybook Island, The Poetry Garden was later moved to Karuna island, and apparently disappeared when Karuna closed. Images of the displays are also posted at: http://www.flickr.com/photos/34068607@N05/6333052222/ and http://www.flickr.com/photos/34068607@N05/6333057176/.

19. For an article on the Poetry Quest and its co-winners and samples of our poems, visit: http://rezlibris.com/old/books-a-publishing/quest-winners/403-a-poetry-quest-for-poetry-month.html. An image of the animated dragon that provided inspiration for "Dragon Small," one of the poems posted on the web page can be seen at: http://www.flickr.com/photos/34068607@N05/6473859993/.

20. An image showing Franchella and Max exploring Storybook Island in *Second Life* is posted at http://www.flickr.com/photos/34068607@N05/6332412669/.

21. "Journeys and Intersections," the fictionalized two-part story of Denise, the physically challenged but determined, and Solomon, the guide dog destined to serve her, can be read at: http://rezlibris.com/old/education/books-a-publishing/quest-winners/428-vision-quest-introduces-virtual-guide-dog-anticipates-new-island.html. Their story is a composite of the journeys and training of countless pairs of humans and support animals who with the help of many others find each other and forge a lifelong bond of companionship and service.

22. A screenshot of the cave that inspired "Dragon's Blood" is at: http://www.flickr.com/photos/34068607@N05/6333112374/.

23. View an image of the 2009 World AIDS Day Poetry Reading in *Second Life* at: http://www.flickr.com/photos/34068607@N05/6332423569/.

24. Explore Uncle D's Quest at http://slurl.com/secondlife/Story%20Quest%20Island/114/246/22.

25. Learn about Karuna's mission at: http://karunahiv.com/home.html. Visit Karuna island in *Second Life* at: http://slurl.com/secondlife/Karuna/162/210/21.

26. The complete "A Child's Wartime in Coal Town PA" poem can be found at: http://www.flickr.com/photos/34068607@N05/6912255750/.

27. Some of the sims the art class visited can still be found in *Second Life*: New Media Center's Arts Simulacra: http://slurl.com/secondlife/Ars%20Simulacra/156/36/26; Dresden

Gallery left *SL*, but tours can be found on YouTube; PiRats Art Network: http://slurl.com/second life/PiRats%20Art%20Network/129/122/29.

28. A photo of the "Heart of the Universe" sculpture is posted at: http://www.flickr.com/photos/34068607@N05/6478380027/.

29. A photo of the "Dream Dancing" composition is posted at: http://www.flickr.com/photos/34068607@N05/6333038760/.

30. Virtual Ability Island (http://slurl.com/secondlife/Virtual%20Ability/128/128/23) offers a well-organized introduction to new users. Other useful options are sims devoted to introduction for students of a particular language. If you have building rights to your organization's *Second Life* island, you may wish to design and build your own introductory program.

31. Moscow's Red Square: http://slurl.com/secondlife/Moscow%20Island/222/166/21.

32. The spectacular *SL* build of the Great Wall of China can no longer be found. For a photo of the Great Wall in *Second Life*, visit: http://www.flickr.com/photos/34068607@N05/6332295441/.

33. An image of Franchella among the roses is posted at: http://www.flickr.com/photos/34068607@N05/6477375919/.

About the Contributors

Julie **Achterberg** (aka Steorling Heron) is a retooled teacher of English and biology. She teaches Guided Study. She is employed by the non-profit WAY (Widening Advances for Youth) Program as an English language arts expert blending writer's workshop and project based learning in an alternative online school and working on curriculum development for the Michigan Education Achievement Authority.

Suzanne **Aurilio** (aka Aurili Oh) is director of technology enhanced instruction and faculty support in the College of Extended Studies at San Diego State University, focusing on distance education. She also freelances as a consultant and learning designer.

Dianna **Baldwin** (aka Zoeb Mcmillan) is the associate Writing Center director at Michigan State University, where she works with undergraduate and graduate consultants. She is also a member of the Writing and Rhetoric graduate faculty. She is responsible for the online Writing Center at MSU.

Christine **Ballengee Morris** (aka Rain Winkler) is a professor of art education and founding director of the Multicultural Center at the Ohio State University. She is the editor of *Art Education* and has served the National Art Education Association as president of the United States Society for Education through Art and vice president of membership. She serves on the editorial boards of *The Journal of Cultural Research in Art Education* and *Journal of Social Theory in Art Education*.

Kara **Bennett**'s (aka Dancers Yao) career in mental health research and practice spans more than 30 years. She received her Ph.D. from the University of California, Los Angeles in 1981, and a psychologist license in 1987. As a post-doctoral scholar, she continued her dissertation research which proposed a dynamic model for how knowledge is represented to help make decisions.

J. A. **Brown** (aka Skyther) is a doctoral candidate in the Graduate School for Gerontology at the University of Kentucky's College of Public Health. With a specialization in gerontechnology, her research focuses upon digital gaming and technology design for older adults. She also serves as a consultant for agencies that cater specifically to older populations.

Meg Y. **Brown** (aka Cupcake Hubbenfluff) graduated from the University of Kentucky with a bachelor of arts degree in telecommunications and intends to pursue a master's degree in public administration at the University of Southern Indiana. Her interests are in telecommunications policy and gender studies.

Patricia A. **Facciponti** (aka Franchella Milena) is an educator, author, poet, photographer, videographer, academic technologist and GIS mapper. She enjoys studying, researching, writing, and sharing information on a broad range of topics and skills.

Phylis **Johnson** (aka Sonicity Fitzroy) is professor of sound and new media studies in the Department of Radio-Television-Digital Media at Southern Illinois University, Carbondale. She is the author of four books and has published in numerous journals.

Susan **Patrice**, M.D. (aka Kasuka Magic) received her medical and public health degrees from Tulane University. With experience in bioethics, clinical medicine and research, she was affiliated with the program in medicine and philosophy at California Pacific Medical Center in San Francisco, and the Kennedy Institute of Ethics at Georgetown University. She was the co-founder of Elder Voices, a 501 (c)(3) charity. She was the editor of the *Full Circle* literary magazine. Dr. Patrice died of a rare cancer while the manuscript was in progress.

Jennifer J. **Reed** (aka Jamie Pluvences) is a doctoral student in sociology at the University of Nevada, Las Vegas, where she is active in graduate student government. Her areas of interest include environment, technology and health, sexuality and gender, and politics, social movements and social change. She is a an avid social justice activist.

Jennifer **Regan** (aka Piper Carousel) is a recent graduate from University of Kentucky, where she majored in integrated strategic communications with a minor in anthropology. She works for an advertising agency in New York City.

Carleen D. **Sanchez** (aka Adventurette Constantine) is an interdisciplinary anthropologist with a variety of interests including ancestral Mesoamerica, Latin American pop culture, comparative ethnic studies, and virtual world research. Her Ph.D. and M.A. were earned at the University of California Santa Barbara and her B.A. from California State University Fullerton.

Amanda Grace **Sikarskie** (aka Ione Tigerpaw) is a visiting assistant professor in the public history program at Western Michigan University, where she teaches a graduate seminar on museum technology. She received her Ph.D. in American studies from Michigan State University. She has worked at the Quilt Index, which provides digital access to over 50,000 historic and contemporary quilts.

Index